THE
COMMON SPIDERS
OF THE
UNITED STATES

By
JAMES H. EMERTON

With a New Key to Common Groups of Spiders by
S. W. FROST
PROFESSOR EMERITUS, THE PENNSYLVANIA STATE UNIVERSITY

DOVER PUBLICATIONS, INC.
NEW YORK

This Dover edition, first published in 1961, is an
unabridged and unaltered republication of the work
originally published by Ginn & Company in 1902,
to which has been added a new key to common
groups of spiders and a selected bibliography, both
especially prepared for this edition by S. W. Frost,
Professor Emeritus, the Pennsylvania State University.

Standard Book Number: 486-20223-2
Library of Congress Catalog Card Number: 61–3981

Manufactured in the United States of America
Dover Publications, Inc.
180 Varick Street
New York, N. Y. 10014

PREFACE

THERE are few books on the American spiders, and these
are either large and expensive works or else special papers
published by scientific societies, and so little known to the
public. Since publishing my papers on the New England and
Canadian spiders in the *Transactions of the Connecticut Acad-
emy* from 1882 to 1894, I have had frequent calls for a smaller
and simpler book to meet the wants of readers who, without
making a special study of the subject, want to know a little
about spiders in general and especially those species that they
often meet with. It is hoped this book will answer the pur-
pose and help to lessen the prejudice against spiders, and lead
to a more general acquaintance with them, like the popular
knowledge of birds and butterflies. The characters used in
the descriptions are, as far as possible, those that can be seen
without microscopic examination and without much experience
in the handling of small animals. The illustrations, which show
the form and markings of every species, are from my own
drawings and photographs, a large part of them made new
for this book.

J. H. EMERTON.

APRIL, 1902.

iii

CONTENTS

INTRODUCTION   PAGE
    NUMBER AND NAMES OF SPIDERS vii
    ANATOMY viii
    SILK AND SPINNING ORGANS x
    COLORS AND MARKINGS xi
    HABITATS OF COMMON SPIDERS . . . . . xii–xiv
    COBWEBS xvi
    CATCHING AND PRESERVING SPIDERS xvii
KEY TO COMMON GROUPS OF SPIDERS xix
THE DRASSIDÆ 1–21
    CLUBIONA 15
THE DYSDERIDÆ 22
THE THOMISIDÆ 24–40
    MISUMENA 25
    XYSTICUS 30
    PHILODROMUS 35
THE ATTIDÆ 41–66
THE LYCOSIDÆ 67–90
    LYCOSA 68
    PARDOSA 78
    DOLOMEDES 85
    OCYALE 88
    OXYOPES 88
THE AGALENIDÆ 91–106
THE THERIDIDÆ 107–133
    THERIDIUM 110
    STEATODA 119
    PHOLCUS 128
    SCYTODES 131

PAGE

THE LINYPHIADÆ 134–153

    LINYPHIA 134

    ERIGONE 148

THE EPEIRIDÆ 154–204

    ROUND WEBS OF THE EPEIRIDÆ 155–159

    SPECIES OF EPEIRA 160–181

    THE THREE SPECIES OF THE GENUS ZILLA . . . 184

    ACROSOMA 188

    ARGIOPE 192–198

    TETRAGNATHA 198–204

THE CINIFLONIDÆ, OR CRIBELLATA 205–220

    DICTYNA 205

    AMAUROBIUS 213

    ULOBORUS 216

    HYPTIOTES 218

    FILISTATA 220

INDEX 223

INTRODUCTION

THIS book is designed to make the reader acquainted with the common spiders most likely to be found over a large part of the United States as far south as Georgia and as far west as the Rocky Mountains. Local collections show that in the neighborhood of any city in the country there are at least three or four hundred species of spiders ; but few such collections have been made, and it is not yet possible to tell all the kinds of spiders that live in any particular place, or how far any species extends over the country. The species which are here described and figured are all of them well known and have been described in other books. Rare and doubtful species are omitted, though some of these may in time prove to be among the most common. A large number of spiders are too small to be easily seen, and most of these are omitted, only a few representative species being described. Spiders have, unfortunately, no common names, except such indefinite ones as "the garden spider," "the black spider," "the jumping spider," and the like. Even "tarantula" has become only a nickname for any large spider. The names of spiders, like those of other animals, have been given to them independently by different persons, so that many of them have more than one name, and the more common the spider the larger the number of names. In this book only one name is usually given to each species, and the name used is one that has been published with a description of the species in some other well-known book. Readers who are interested in the names of species and in comparing the classifications of different naturalists are referred to a

"Catalogue of the Described Araneæ of Temperate North America," by George Marx, in the *Proceedings of the United States National Museum,* 1890, which is a useful index to what has been published on American spiders.

The front half of a spider's body, called the cephalothorax, contains in one piece the head and thorax, the only outward division between them being shallow grooves from the middle of the back to the front legs. In the middle of the cephalothorax is usually a groove or depression, under which, inside, is a muscle that moves the sucking apparatus by which food is drawn into the mouth. At the sides of the thoracic part are four pairs of legs, and on the head part are a pair of palpi and a pair of mandibles. The legs have seven joints : (1) the coxa, the thick basal joint, having little motion ; (2) the trochanter, a short joint moving very freely on the end of the coxa ; (3) the femur, the largest joint of the leg, moving with the trochanter in all directions ; (4) the patella, moving up and down on the end of the femur ; (5) the tibia, joined closely to the patella and moving with it up and down ; (6) the metatarsus ; and (7) the tarsus, moving together on the end of the tibia. The palpi are like small legs and have one less joint than the walking legs. The mandibles are close together at the front of the head (fig. 2). They are two-jointed, the basal joint stout and the end joint or claw slender and sharp-pointed. The claw has near its point a small hole, which is the outlet of the poison gland. The poison kills or disables the insects which are captured by the spider. Its effect on the human skin varies in different persons ; sometimes it has no effect at all ; oftener it causes some soreness and itching like the stings of mosquitoes and bees, and cases have been known in which it caused serious inflammation which lasted a long time. Spiders seldom bite, and only in defense, the bites so commonly charged to them being often the work of other animals.*

*The black widow spider *(Latrodectus mactans)* is the most poisonous North American spider; its bite has been known to be fatal to man.

On the front of the head are the eyes, usually eight in number, differing in size and arrangement according to the

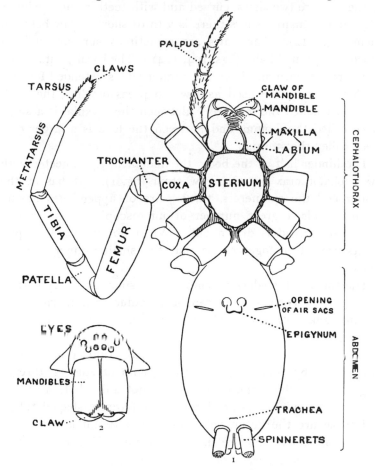

FIG. 1. Diagram of the under side of a spider, with the legs removed except one.
FIG. 2. Front of head, showing the eyes and mandibles.

kind of spider. The sight of spiders is distinct for only short distances. Spiders of middle size can see each other, and the insects which they eat, at a distance of four or five inches, but beyond that do not seem to see anything clearly. At the ends of the feet are two claws, curved and with teeth along the inner edge, and in many spiders there is a third shorter claw between them (fig. 212). The claws are sometimes surrounded by a brush of flattened hairs (figs. 104, 114). The basal joints of the palpi are flattened and have their inner edges extended forward so that they can be used as jaws to press or chew the food. These are called the maxillæ. Between the maxillæ is a small piece called the labium, and between the legs is a larger oval piece called the sternum.

The hinder half of the body, the abdomen, is connected with the cephalothorax by a narrow stem (fig. 1). It has at the hinder end the spinnerets, three pairs of appendages having at their ends a great number of microscopic tubes through which the thread is drawn out. When not in use the spinnerets are folded together, so that the smaller inner pair are concealed.

The thread of spiders resembles that spun by caterpillars in making their cocoons, and can be manufactured in the same way into silk cloth. The spider's thread is composed of a great number of finer threads passing from the body through separate tubes and uniting into one before they have time to dry. This can be seen by examining the attachments of spiders' threads to glass. All the spinning tubes are not alike, but on certain parts of the spinnerets are larger or differently shaped tubes, and these are the outlets of glands of different kinds in the spider's abdomen, and are used in making different kinds of threads for certain parts of the webs, nests, or cocoons.

In front of the spinnerets on the under side is a small opening to the tracheæ, or air-tubes (fig. 1). At the front of the abdomen on the under side is a transverse fold of the skin, at the ends of which are the openings of the air-sacs or lungs, and between them the opening of the reproductive organs (fig. 1). The latter is covered in females by an apparatus, sometimes large and complicated, called the epigynum. Its presence shows that the female is full grown. Young spiders do not have it. Male spiders have the ends of the palpi enlarged, and under the terminal joint what is known as the palpal organ, sometimes very complicated in shape. The presence of these organs shows that the male is full grown. Young males that have nearly reached maturity have the ends of the palpi simply enlarged. Male spiders almost always have the body smaller and the legs longer than females of the same species.

The colors of spiders are partly in the skin itself and partly in the hairs and scales that cover it. Almost all spiders are covered with hair of some kind, but in some species it is so fine and short that it has little effect on the color. In others the skin is entirely covered with hairs of various lengths and sometimes with scales somewhat like those of butterflies, flattened and feathered or toothed on the edges. The colors of spiders are very varied, and in many species, especially of the jumping spiders, as brilliant as those of butterflies. The most common colors are grays and browns, resembling the ground or plants and stones among which the spiders live. Sometimes the color is uniform all over the body, except that it is a little darker toward the head and the ends of the feet. The most common marking is a spot on the front of the abdomen over the spider's heart, sometimes merely a translucent part of the skin and sometimes a definite color spot darker in the middle and outlined with a lighter shade or white. The hinder half of the abdomen is often marked with several pairs of spots, becoming smaller toward the end, and these spots may be united into a pair of stripes or a more complicated pattern. (See figures.) The legs are often marked with rings of color, almost always at the ends of the joints.   Besides these common markings there are in some spiders strong contrasts of color, such as bright red or yellow spots on a black ground.   In the males, especially among the Attidæ, there are often shining scales that reflect different colors in a bright light, and tufts of black or white hairs about the head and front legs.

Spiders live in all kinds of places.   Certain species are attached to houses and seldom found far from them, and many of these occur over a large part of the world.   The light webs in the corners of rooms are chiefly the work of *Theridium tepidariorum* (p. 112), occasionally of *Steatoda borealis* (p. 119) and *Steatoda triangulosa* (p. 121).   In cellars the thin webs about the stairs and shelves are those of the long-legged *Pholcus phalangioides* (p. 129) or of *Linyphia nebulosa* or *minuta* (pp. 144, 145), and the thick flat webs in corners and between the beams are those of *Tegenaria derhamii* (p. 96).   On the outside of houses live two jumping spiders, the most common being *Epiblemum scenicum* (p. 60), a small gray species the color of weathered wood, and the other, *Marptusa familiaris* (p. 61). Some of the round-web spiders live in great numbers about houses.   The three brown species, *Epeira sclopetaria* (p. 160), *patagiata*, and *strix*, hide in cracks and at night make their round webs in porches, barns, and bridges.   In the northern part of the country *Epeira cinerea* (p. 165) has the same habit. *Epeira globosa* (p. 174) is often found on the outside of houses, and so are *Zilla atrica* and *Zilla x-notata* (p. 185).   *Amaurobius ferox* (p. 215), a large imported species, is sometimes found in cellars, and several Dictyna (p. 206) live in great numbers on the outside of houses, in corners of windows, under the edges of shingles, or in cracks of walls, spreading their webs wherever there is room for them and gathering dust so that they often make a distinct spot on the wall.   In the southern states *Filistata hibernalis* (p 220) is one of the most common

spiders about houses. Its webs often make a round spot of
dust a foot or more in diameter. Stones and sticks lying on
the ground furnish shelter for a great number of spiders.
Steatoda borealis (p. 119), *marmorata* (p. 121), and *guttata*
(p. 120) and *Asagena americana* (p. 122) are found in such
places, and so, especially in the South, is *Latrodectus mactans*
(p. 122). The large jumping spiders, *Phidippus mystaceus*
(p. 50) and *tripunctatus* (p. 51), make large nests of white
silk under stones near the ground. The ground spiders,
Drassus saccatus (p. 6), *Gnaphosa conspersa* (p. 2), and *Prosthesima atra* (p. 5), run on the ground and hide under stones.
Lycosa nidicola (p. 69), *Lycosa communis* (p. 75), *Lycosa pratensis* (p. 69), *polita* (p. 70), and *cinerea* (p. 74) are often found
under shelters of this kind. The crab spiders of the genus
Xysticus live under stones, but oftener under bark farther
from the ground.

In the summer, plants of all kinds from grass to trees are full
of spiders. The Lycosas (pp. 68 to 84) run among the short
grass. The small species of Linyphia (p. 134) and Erigone
(p. 148) make their flat webs close to the ground among small
plants. *Linyphia marginata, communis, coccinea,* and *phrygiana*
make theirs among plants and rocks, a foot or two above the
ground. The Theridiums (p. 110) live between leaves and on
the ends of twigs, covering them with webs that only show
when the dew is on them. *Agalena nævia* (pp. 91 to 95) makes
its flat webs on the grass and anywhere else where it can find a
place to fasten them. The jumping spiders (p. 41) run about
for their prey on plants, and some of them have silk nests
among the leaves. The Misumenas (p. 25) live among flowers
and wait for insects to alight within reach. The webs of
Dictyna (p. 206) are commonest on the ends of grass and
twigs, and are known by the dust that they gather. The
round-web spiders mature in the middle of the summer, and

then *Epeira trivittata* (p. 166) is found on all kinds of bushes and grass, and later *Epeira insularis* (p. 169) and *Epeira trifolium* (p. 171) in hidden nests near their webs. *Epeira angulata, sylvatica,* and *nordmanni* (p. 162) live among bushes and trees. *Cyclosa conica* (p. 183), *Acrosoma spinea* (p. 190), and Uloborus (p. 216) live among low bushes in openings of the woods. Hyptiotes (p. 218) lives among the lower dead branches of pines, perching on the end of a twig which it exactly matches in color.

The marshes are the home of great numbers of spiders. The Tetragnathas (p. 198) live there, especially along the streams and ditches. *Epeira gibberosa* (p. 175) and *placida* (p. 176) make their horizontal and oblique webs among the tall grass in open places. The two species of Argiope (pp. 193 to 198) swarm in marshes and open fields and in autumn become conspicuous by their size and bright colors, and when they disappear leave over winter their brown cocoons (pp. 197, 200) fastened to the grass.

The moss and dead leaves in the woods are alive with spiders ; even in summer some species always live there, and in winter the young of those that in warm weather live among the bushes find shelter where they can remain torpid through the cold season without freezing.

The eggs of spiders are covered with silk, forming a cocoon which varies much in shape and color in different species. Some spiders hang it in the web, others attach it to plants or stones, and others carry it about with them either in the mandibles or attached behind to the spinnerets. The young remain in the cocoon until they are able to run about, and after coming out of the cocoon keep together for a short time, sometimes in a web which they make in common, sometimes in a nest made by the mother, and in some species on the mother's back, but they soon scatter and hunt their own food or make cobwebs, according to the habits of the species.

Different kinds of spiders mature and breed at different times of the year, most of them living only one season. Those that mature late, like *Agalena nævia* and Argiope, pass the winter as eggs, while those that mature early, like *Epeira sclopetaria* and *Lycosa nidicola*, pass the winter half grown. Some species, like *Theridium tepidariorum* (p. 112), breed several times in the year, and old and young are found at all seasons.

The spiders are naturally divided into two groups of families: (1) the hunting spiders, which run on the ground or on plants, catching insects wherever they find them, or waiting among leaves and flowers until insects come within their reach; (2) the cobweb spiders, which make webs to catch insects and live all the time in the web or in a nest near it.

The hunting spiders include: (1) the Dysderidæ (p. 22), a few species with six eyes only and with four breathing holes at the front end of the abdomen; (2) the Drassidæ (p. 1), or ground spiders, which live among stones and dead leaves or among plants, making tubular nests and flat egg cocoons but no cobwebs; (3) the Thomisidæ (p. 24), the flat and crab-like spiders living on plants or under bark and stones; (4) the Attidæ (p. 41), the jumping spiders, with wide heads and large front eyes, many of them brightly colored and active in their habits; (5) the Lycosidæ (p. 67), the long-legged running spiders, living on the ground and, a few of them, in holes and carrying about their round egg cocoons attached to the spinnerets.

The cobweb spiders include: (1) the Agalenidæ (p. 91), making flat webs on grass or in corners of houses, with a tube at one side in which the spider lives; (2) the Therididæ (p. 107), round spiders with flat or irregular webs in corners and on plants; (3) the Linyphiadæ (p. 134), with flat webs, small spiders of a great number of species living near the ground and in shady places ; (4) the Epeiridæ (p. 154), the round-web spiders ; (5) the Cribellata, having a calamistrum (see p. 205) on the hind legs and making rough webs that gather dust.

Cobwebs are of four principal kinds :

1. The flat webs, closely woven of long threads crossed by finer ones in all directions and connected with a tubular nest where the spider hides, and from which it runs out on the upper side of the web after insects that may fall upon it. These are made by Agalena and Tegenaria (pp. 91 to 104).

2. The net-like webs, made of smooth threads in large meshes, sometimes in a flat or curved sheet held out by threads in all directions. The spider lives on the under side, back downward. These are made by Therididæ and Linyphiadæ (pp. 107, 134).

3. The round webs, made of threads radiating from a common center and crossed by circular loops and spirals, part of which are adhesive.

4. The webs of the Ciniflonidæ, composed in part of loose bands of silk (p. 205).

The simplest and best way to preserve spiders for examination is to put them in alcohol. It kills them immediately and keeps their form and markings and, to a great extent, their colors. They may be kept alive for a few days in glass bottles or jars. It is not necessary to make holes in the covers, or to feed the spiders often. They need water, and this can be furnished them conveniently by putting a piece of wet paper or rag in the bottle.

If one wishes to find what spiders live in his neighborhood, they must be looked for at all times and in all kinds of places. The house and cellar should be looked over and the spiders watched until they are fully grown. The outside of the house and fences should be looked over occasionally in the same way, only those spiders being taken that are full grown, unless they

are of new or rare kinds. A great many spiders may be found
on the garden fences of a shady street, especially in the early
summer and again in the autumn. At both seasons they are
more active in the middle of the day and more likely then
to be wandering about. The writer always carries two small
bottles, one a common homeopathic medicine vial, holding one
or two drams and half full of alcohol, the other a straight tube
vial, without any neck and about the same size, that is kept
always dry and occasionally wiped out to remove the threads
that are made in it. The dry bottle is placed quickly over the
spider and moved about until the spider is coaxed to go into it.
The bottle is then turned up and closed with a finger until the
other bottle can be uncorked and the spider shaken into the
alcohol. In the fields and along the country roads the stones
and sticks that have been lying for some time on the ground
should be carefully lifted and searched, both on the under surface and on the ground below. The stones and sticks should
be turned back into the same places so that other spiders
may find at once comfortable places to hide under. If they
are dropped on new ground, it may be a year before they
are fit to use again. Among trees and shrubs the best
things are to be found by moving slowly about and watching
for spiders, nests, and cobwebs without disturbing them. The
webs can be best seen when moving toward the light. The
greatest number of spiders can usually be found along paths
and the edges of woods, and paths through the woods are the
best places for many ground spiders.

Spiders should be looked for in the same way in grass, by
creeping along on the ground or by sitting down and watching
until something walks into view ; or the grass and weeds may
be swept with a cotton bag, fastened on a hoop like a dip net,
with a short handle, and the spiders picked out with a dry
bottle from among the leaves and insects that will be gathered

with them. Bushes may be swept in the same way, or may be shaken over an open umbrella, or a piece of cloth or paper. In winter, when spiders are torpid, great numbers can be found by sifting the dead leaves that have been lying for some years in the woods. A common coal sieve is fine enough to hold the leaves while the spiders and sticks and dirt pass through, and may be picked over on a cloth or carried home in a bag and examined in the house. The sifting should be repeated several times, as many of the spiders hold to threads among the leaves and become loosened only after much shaking.

In the following pages a general description is given of each family, followed by descriptions of the species belonging to it, with a figure of each species placed as near as possible to the description. In some cases, where the genera are large and well defined; separate descriptions are given of each genus, but where the genus is not easy to distinguish or represented by only a few species, there is no separate generic description, and the species are placed next to those of other genera to which they are most closely related. If the names of spiders are known, they can readily be found by the index at the end of the book. If information is sought about an unknown spider, the illustrations through the book furnish the most convenient index, as the general form and proportions of spiders and the arrangement of their eyes usually show to what family they belong. The ground spiders and those without cobwebs are described first, and the sedentary species living in webs in the last half of the book. Readers unfamiliar with the subject are advised to read first the descriptions of the families and compare with them the spiders that they find in their own neighborhoods. The figures are in most cases enlarged for the sake of distinctness, and spiders of much smaller size must be looked for.

KEY TO COMMON GROUPS OF SPIDERS

§No.	Characteristic	Group	see
	With a cribellum*	(*Ciniflonidae*)	p. 205
	Without a cribellum		§1
§1	Tarsi with two claws		§2
	Tarsi with three claws		§5
§2	First and second pairs of legs stouter and longer than third and fourth pairs, and extending sidewise	Crab spiders (*Thomisidae*)	p. 24
§3	Eyes unequal in size and arranged in three or four rows	Jumping spiders (*Attidae*)	p. 41
	Eyes equal in size and usually arranged in two rows		§4
§4	Fore spinnerets widely separated	The drassids (*Drassidae*)	§1
	Fore spinnerets contiguous	Crab spiders (*Thomisidae*)	p. 24
§5	Without eyes	Cave spiders (*Linyphiidae*)	p. 134
	With eyes		§6
§6	With six eyes	Funnel-web spiders (*Agelenidae*)	p. 91
	With eight eyes		§7
§7	Eyes similar in color		§8
	Eyes dissimilar in color		§11
§8	Eyes pearly white		§9
	Eyes dark in color		§10

*A peculiar spinning organ located in front of the spinnerets and described on page 205. A composite group including the families *Uloboridae, Amaurobiidae, Filistatidae,* and *Dictynidae.*

§No.	Characteristic	Group	see
§9	Hind spinnerets very long	Funnel-web spiders (*Agelenidae*)	p. 91
	Hind spinnerets short	Orb weavers (*Argiopidae, Epeiridae*)	p. 154
§10	Eyes equal in size		§12
	Eyes unequal in size	Wolf spiders (*Lycosidae*)	p. 67
§11	Tarsi of fourth pair of legs armed on inside with a row of from six to ten strongly curved setae	Comb-footed spiders (*Therididae*)	p. 107
	Tarsi not so armed		§13
§12	Lateral condyle of chelicerae present	Funnel-web spiders (*Agelenidae*)	p. 91
	Lateral condyle of chelicerae lacking		§13
§13	Tarsi of fourth pair of legs clothed beneath with numerous serrated bristles	Orb weavers (*Argiopidae, Epeiridae*)	p. 154
	Tarsi not so clothed	Cave spiders (*Linyphiidae*)	p. 134

THE COMMON SPIDERS

THE DRASSIDÆ

THE Drassidæ, like the Lycosidæ (p. 67), are ground spiders, though some genera, like Anyphæna (p. 12) and Clubiona (p. 15), are equally common in summer on bushes. They make nests in the form of a bag or flattened tube, but no cobwebs for catching insects, and are commonly found running about among dead leaves and short grass and sometimes even on bare ground and sand. In form they are usually two or three times as long as they are wide, like the Lycosidæ (p. 67), but more often flattened on the back. The legs differ but little in length, and the first and second pairs are directed forward, the third and fourth backward. Their hairs and spines are short, giving them a smooth, velvet-like appearance. The feet have two claws, with a brush of flattened hairs under them, like the Thomisidæ and Attidæ (p. 41), but unlike the Lycosidæ (p. 67), which have three claws. The mandibles are large and strong and are together as wide as the head. The eyes are all about the same size and arranged in two rows of about the same length and not far apart, but between different species there are slight differences in their arrangement. The colors are usually dull gray, brown, and black, with few markings or none. A few species are very brightly marked, as in Micaria (p. 9) and Pœcilochroa (p. 4).

There are three groups among the Drassidæ :

1. Prosthesima, Gnaphosa, Pœcilochroa, Pythonissa, and Drassus, which are generally dark in color and flattened above,

with the cephalothorax narrow in front and the eyes covering about half the width of the head and differing in their relative positions among the different genera.   The labium is long and the maxillæ slightly widened at the end, or with the outer

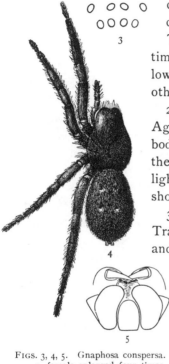

corners rounded off and sometimes a crease or depression in the middle. The joints of the first legs are sometimes thickened in the middle. The lower spinnerets are longer than the others and flat on the end.

2. Micaria, Geotrecha, Phrurolithus, Agrœca, and Anyphæna, in which the body is less flattened, the legs longer, and the movements quicker.   The colors are lighter and more varied.   The labium is short and the maxillæ with straight sides.

3. Clubiona, Chiracanthium, and Trachelas, in which the colors are plain and light, the eyes spread over more than half the front of the head and close to its front edge.   The labium is as long as it is in Drassus, but contracted at the base.   The maxillæ are narrow in the middle and flat and wide at the ends.

FIGS. 3, 4, 5.   Gnaphosa conspersa. — 4, female enlarged four times. 3, the eyes seen from in front. 5, the maxillæ, labium, and ends of the mandibles from below.

Gnaphosa conspersa. — Half an inch long and rusty black in color.   In alcohol the legs and cephalothorax are dark reddish brown and the abdomen gray.   The whole body is covered with fine black hairs.   The cephalothorax and abdomen are about the same size and a little flattened.   The legs are stout and all nearly the same length.   The upper row of eyes is nearly straight and the lateral eyes much farther from the middle pair than these are from each other (fig. 3). The middle eyes are oval and oblique, diverging toward the front. The maxillæ are large, and rounded on the outer corners. The mandibles are large and strong, with a wide, flat, serrated tooth (fig. 5) under the claw. The cocoon is white and flat, with a diameter as great as the length of the spider. The female, as far as I have observed, makes no nest, but partly lines with silk a shallow hole, in which she nurses her cocoon. It lives under stones and leaves as far north as the White Mountains and west to the Rocky Mountains in British Columbia, and on the Pacific coast in Oregon. A smaller and similar species, *Gnaphosa brumalis*, lives on the top of Mount Washington and as far north as Labrador.

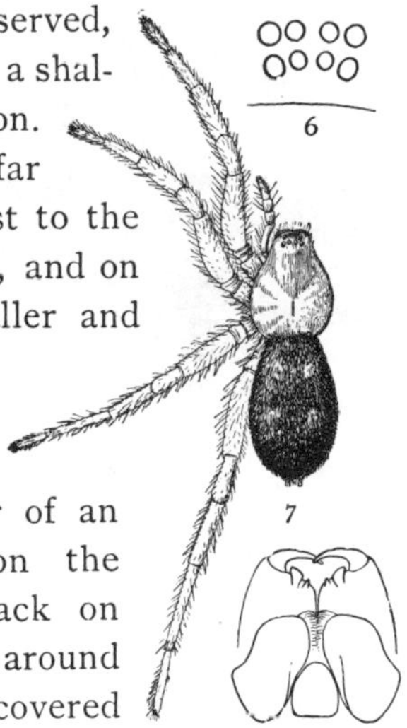

Pythonissa imbecilla. — About quarter of an inch long, bright orange brown on the cephalothorax and legs and blue black on the abdomen, with a few white hairs around the muscular spots. The legs are covered with fine long hairs a little darker in color than the skin. The cephalothorax is wide behind and more narrowed in front than in Gnaphosa. The eyes (fig. 6) are close together, and the lateral eyes of both rows are larger than the middle pairs and a little farther back on the head. The maxillæ (fig. 8) are short and wide, and bent toward each other so that they nearly meet in front of the labium. The front edges are nearly straight and the outer corners only slightly rounded. The sternum is wide and almost circular. The tarsus of the female palpi tapers from the base to the tip.

Figs. 6, 7, 8. Pythonissa imbecilla, female enlarged four times. 6, the eyes seen from in front. 8, the maxillæ, labium, and ends of mandibles from below.

Pœcilochroa variegata. — This is one of the most brightly colored of the family. The cephalothorax is bright orange,

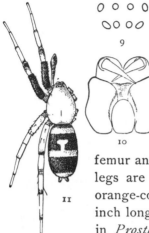

a little darker toward the eyes. The abdomen is black, with three transverse white stripes and a T-shaped white mark between the first and second stripes. On the front of the abdomen the white stripes are sometimes tinged with orange. The femora of the first and second legs are black. The distal end of the femur and both ends of the tibia of the fourth legs are black. Other parts of the legs are orange-colored. The female is quarter of an inch long. The cephalothorax is narrower than in *Prosthesima atra* and *Gnaphosa conspersa*, and the sternum longer and narrower. The maxillæ (fig. 10) are long and widened at the outer corners. The two rows of eyes (fig. 9) are almost straight, the upper one longer than the lower.

FIGS. 9, 10, 11. Pœcilochroa variegata. — 11, female enlarged four times. 9, eyes from in front. 10, maxillæ, labium, and ends of mandibles from below.

Pœcilochroa bilineata. — A little smaller than *P. variegata*, but with the abdomen longer. Cephalothorax and abdomen both white at the sides and in the middle, with two black stripes from the eyes nearly to the spinnerets. The abdomen is covered with long hairs, black in the stripes and silvery white in the light portions. The legs are gray, with white hairs. The under side is light gray, with two black stripes at the sides of the abdomen that do not quite reach the spinnerets. The spinnerets are unusually

FIG. 12.   FIG. 13.

Pœcilochroa bilineata. — Upper and under views of female without the legs, enlarged four times.

long. The eyes are arranged as in *variegata*, the middle eyes being even more distinctly farther apart than they are from the lateral eyes.

Prosthesima atra. — Black, and less than a third of an inch long. It may be mistaken for a small *Gnaphosa conspersa*, but, besides the small size, the abdomen is usually longer in proportion and the head is narrower than in Gnaphosa. The color is usually a deeper black and less likely to be gray in the young and rusty in the old, but the feet and under side of the abdomen are sometimes yellowish in the young. The eyes (fig. 14) are closer together and the two rows more nearly of the same length. In alcohol the cephalothorax and legs are blacker than in Gnaphosa and less brown. The maxillæ (fig. 15) are a little longer and less rounded at the outer corners than in Gnaphosa or Pythonissa. The mandibles (fig. 15) are without the large teeth under the claw that Gnaphosa and Pythonissa have, and they are turned forward more than in those genera. It lives on the ground and under stones. The cocoon is white or pink, attached by the under surface, with the upper side convex and thickened in the middle, sometimes with a little dirt attached to it.

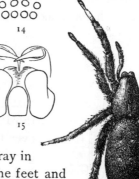

FIGS. 14, 15, 16. Prosthesima atra.— 16, female enlarged four times. 14, eyes seen from in front. 15, maxillæ, labium, and ends of mandibles from below.

Prosthesima ecclesiastica. — Black, with white markings along the middle of the back. One-third of an inch long, a little

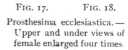

FIG. 17.   FIG. 18.
Prosthesima ecclesiastica.— Upper and under views of female enlarged four times.

larger than *P. atra* and smaller than *Gnaphosa conspersa*. The cephalothorax is proportionally longer and narrower and the sternum narrower and less round than in *P. atra* (fig. 18). The cephalothorax is dull black at the sides, with a whitish stripe in the middle. The legs are also dull black and, like the cephalothorax, turn brown in alcohol. The abdomen is black, with a bright white stripe in the middle that extends from the front end about two-thirds its length; and at the hinder end, just over the spinnerets, is another white mark (fig. 17). The under side of the abdomen is dark at the sides and light in the middle. The eyes and maxillæ are as in *P. atra*, the maxillæ a little less rounded at the ends.

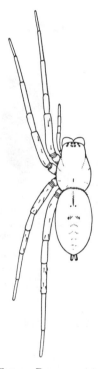

FIG. 19. Drassus saccatus. — Female enlarged three times. For eyes and mouth parts see figs. 1 and 2 in Introduction.

Drassus saccatus. — Four-fifths of an inch long, and pale, without markings. The head is shorter and wider than in *Gnaphosa conspersa* and *Prosthesima atra*, and the eyes cover a larger part of the head. Both rows of eyes (figs. 2, 19) are curved, with the middle highest. The middle upper pair are oval and turned apart toward the front. The lateral eyes are twice their diameter from the middle pair. The maxillæ (fig. 1) are widened at the ends on both sides. The labium is as wide as it is long, narrowed toward the end but truncated at the tip. The color is light gray, with short fine hairs all over the body. The front of the head, the feet, and the mandibles and maxillæ are darker and browner. The abdomen is marked only with the usual four muscular spots and sometimes a few transverse dark markings toward the hinder end. The legs are long and tapering in both sexes. The male is smaller and more slender than the female, and the male palpi are long, with the end very little enlarged. They live under stones, and make a large transparent bag of silk in which the female makes her cocoon of eggs, and stays with it until the young come out. Early in the summer a male and female often live together in the nest, even before the female is mature.

Geotrecha crocata. — Black, with the ends of the legs light yellow and a bright red spot on the end of the abdomen. It is about a third of an inch long. The legs are slender and the body is not at all flattened. The cephalothorax is two-thirds as wide as long, oval behind and narrowed in front of the legs, where the sides of the head are nearly parallel. The abdomen is oval and nearly twice as long as wide. The spinnerets are so far under the body that they show but little from above. At the front end of the abdomen is a spot larger below than above, where the skin is thicker and harder and browner in color than the rest. The cephalothorax is dark brown or black, as are also the femora of all the legs and of the palpi. The ends of the third and fourth legs are a lighter brown and the ends of the first and second legs and palpi light yellow. The abdomen is deep black except a bright red spot at the hinder end, which varies in size, is sometimes broken into several spots, or is sometimes wanting altogether. The eyes (fig. 20) are near together, the upper row curved

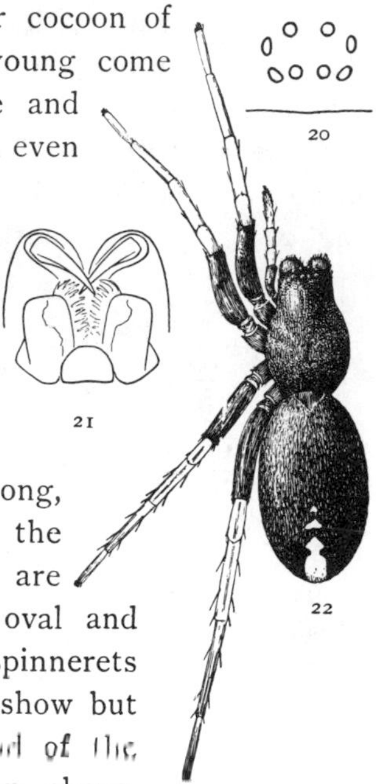

Figs. 20, 21, 22. Geotrecha crocata. — 22, female enlarged four times. 20, eyes seen from in front. 21, maxillæ, labium, and ends of mandibles from below.

down at the ends. The maxillæ are straight, with the sides
nearly parallel, and the labium is shorter than wide. The
males are usually smaller than the females and have the red
spot larger. These spiders live among stones in dry open
places. They are easily alarmed and move very rapidly. The
flat, parchment-like cocoons found on stones are probably made
by this species.

Geotrecha bivittata. — The same size as *G. crocata* but much
lighter colored, and with two white stripes across the abdomen
(fig. 23). The cephalothorax is a little narrower behind than

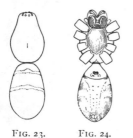

it is in *crocata*. Its color varies from
orange to dark brown. The femora of
all the legs are striped lengthwise with
brown and yellow. The hind legs are
brown, with a little yellow on the upper
side of the patella and tibia. The other
legs are yellow, sometimes with brown
stripes on the under side. The white
marks on the abdomen extend underneath halfway to the middle line. The
sternum and under side are light brown.

FIG. 23.   FIG. 24.

Geotrecha bivittata. — Upper
and under views of female
enlarged four times.

It lives under leaves at all seasons.

Micaria longipes or **aurata.** — A quarter of an inch long or less,
and resembling an ant both in size and color (fig. 28). The
cephalothorax is twice as long as wide, and only a little widened
in the middle. It is highest in the middle, curving downward
at both ends. The front row of eyes (fig. 25) is nearly straight
and the upper row curved, with the middle eyes highest and
the eyes all farther apart than in the lower row. The abdomen is one-half longer than the cephalothorax and about as
wide, blunt at both ends and drawn in a little at the sides and
above at a point a third of its length from the front. The
legs are long and slender, the fourth pair longest. The colors

are light yellow brown, with gray hairs and scales which on the abdomen have green and red metallic reflections. The legs are darker from before backward, the front pair all light yellow except the femur, and the third and fourth pairs with longitudinal brown stripes that nearly cover the tarsal joints. The abdomen has a pair of transverse white stripes near the constricted part and another pair less distinct at the front end. The under side is as dark as the upper. The white markings extend underneath halfway to the middle line. The maxillæ are nearly straight on the outer edge and a little widened toward each other at the ends. The labium is narrowed at the end and a little longer than wide (fig. 26).

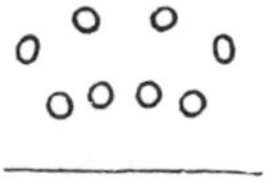

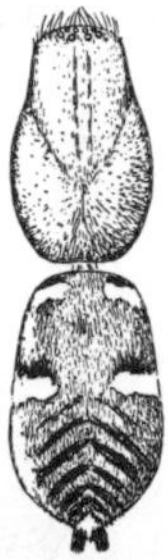

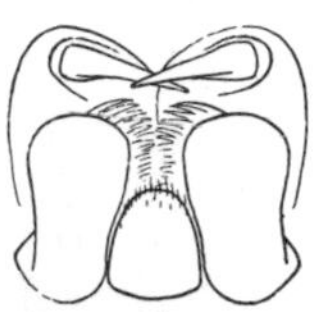

There is an orange-colored Micaria from Long Island, N.Y., and farther south (probably what is described by Hentz under the name *Herpyllus auratus*), that seems to belong to this species (fig. 27). Its size and markings are the same, and the epigynum is like that of *longipes*. The cephalothorax, abdomen, and femora of all the legs are bright orange color, with brilliant yellow and green reflections. The spinnerets are black, and there are five or six transverse black marks on the hinder half of the abdomen and some irregular black spots around the white bands.

Phrurolithus alarius. — A small and very active spider marked with gray and white and having on the abdomen iridescent green scales (fig. 31).

FIGS. 25, 26, 27, 28. Micaria longipes. — 28, Male enlarged four times. 25, eyes seen from in front. 26, maxillæ, labium, and ends of mandibles from below. 27, Southern variety, Micaria aurata. Colored orange, with black and white markings.

The cephalothorax is nearly as wide behind as it is long.   The
head is about half as wide as the thorax.   The eyes (fig. 30)
are large for so small a spider, and cover more than half

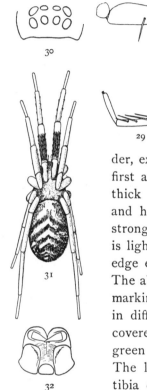

30

31

32

Figs. 29, 30, 31, 32. Phrurolithus alarius. — 31,
female in a natural posi-
tion, with legs drawn up
over the back, enlarged
eight times.   29, one of
the front legs to show
spines.   30, eyes from
in front.   32, maxillæ,
labium, and ends of
mandibles.

the width of the head.   The
middle eyes of the upper
row are oval and turned obliquely, diverging toward the
front.   The labium is short
and the maxillæ straight, as
in Agrœca and Anyphæna,
but wider at the base (fig. 32).
The legs are long and slen-
der, except the tibia and metatarsus of the
first and second pairs, which are twice as
thick as the same joints of the other legs
and have on the under side two rows of
strong spines (fig. 29).   The cephalothorax
is light yellowish, with a black line on the
edge each side, and two light gray stripes.
The abdomen is gray, with transverse white
markings that vary greatly in size and shape
in different individuals.   The abdomen is
covered with scales that change from grayish
green to pink with the motions of the spider.
The legs are pale, except the patella and
tibia of the first pair, which are black or
dark gray, with the tip of the tibia white.
The tibia and patella of the second pair are
marked with lighter gray in the same way.
It lives among stones in open ground, and
runs short distances with great swiftness.
When still it lies close to a stone, with the
tibiæ drawn up over the back.

Agrœca pratensis. — A little light-colored spider, resembling the next species, *Anyphœna incerta*. It is about a fifth of an inch long. The cephalothorax is wide behind and low in front and highest near the dorsal groove. The head is contracted in front of the legs more than it is in *incerta*. The front row of eyes is nearly straight, the middle pair only a little the higher (fig. 33). The upper row is longer and more curved, with all the eyes about the same distance apart, the middle pair not so much separated as in *incerta*. The abdomen is widest behind, but not as wide as in *incerta*. The spinnerets are two-jointed, as in Anyphæna. The legs are long, the fourth pair longest, and are a little thicker than those of *incerta*. The coxæ of the hind legs almost touch, and the sternum is short and nearly round (fig. 36). The labium is short and the maxillæ straight, as in Anyphæna. The cephalothorax, legs, and mouth parts are light brownish yellow. The cephalothorax has a fine dark line on each side and two broken longitudinal stripes made up of gray marks radiating from the dorsal groove. The abdomen has two rows of gray oblique markings on a light ground. The general appearance is like a small Lycosa. It lives among leaves and short grass. There is little difference between male and female.

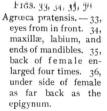

FIGS. 33, 34, 35, 36. Agrœca pratensis. — 33, eyes from in front. 34, maxillæ, labium, and ends of mandibles. 35, back of female enlarged four times. 36, under side of female as far back as the epigynum.

Anyphæna incerta. — About a fifth of an inch long, light yellow, with gray markings. The cephalothorax is three-quarters as wide as long, rounded at the sides and highest in the middle. The front of the head is very low, so that the eyes nearly

touch the mandibles. The front row of eyes is nearly straight.
The upper row is longer and more curved, with the middle eyes

highest and farthest apart (fig. 39).
The abdomen is large in the female,
widest behind the middle, and a little
pointed behind. The labium is not
longer than wide, and the maxillæ are
straight, with the sides parallel. The
sternum is oval, not so short and wide
as in *pratensis*. The opening of the
air-tubes is halfway between the epigynum and spinnerets (fig. 38), instead of
just in front of the spinnerets, as it is in
most spiders. The spinnerets are two-jointed.
The legs are slender and tapering, the fourth
longest in females and the first in males. The
cephalothorax has two longitudinal broken
gray bands. The abdomen has a double row
of spots in the middle and oblique rows of
smaller spots each side. The oblique lines
of spots extend under the abdomen halfway
to the middle.

Anyphæna calcarata. — The same size and
color as *A. incerta*, with longer legs. The
markings are the same in both species.
The plainest difference between the females
is in the epigynum, the hard and dark parts
of which are larger and longer in *incerta*.
Another slight difference is in the shape
of the sternum, which in *calcarata* extends
farther between the hind legs (fig. 42). In
incerta it is more pointed at the hinder end
and shorter (fig. 38). The difference between

FIGS. 37, 38, 39, 40, 41.
Anyphæna incerta. —
37, palpus of male.
38, under side of fe-
male as far forward as
end of sternum. 39,
eyes from in front.
40, female enlarged
four times. 41, max-
illæ, labium, and ends
of mandibles.

the length of the legs in the two species, which is slight in the females, is greater in the males, the legs of *calcarata* being the longer. The palpi of the males differ considerably. In *incerta* (fig. 37) the tibia of the palpus has a large process on the outer side close to the tarsus and extending

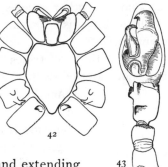
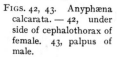
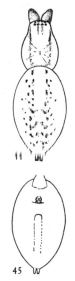

along its edge a third of its length. In *calcarata* (fig. 43) the corresponding process is small and does not lap over the tarsus. The coxæ of the third and fourth legs of the male *calcarata* have little processes on the under side (fig. 42), one on the fourth and two on the third. These do not occur in *incerta*. It lives on plants like *saltabunda* (p. 14).

FIGS. 42, 43. Anyphæna calcarata. — 42, under side of cephalothorax of female. 43, palpus of male.

Anyphæna rubra. — Larger than the other species, with the legs shorter. The female is about a third of an inch long, with the abdomen longer and narrower than in *incerta* or *saltabunda*. The opening of the air-tubes (fig. 45) is farther forward than usual, twice as far from the spinnerets as from the epigynum. The legs are comparatively short, the longest, the fourth, being about as long as the body. The maxillæ are a little widened at the end. The sternum is widest at the second legs and narrows to a point behind. The head is a little wider than usual, and the whole appearance more like

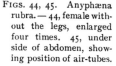

FIGS. 44, 45. Anyphæna rubra. — 44, female without the legs, enlarged four times. 45, under side of abdomen, showing position of air-tubes.

Clubiona than the other species.   The color is the usual pale
yellow, a little brownish on the head and legs, and with two
longitudinal stripes on the cephalothorax.   The abdomen is
nearly white, with two stripes made up of gray spots, and
scattered spots at the sides.   The spots turn red in alcohol.

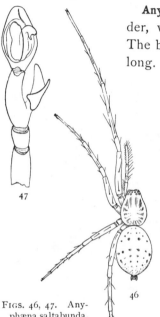

47

FIGS. 46, 47.   Any-
phæna saltabunda.
— 46, female en-
larged six times.
47, palpus of male.

Anyphæna saltabunda. — A pale short spider, with long and slender legs (fig. 46).
The body is an eighth to a sixth of an inch
long.   The abdomen is oval, two-thirds as
wide as long, and nearly as high as it
is wide.   The cephalothorax is three-
fourths as wide as long, widest across
the dorsal groove and narrowing gradually to half as wide in front.   The
eyes of the upper row are twice as
large as those of the front row.   The
first legs are longest in both sexes,
measuring in the female over twice
the length of the body and in the
males three times.   The spines are
very long on the legs and palpi but
only a little darker in color.   The
general color is pale yellow or white,
with two broken gray stripes on the cephalothorax and two middle and several lateral
rows of light gray spots on the abdomen.
The spinnerets are slender and two-jointed.   The opening of
the air-tubes is halfway between the spinnerets and the
epigynum.   The palpi of the male (fig. 47) are long and
slender, and the tibia is slightly curved and has a large thin
process on the outer side.

THE GENUS CLUBIONA

These spiders are all pale and most of them without markings. The eyes are close to the front edge of the head and cover more than half its width (figs. 50, 54, 56). The upper row is longer and the eyes larger and the middle pair farthest apart. The distance between this pair varies according to the species. In *crassipalpis* and *canadensis* it is little more than that between the middle and lateral eyes, while in *rubra* it is nearly twice as great. The mandibles of the females are swelled at the base in front, and this swelling is greatest in *canadensis* (fig. 55). The mandibles of the males are longer and are shaped in a variety of ways according to the species. The shape of the epigynum is indistinct and variable, and females of different species are difficult to distinguish. The females of *ornata* and *excepta* are known by their markings and those of *rubra* by their size and resemblance to the male.

FIG. 48.   Female Clubiona crassipalpis, enlarged four times.

The females of *crassipalpis* and *tibialis* are doubtful. The palpal organs and male palpi are of great variety and distinguish the males of all species without much difficulty.

The Clubionas live in flat tubes of silk on leaves of low plants in summer and under bark and stones at all seasons.

Clubiona crassipalpis. — A quarter of an inch long and pale, without markings. The head is sometimes a little darker than

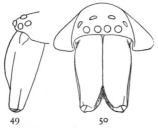

the rest of the body, and the mandibles and ends of the male palpi are always darker. The eyes of the upper row are almost equidistant, the middle pair only a little farther apart than they are from the lateral eyes. The mandibles of the male (figs. 49, 50) are elongated as usual, narrowed toward the end, and thickened in front just above the middle. On the outer side in front is a sharp ridge that extends from the base of the claw halfway up the mandible. The inner edges of the mandibles are thin and inclined backward toward the mouth, but there is no line or ridge between the thick and thin portions as in some other species. The palpi of the male (fig. 51) have the patella and tibia both short. The tibia is widened on the outer side and laps over the tarsus,

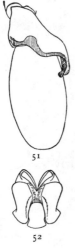

FIGS. 49, 50, 51, 52. Clubiona crassipalpis.—49, head and mandibles of male from the left side. 50, head and mandibles of male from in front. 51, palpus of male. 52, maxillæ, labium, and ends of mandibles.

FIGS. 53, 54. Clubiona tibialis. — 53, end of palpus of male, showing large tibia. 54, head and mandibles of male.

extending in a blunt hook for half its length.

Clubiona tibialis. — Quarter of an inch long, the same size and color as *crassipalpis*, with no markings and no dark color except on the mandibles and male palpi. The middle eyes are a little farther apart than in *crassipalpis*. The male mandibles (fig. 54) are narrower than in *crassipalpis* and without the sharp ridge on the outer side, but on the inside they are sharply hollowed out with a ridge between the thick outer and thin inner portions. The male palpi (fig. 53) have the patella about as long as wide, as it is in *crassipalpis* and *canadensis*, but the tibia is very large, with a hook in the usual place on the outer side and a much larger process, which extends forward over the tarsus. The tarsus is long and thickened in the middle where it rests against the process of the tibia.

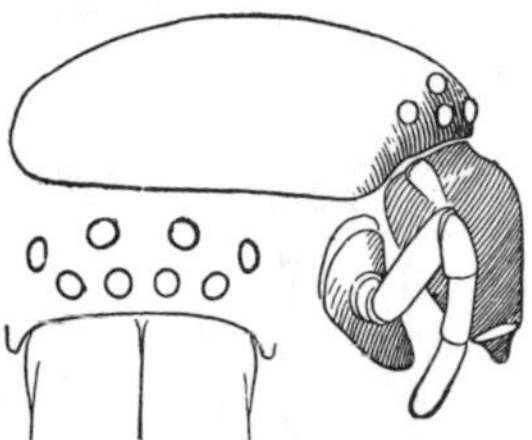

Clubiona canadensis. — Quarter of an inch long and without markings. The upper eyes are nearly equidistant, as they are in *crassipalpis*, but the legs and palpi are shorter. The male mandibles (fig. 56) are much like those of *crassipalpis*, but have not so sharp a ridge on the outer side. The male palpi (fig. 57) have the patella longer than wide and the tibia wider than long, with two processes on the outer side. The upper tibial process is a simple point extending along the outer side of the tarsus for quarter of its length. The under process is twice as long, with a projecting corner at its base and running forward to a sharp point, with a round notch halfway between the point and base. The female has the head wider and the mandibles very much swelled in front at the base (fig. 55). The fourth leg is longest and about as long as the body.

FIGS. 55, 56, 57. Clubiona canadensis. — 55, head of female, showing the swelled mandibles. 56, head and mandibles of male. 57, palpus of male.

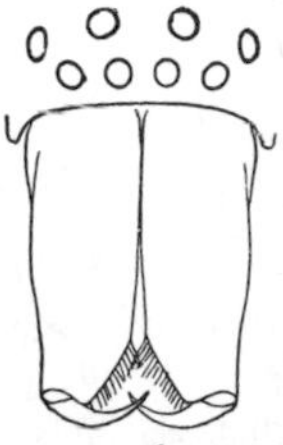

Clubiona rubra. — Smaller than the other species, a sixth to a fifth of an inch long. Cephalothorax light yellow brown, darker toward the front. Abdomen pale in front and darkened with brownish red at the sides and behind and along the middle of the back. The hind middle eyes are nearly twice as far apart as they are from the lateral eyes. The fourth legs are longest in both sexes, and there is little difference in the length of the legs of the

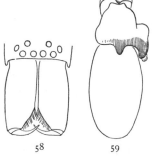

FIGS. 58, 59. Clubiona rubra. — 58, front of head and mandibles of male. 59, palpus of male.

two sexes. The mandibles of the female are but little swelled in front, not much more than those of the male, and the male mandibles (fig. 58) are only a little narrowed at the ends. The male palpi (fig. 59) have the tibia very much widened on the outer side, with a short tooth in the middle and two larger short processes on the outer side. The palpal organ has a large dark-colored process in the middle. The epigynum is pointed behind, with a notch in the middle and two black spots under the skin toward the front of the abdomen.

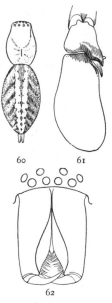

FIGS. 60, 61, 62. Clubiona ornata. — 60, back of female enlarged four times to show markings. 61, palpus of male. 62, front of head and mandibles of male.

Clubiona ornata. — This is one of the few Clubionas that have markings on the abdomen. The general color is pale as usual, but the abdomen has a dark stripe in the middle, broken into spots behind and bordered by pale yellow. At the sides are oblique dark and light transverse markings. These marks are of different sizes in different individuals and connected in different ways. The length is from a third to half an inch. The abdomen is wide across the middle and more pointed behind than in most species. The front middle eyes are about as far apart as in *tibialis* and nearer than in *rubra*. The mandibles are not much swelled in front. The legs of the male are longer than those of the female, with the first pair longest, while in the female the fourth pair is longest. The male mandibles (fig. 62) are narrow at the end and hollowed on the inner edges as in *tibialis*, with a sharp ridge between the thick and the thin portions. The male palpi (fig. 61) have two processes on the outer side of the tibia longer than in *rubra* and shorter than in *canadensis*. The tibia is a little widened toward the end and curved outward.

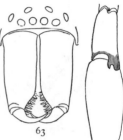

FIGS. 63, 64, 65. Clubiona excepta. — 63, front of head and mandibles of male. 64, palpus of male. 65, back of female enlarged four times to show markings.

Clubiona excepta. — A third of an inch long and with very distinct gray markings on the abdomen. The cephalothorax is light yellow brown, and the legs are more deeply colored with yellow than in most species. The abdomen is white, with sometimes a yellow mark on the front of the abdomen, and on the hinder half of the abdomen is a middle row of gray spots and a row of larger transverse spots on each side. The fourth legs are longest in both sexes. The male palpi have the tibia longer than usual and patella and tibia about the same length. The tibia has a small process with two teeth (fig. 64). The tarsus is oval and narrow and the palpal organ small.

Trachelas ruber. — One-third of an inch long, with the cephalothorax short and wide like Clubiona, and the deep orange-brown

color of Dysdera.   The cephalothorax is almost as wide as long,
and widest opposite the second legs.   The head is three-
quarters as wide as the thorax and as
high in the middle halfway between

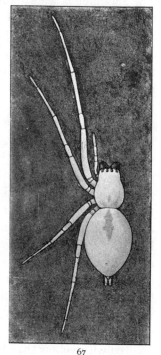

the eyes and the dorsal
groove.   The front of
the head is low, as in
Clubiona.   The front
row of eyes is a
little curved, so
that the middle
pair are half
their diameter
higher than the
lateral.   The
upper row is
much longer
and the lateral
eyes are farther
from the mid-
dle than these
are from each
other.   The

FIG. 66.   Tra-
chelas ruber,
enlarged four
times.

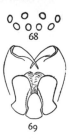

67

labium and maxillæ are like those of
Clubiona and the palpi very slender.
The first pair of legs are thicker than
the others and as long as the fourth.
The second pair are also somewhat
thickened.   The legs are orange
brown, darkest on the front pair.   The cephalothorax is dark brown and finely roughened over the
whole surface, without hairs except in front.   The abdomen is
pale, with no markings except over the dorsal vessel and the

FIGS. 67, 68, 69. Chi-
racanthium viri-
de. — 67, female
enlarged four
times.   68, eyes
from in front.
69, maxillæ, labi-
um, and mandi-
bles from below.

muscular spots. Some light-colored individuals have all the colors paler. Under stones and leaves.

Chiracanthium viride. — This has the color and general appearance of the Clubionas, but the legs are longer and the first legs are considerably longer than the fourth. The body is shorter and the abdomen is wider and thicker in the middle. The female (fig. 67) is a third of an inch long and the front legs two-fifths of an inch. The eyes (fig. 68) are arranged as in Clubiona. The maxillæ and labium are like those of Clubiona, but the sternum is shorter and rounder. The head is but little narrowed and the eyes cover almost its whole width. The upper spinnerets are longer than the lower and distinctly two-jointed. The spines of the legs are small and inconspicuous. The color in life is greenish white, the mandibles brown, and the stripe over the dorsal vessel darker than the rest of the abdomen.

The male has the front legs nearly three times as long as the body, though the other legs are not much longer than in the female. The mandibles are also elongated, as in the males of Clubiona. The male palpi have the tarsus long, with a pointed process that extends backward over the tibia between two processes on that joint.

THE DYSDERIDÆ

THE Dysderidæ are a small family of spiders resembling in their general appearance the Drassidæ, but differing from them in several important characters. They have only six eyes instead of the usual eight, and they have four breathing holes in the front of the abdomen, two of them leading to the usual lungs and the others to the air-tubes, which in most spiders open just in front of the spinnerets.

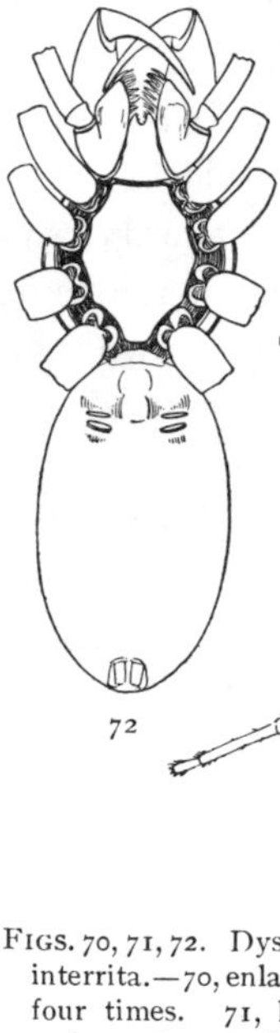

Dysdera interrita. — Six eyes close together on the front of the head. Length half an inch, with the abdomen a little longer than the cephalothorax. The coxæ and patellæ are unusually long, especially on the front legs, and the tarsi are unusually short (fig. 70). The mandibles are long and inclined forward. The maxillæ are long, a little widened in the middle and pointed at the ends. The labium is long and narrow, and forked at the end (fig. 72). The skin around the base of the legs is thick and hard, so that the sternum appears to extend between them (fig. 72). There are two tracheal openings just behind

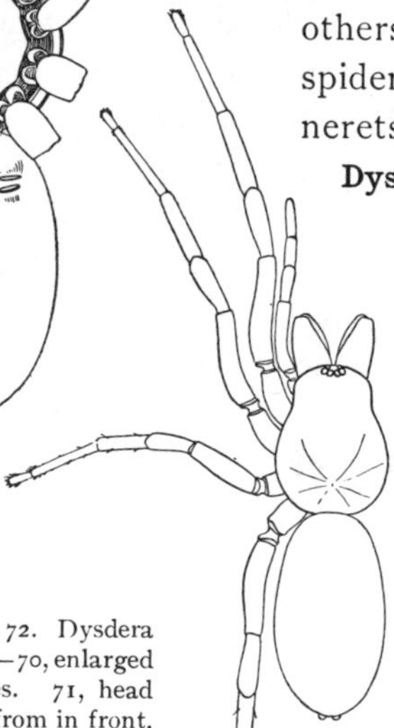

FIGS. 70, 71, 72. Dysdera interrita.—70, enlarged four times. 71, head and eyes from in front. 72, under side enlarged six times.

72

70

71

the openings of the lungs. The cephalothorax and legs are orange brown, darker toward the front. The abdomen is the same color, but so pale as to be almost white.

Ariadne bicolor. — Six eyes in three pairs, the side pairs separated by their diameter from the middle pair. The length is about a third of an inch, the cephalothorax and abdomen about the same length. The cephalothorax is long and the head wide. The maxillæ are long and narrow. The sternum is widest opposite the third legs (fig. 74), and ends behind in a blunt point. The first, second, and third legs are directed forward,

the first pair longest and stoutest. The tibiæ of the first and second legs are a little thickened in the middle and have four pairs of spines on the under side, and the metatarsus of the same legs eight pairs. The hinder pairs of spinnerets are very small. The cephalothorax and legs are yellow brown, darker toward the front. The abdomen is purplish brown, darker in the middle and toward the front. In the male the head is more narrowed and the front legs longer. The front metatarsi are curved at the base and have a tooth each side, the inner one farthest from the tibia. The palpal organ is outside the tarsal joint, as it is in the Mygales.

Figs. 73, 74. Ariadne bicolor. — 73, upper side enlarged four times. 74, under side.

THE THOMISIDÆ

THE Thomisidæ are generally flat, short, and widened behind, and have a sidewise gait and crab-like appearance. The first and second legs are often much larger than the third and fourth, and all the legs extend sidewise from the thorax and not forward and backward, as they do in the Drassidæ (pp. 1–21). The feet have two claws and a thick brush of hairs. They are generally smooth or covered with very short and fine hair, and often have coarser hairs scattered at considerable distances from each other over the back. The eyes are small and in two slightly curved rows, the upper one longest and often much longer than the front row. The mandibles are small and narrowed toward the end. The maxillæ are narrow at the end and slant inward. Most of the species belong to the three following genera :

Xysticus (p. 30) is flat, with short legs, and marked with gray and brown, like bark and stones.

Misumena (p. 25) is white or brightly colored. The first and second legs are much longer than the third and fourth, and there is great difference between the sexes, the females being large and light colored, while the males are small, and yellow or green, with red and brown markings.

Philodromus (p. 35) is generally small, with long slender legs, the second pair longest. The colors are generally light gray and brown, sometimes with iridescent scales.

Besides the larger genera are several other spiders belonging to this family. *Tmarus caudatus* (p. 38) resembles Philodromus in color and outline, but has besides the caudate abdomen a very different head and thorax, and the hind legs much shorter than the first and second. *Ebo latithorax* (p. 38) is a small Philodromus, with a wide body and exaggerated second legs. *Thanatus lycosoides* (p. 40) is like a stout Philodromus, with rough hairs and markings, resembling some Lycosidæ. *Tibellus duttonii* (p. 39) is a long straw-colored spider, resembling Philodromus in its feet and head, but having a long slender abdomen, with two black spots.

THE GENUS MISUMENA

The Misumenas are the most conspicuous spiders of their family, and are among the few that are popularly noticed. They grow to a large size and are white or brightly colored, and live in open places on flowers. The males and females differ widely. The males mature early and remain small, and are marked with a variety of colors in spots and bands, while the females grow several times as large, lose in great part their markings, and become white or yellow. In both sexes the two front pairs of legs are much longer than the two hinder pairs, and often differently colored. In the young the colors are variable and

FIG. 75. Misumena aleatoria. — Natural size, among flowers of thoroughwort, holding a fly in her mouth.

there is less difference between the sexes. The Misumenas live on plants, among the flowers, especially on large flat clusters, like those of carrot and

thoroughwort. They stand among the flowers, holding by the
hind legs, with the front legs extended or bent in stiff and
awkward positions, and wait for insects to alight on the flowers
within their reach. Whether spiders prefer flowers colored
like themselves is an unsettled question ; at any rate, Misumenas of all colors and both sexes have been found on white
flowers. Occasionally individuals are
found on flowers of exactly the same
color as themselves ; for
example, deep yellow *M.
aleatoria* on the wild indigo,
Baptisia tinctoria, and the
reddish *M. asperata* on the
flowers of sorrel, *Rumex
acetosella*. The adult females of *vatia* and *aleatoria*
are easily mistaken for
each other. Both vary in
color from white to deep
yellow, and grow to a large
size, but they can be distinguished by the differ-
ence in the shape of the
head. *Asperata* is perhaps
the most common species.

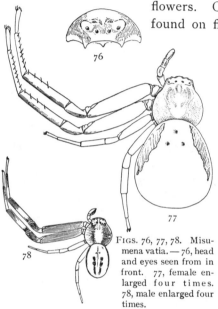

FIGS. 76, 77, 78. Misu-
mena vatia. — 76, head
and eyes seen from in
front. 77, female en-
larged four times.
78, male enlarged four
times.

The female seldom grows as large as the others, and does
not lose entirely the red markings of the abdomen and legs.
The scattered stiff hairs also distinguish it from the others.
The males of the different species are distinct enough one
from the other, though they differ widely from the females. The
shape of the head and the markings around the eyes are much
the same in both sexes, and by these males and females of the
same species may be recognized.

Misumena vatia is the largest species and lives all over this country and Europe. It is sometimes half an inch long, and the first legs spread an inch and a half (fig. 77). It is white, with sometimes a crimson spot on each side of the abdomen and another on the front of the head between the upper eyes. The sides of the thorax are a little darkened with yellow or brown, which extends around the head to a distinct opaque white spot under and between the eyes (fig. 76). This white spot widens below over the mandibles and above under the eyes and around the eyes of the upper row. The shape of this mark and the greater height of the head distinguish this species from *aleatoria* (figs. 79, 80). On the back of the thorax is also a distinct opaque white spot. The first and second legs have usually a light brown mark on the upper side, but this is sometimes absent.

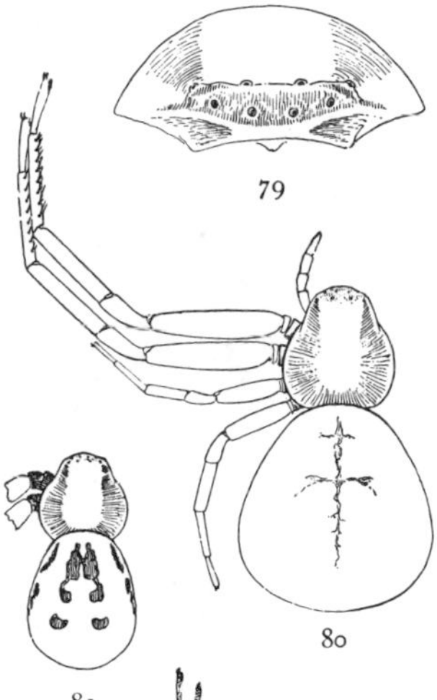

The male (fig. 78) is only a quarter or a third as long as the adult female. The front legs are proportionally longer than in the female, and the abdomen smaller and more pointed behind. The males

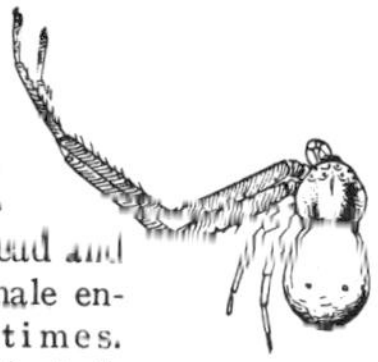

FIGS. 79, 80, 81, 82. Misumena aleatoria. — 79, front of head and eyes. 80, female enlarged four times. 81, female with dark markings. 82, male enlarged four times.

are strongly marked with reddish brown on a light ground. The thorax is dark at the sides, while the front of the head is white like that of the female.

Misumena aleatoria. — The female of this species grows nearly as large as *vatia*, and in some places is much more common. It is white or yellow, but does not have the crimson markings at the sides of the abdomen or between the eyes. The head (fig. 79) is rounder than in *vatia* and much lower in front, and there is a narrow white stripe under the eyes that divides at the sides, one branch passing around over the mandibles and the other close under the eyes.   The sides of the

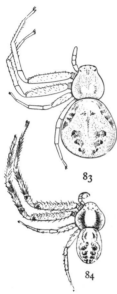

cephalothorax are gray or green.   The abdomen usually has no markings except a little gray color in the middle, but sometimes it has two rows of dark brown spots (fig. 81), and in such individuals the legs are also marked with brown at the ends of the joints. The males are very small and strikingly colored (fig. 82).   The two front pairs of legs are brown, the cephalothorax green, and the abdomen yellow.   The shape of the head and the white under the eyes are the same as in the female.

Misumena asperata. — The males and females of this spider are more alike than in *vatia* and *aleatoria*.   The adult females are always pale and sometimes white, but seldom lose entirely the reddish bands around the legs.   Both sexes are covered with short stiff hairs about their length apart all over the upper part of the body and legs.   The usual color is pale yellow, with dull red

FIGS. 83, 84. Misumena asperata. — 83, female enlarged four times. 84, male enlarged four times.

markings.   The thorax is reddish at the sides.   The abdomen has two red bands or rows of spots on the hinder half, meeting behind.   In front are a middle pair of spots and two side bands that spread apart in the middle and meet again at the spinnerets.   The tibia and tarsus of the front legs are marked with a narrow red ring at the base and a wider ring near the end of each joint.   The female is a quarter of an inch long and the male about half that length. The markings of the male are like those of the female, but the spots are larger and more deeply colored. The male palpi are larger than in the other species.

The male *M. spinosa* of Georgia resembles *asperata*, but the legs are much longer and the ends of the palpi smaller.

Synema parvula. — A common species in the South. Length about one-eighth of an inch. The thorax is as wide as long, round and high in the middle. The abdomen is as wide as long, widest across the middle, and a little pointed behind. The third and fourth legs are not more than two-thirds as long as the first and second, and lighter colored. The thorax is orange-colored, a little darker at the sides, and with a dark brown line on the edges over the legs. There are light rings around the eyes. The abdomen is white or light yellow in front, and has a wide black or brown band across the hinder half, not reaching back

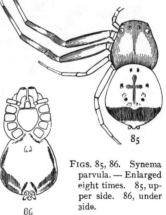

85

FIGS. 85, 86. Synema parvula. — Enlarged eight times. 85, upper side. 86, under side.

to the spinnerets, and sometimes partly divided by a notch in front. On the front half of the abdomen are some small dark spots and usually several opaque white marks. On the under side of the abdomen there is a dark band on each side extending back to and partly surrounding the spinnerets. The front legs are orange brown, with the femora darker on the front and rear edges. The other joints are a little darker at the ends. The males are a little smaller and darker in color, but differ little from the females.

THE GENUS XYSTICUS

In these spiders the general appearance is crab-like. The abdomen is not much larger than the thorax, and both are flat and wide. The first and second legs are a third longer than the third and fourth. The colors are usually various shades of brown and gray, in small spots and bands. On the upper side of each leg is usually a light line, with dark lines on each side of it. The gait is often sidewise, the legs kept close to the ground, so that the spider can move in a narrow crack. They live under stones and bark and leaves, and some, like *triguttatus*, on low plants. The males have longer legs and smaller abdomen and all the dark markings larger and darker than the females. In *triguttatus* there is great difference between the sexes, but in most species very little, as in *limbatus* and *stomachosus*. The head is generally low, and the four middle eyes form a rectangle a little wider than high (fig. 97).

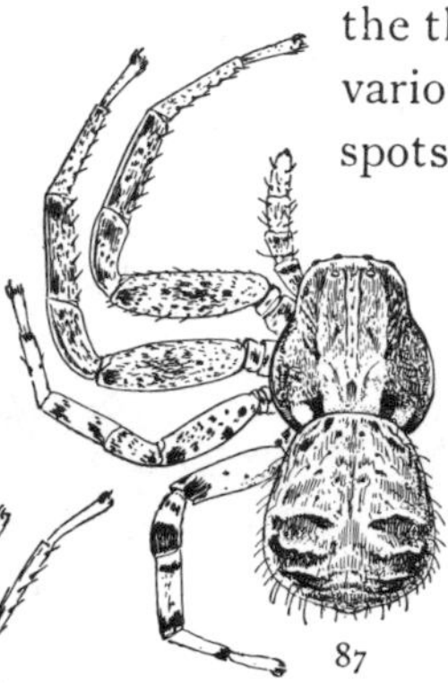

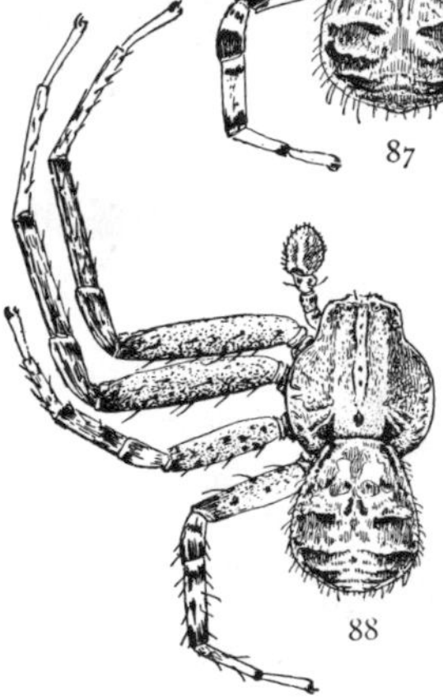

Figs. 87, 88. Xysticus stomacho-sus. — 87, female. 88, male. Both enlarged four times.

Xysticus stomachosus. — A middle-sized and light-colored species, with gray markings on a light ground, the markings most distinct on the hinder legs and abdomen. The middle of the thorax is lighter than the sides, and there is a small dark spot in the middle and a larger one on each side toward the hinder end (figs. 87, 88). The third and fourth legs have a distinct dark spot at the ends of femur, patella, and tibia. The abdomen is light, with a few small spots at the front end and three pairs of dark transverse bands on the hinder half. The hairs are short and fine. The male has longer legs and is marked in the same way, with the spots on the abdomen larger and extended farther forward.

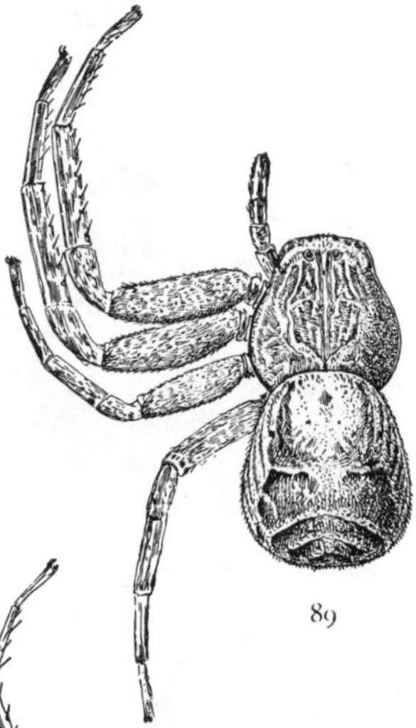

Xysticus limbatus. — This is one of the largest species, the females reaching a length of a third to half an inch (figs. 89, 90). The thorax is one-eighth of an inch wide and nearly as long. The abdomen is a little wider at the hinder end. The legs are short, the longest about half an inch in length. The whole body is hairy. The color is brown, the markings dark on a light ground, best shown by the figures. The middle of the head and thorax is more fully covered by the dark markings than in other species. There is great variation in the color, and young spiders are usually lighter than adults. Adult males and females in June and July.

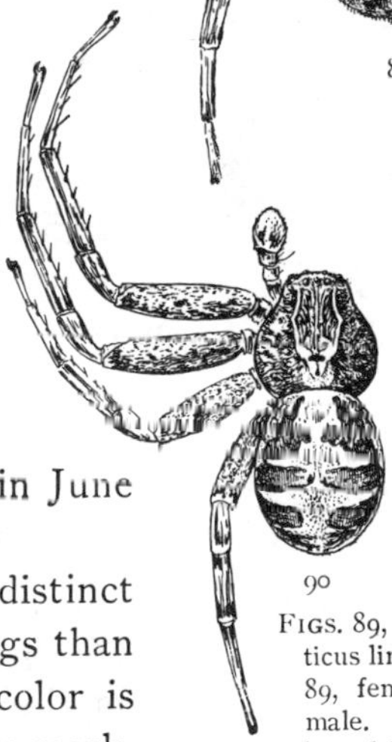

Xysticus gulosus. — This is a very distinct species and less variable in markings than *limbatus* and *stomachosus*. The color is brown or gray, with indistinct darker markings (figs. 91, 92). The whole body is covered with fine brown spots and has at the hinder end of the thorax and on the legs traces of the same markings that show more distinctly in *stomachosus*. There are a few transverse

89

90

FIGS. 89, 90. Xysticus limbatus. — 89, female. 90, male. Both enlarged four times.

dark lines on the hinder half of the abdomen and less distinct longitudinal lines at the sides of the front half.

The male is a fourth smaller than the female, with a smaller abdomen and more slender legs, but the same colors and markings. It is usually found under bark or stones which it closely resembles in color.

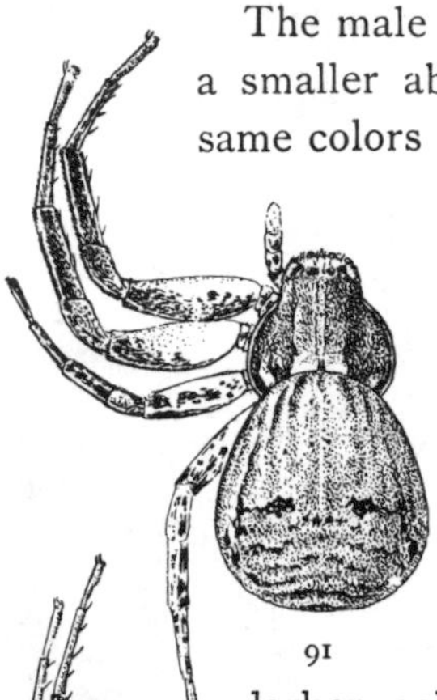

Xysticus nervosus. — This is a pale species, the females of which are nearly as large as *limbatus*. The color is light brownish yellow, with small spots of lighter and darker color scattered all over the body, and there are traces of the markings which are more distinct in other species (figs. 93, 94). On the hinder half of the abdomen are three or four pairs of very indistinct transverse markings. The legs are marked with irregular dark and light spots, without any distinct rings or markings, and the first and second pairs are darker than the others. In the male the first and second legs are twice as long as the third and longer and more slender than in the other species. It lives on fences and under bark.

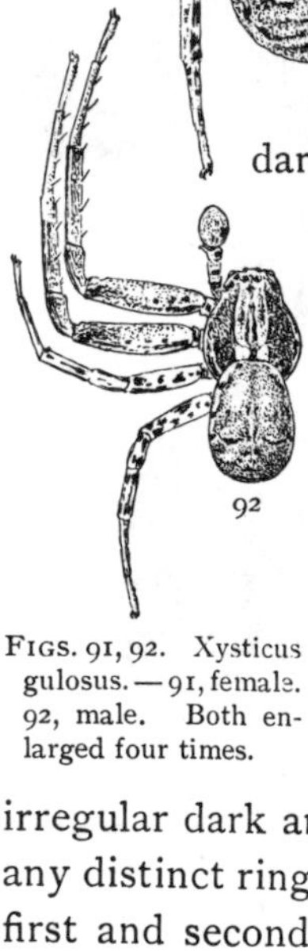

FIGS. 91, 92. Xysticus gulosus. — 91, female. 92, male. Both enlarged four times.

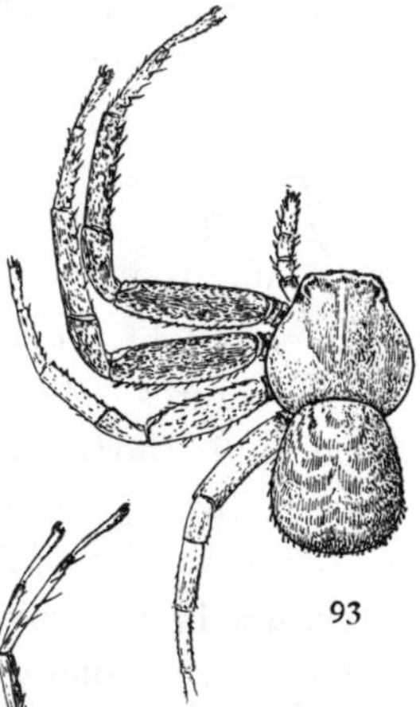

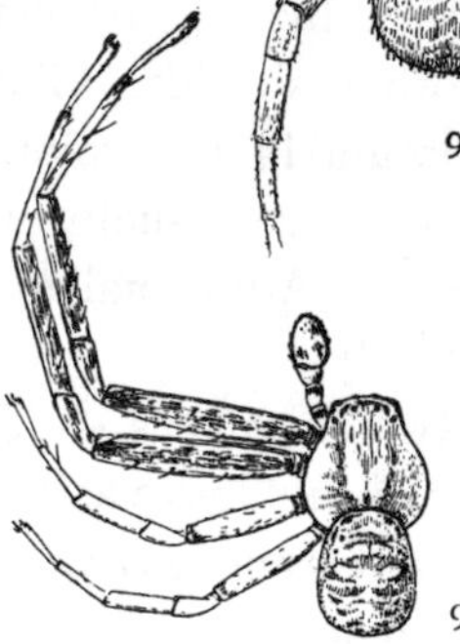

FIGS. 93, 94. Xysticus nervosus. — 93, female. 94, male. Both enlarged four times.

Xysticus triguttatus. — This is a small and very common spider living on grass and low bushes. The female is about a fifth of an inch long and the male as large but with a smaller abdomen. The difference in the color of the sexes

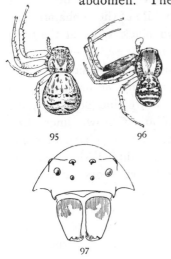

is so great that they may easily be mistaken for different species. The females (fig. 95) are straw-colored, the abdomen almost white, and the thorax and legs brownish yellow. There are three black spots at the back of the thorax and indistinct darker bands at the sides. On the abdomen are two black spots near the front end and three pairs of broken transverse stripes behind.

95   96

97

Figs. 95, 96, 97. Xysticus triguttatus. — 95, female. 96, male. Both enlarged four times. 97, front of head much enlarged to show eyes and mandibles.

The male (fig. 96) has the femora of the two front legs dark brown, the rest like the female or a little darker. The thorax is dark brown, except in the middle, where it is a little lighter, as in the female. The abdomen of the male is strongly marked with transverse black and white stripes, irregular toward the front end.

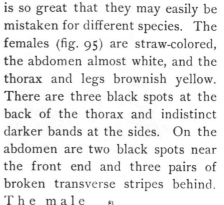

Fig. 98. Xysticus quadrilineatus, enlarged four times.

Xysticus quadrilineatus. — Quarter of an inch long, with the thorax a tenth of an inch wide and the head unusually wide in front. The color is light yellow, with light brown markings and black spots. The cephalothorax has four narrow brown stripes, one on each side close to the edge and the others running back from the lateral eyes (fig. 98); there are also two fine brown lines sometimes extending from the middle eyes to the dorsal groove, but usually broken in the middle. There is a brown spot just behind the dorsal groove and two others in the middle of the cephalothorax. On the abdomen there are two black spots at the front end, two in the middle and two near the hind end, besides

99

100

FIGS. 99, 100. Xysticus versicolor. — 99, female. 100, male. Both enlarged four times.

several smaller ones along the sides. There are four light brown lines across the hinder half, each with a white line behind it, and at the sides are oblique brown lines alternating with white. The legs have a distinct light line along the dorsal side and are covered with fine brown spots without any other markings.

Xysticus (Coriarachne) versicolor. — The thorax, abdomen, and legs are all much flattened, the head is low, and the upper and lower eyes nearer together than in the other species. The colors are black and gray in irregular spots on a light ground (figs. 99, 100). On bark or unpainted wood these spiders can hardly be seen. Light individuals have black spots on the legs at the end of each joint and the usual three pairs of dark marks on the abdomen. On the thorax is a white spot in the middle under the front of the abdomen. Around this spot and behind the eyes is black extending in spots along the sides. In dark females and in most males the dark spots are so large that the whole spider is nearly black.

This is a common spider, and a similar species, *Coriarachne depressa*, is equally common in Europe.

THE GENUS PHILODROMUS

In these spiders there is less difference in length between
the front and hind legs than in Misumena or Xysticus. The
legs are long and slender, the
second pair longest, and the
body is small and flat, and
the abdomen pointed behind.
The colors are brown and gray,
and the whole body is often
covered with fine flattened hairs
that in the males are iridescent.
Philodromus vulgaris lives usually on houses and fences, but
the other species on plants.

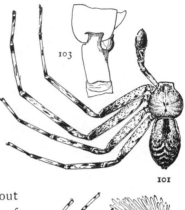

Philodromus vulgaris. — About
quarter of an inch long, the legs of
the female spreading over an inch
and those of the male an inch and
a quarter (figs. 101, 102). They
often stand with all the legs extended
sidewise, flat against a wall or fence
which they closely resemble in color.
When freshly molted they are covered with fine gray hairs of the color
of weathered boards, that obscure
most of the markings. Older spiders
or those wet with alcohol are covered
with small gray spots forming a
stripe in the middle of the front of
the abdomen and a herringbone
pattern on the hinder half.

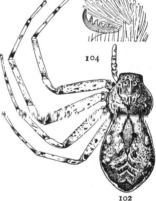

FIGS. 101, 102, 103, 104. Philodromus
vulgaris. — 101, male. 102, female.
Both enlarged four times. 103, tibia
of the male palpus. 104, one of the
feet.

The edges of the back of the
abdomen are dark and form a sharp line against the light

color of the under surface. The thorax is darker in the middle and at the sides in irregular spots of gray. The legs are spotted and darker toward the ends of the joints. The under side of body and legs is light colored.

Philodromus ornatus. — This is a small species about one-eighth of an inch long. The female is very distinctly marked with dark brown on a white ground (fig. 105). The middle of the thorax is white and the sides brown nearly to the edge. The abdomen is white, with a distinct brown band on each side from the front more than half its length backward. Sometimes there is also an indistinct brownish pattern in the

FIG. 105. Philodromus ornatus. — Female enlarged six times.

middle, but this is usually absent in adults, and the middle is entirely white. Under the abdomen the lateral brown bands extend backward and meet around the spinnerets. The abdomen is wider than in most species, — nearly as wide as it is long across the hinder half. The male is very differently colored. The legs and thorax are orange brown, darker at the sides of the thorax and toward the ends of the legs. The abdomen is darker brown and strongly iridescent with red and green in a bright light. In alcohol it shows indistinctly

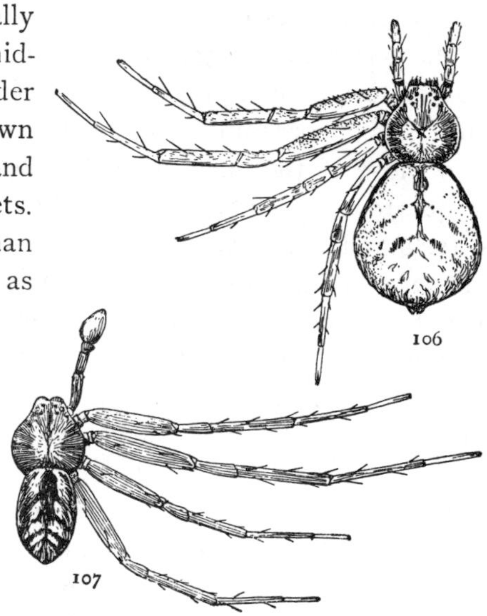

106

107

FIGS. 106, 107. Philodromus lineatus. — 106, female. 107, male. Both enlarged six times.

the same markings as the female. The legs are longer and the abdomen narrower, as in males of other species.

Philodromus lineatus. — The female of this species is a little larger than *ornatus*, the brown markings are lighter, and, in life or when freshly killed, purplish in the lighter parts. The markings are less distinct than in *ornatus*, the brown and white running into each other. The abdomen has a brown band each side, often broken into several spots, and a brown band in the middle extending back half its length, behind which are several lighter marks (figs. 106, 107). Between these are several oblique lighter markings and rows of spots. The legs are light gray, darker toward the ends of the joints.

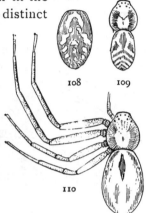

FIGS. 108, 109, 110. Philodromus pictus. — 110, adult female. 109, male without the legs. 108, markings of the abdomen of a young female. All enlarged six times.

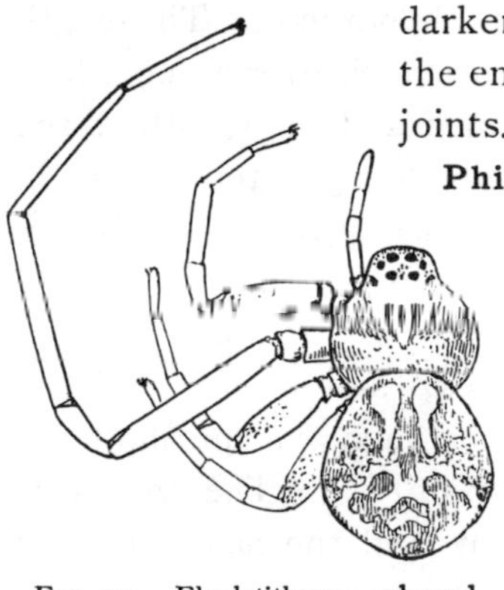

Philodromus pictus. — Female about one-fifth of an inch long, the abdomen nearly twice as long as the thorax, with the widest part across the middle farther forward than in most species (fig. 110). Legs and palpi pale yellow with fine brown spots. Thorax light yellow in the middle and reddish brown at the sides, covered with fine spots. Abdomen dull red at the sides and bright yellow in the middle, with a dark mark in the middle of the front half and two dark marks behind it on the hinder half. The eyes are

FIG. 111. Ebo latithorax, enlarged twelve times.

surrounded by distinct light rings.   In some specimens, usually
immature, the abdomen has a more distinct yellow and red
pattern (fig. 108).   The male (fig. 109) has the thorax and legs
darker and the abdomen less bright red and yellow than the
female, sometimes gray and iridescent.

Ebo latithorax. — In color and general appearance this resembles Philodromus, but is at once distinguished by the length
of the second legs, which are more than twice as long as any
of the others (fig. 111).   The thorax is wider
than long, and the abdomen is wider than in

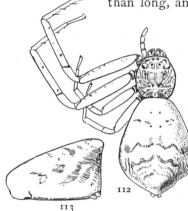

Philodromus.   The head is narrow and rounded in front.   The
front middle eyes are largest
and farthest forward.   The
colors are gray and white, with
black spots in the darker parts,
as in Philodromus.   The length
is not much over an eighth of
an inch and the length of the
longest legs quarter of an inch.

FIGS. 112, 113.   Tmarus caudatus.— 112,
female enlarged six times.   113, left side
of the abdomen.

Tmarus caudatus. — This spider is about as large as *Philodromus vulgaris* and similarly
colored, but may be distin-
guished from it by the height of its abdomen and the short tail
or projection over the spinnerets (fig. 113).   The thorax is
round at the sides and square in front, and the mandibles are
inclined forward so that they can be seen from above.   The
two rows of eyes are farther apart than in Philodromus, and
the lateral eyes of both rows are raised on tubercles.   Among
the eyes are several black spots that may be mistaken for
extra eyes, and there are similar spots on the legs, most
thickly on the front pairs.   On the back of the thorax are

radiating white lines. The abdomen is light in front and marked behind with two or three pairs of indistinct transverse lines (fig. 112). On the under side the whole body and legs are pale, without spots except a wide middle band of gray under the abdomen. The third and fourth legs are shorter than the first and second, the difference being greater than in Philodromus and less than in Misumena.

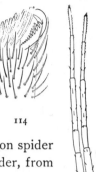

114

Tibellus duttonii. — This is a very common spider on bushes and grass. The body is slender, from a third to half an inch long, and a tenth of an inch wide (fig. 115). The thorax is an eighth of an inch long, widest across the hinder half and narrowed toward the front, where it is cut off nearly straight over the mandibles. Both rows of eyes are strongly curved (fig. 116). The hinder row is twice as long as the front row and all the eyes larger. The abdomen is straight at the sides and a little pointed behind. The color is light gray or yellow, with a darker gray line in the middle, divided into two toward the eyes. At the sides of the thorax are other longitudinal lines. On the abdomen, one-third its length from the hinder end, is a pair of small round or oval black spots. The legs are light gray, with no markings except a few black hairs.

116

FIGS. 114, 115, 116. Tibellus duttonii. — 115, female enlarged four times. 114, one of the feet. 116, front of head, showing eyes and mandibles.

Thanatus coloradensis or **lycosoides.** — In color and general appearance this resembles Philodromus, but is not as flat, and

the legs are not as long and slender. The general color is
light gray, with a distinct wide light stripe in the middle of
the thorax, and a dark brown pointed stripe with white edges
in the middle of the front half of the abdomen (fig. 117).   The
head is a little longer and higher than in most Thomisidæ, and
the abdomen is a little longer and not so much widened behind.
The eyes are much as in Philodromus, but larger and nearer
together.   The whole body is hairy, with longer and darker
hairs scattered among the short ones.   The males differ but
little from the females except in having a little longer hairs
and darker color.   They live on plants and may be mistaken
for Philodromus (p. 35) or for *Ocyale undata* (p. 88).

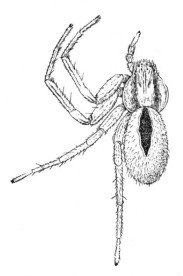

FIG. 117.   Thanatus coloradensis, enlarged four times.

THE ATTIDÆ

THE Attidæ are jumping spiders, many of them brightly colored and quick in their movements and living in open places among the tops of low plants. They are usually short and stout spiders, with a large cephalothorax, which is wide in front, where the eyes have a peculiar arrangement in three rows (fig. 118), somewhat as in the Lycosidæ, but with the middle eyes of the front row much the largest, so that at first sight many of them appear to have only two eyes. The eyes of the second row are very small and hard to see, and those of the third row are far back on the head and usually turned a little backward. The front legs are usually thicker than the others, especially in the males. The relative length of the legs is variable, the first pair being commonly the longest, but sometimes the fourth and even in some species the third pair. The feet have two claws, with many fine teeth and a thick brush of hairs.

FIG. 118. Front of head of Phidippus mystaceus, showing eyes and mandibles.

The Attidæ are usually thickly covered with hair or scales, often brightly colored or iridescent, and their appearance is often entirely changed by rubbing or wetting.

They walk backward or sidewise as well as forward, and many of them jump great distances. They make no cobwebs, but some species make silk tubes or bags on plants or under stones in which they hide to molt or lay their eggs or to pass the winter. There are often great differences in color and markings between the sexes, and the males have peculiar bunches of hairs and color spots on the legs and head.   At the mating time some of the males have peculiar ways of approaching the female, holding their legs extended sidewise or over their heads

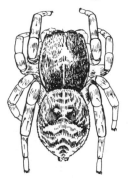

in such ways as to display their ornaments.   These mating habits have been well described by G. W. Peckham, who has made a special study of this family, in the *Occasional Papers of the Wisconsin Natural History Society*, of Milwaukee, in 1889. This family is largely represented in more southern countries, and our species belong to a great number of genera most of whose members live farther south.

Fig. 119.   Attus palustris,
enlarged six times.

Attus palustris. — Large females are quarter of an inch long, the males a little smaller.   The cephalothorax is a quarter longer than wide, shorter in proportion to its width than in the next species, *Saitis pulex*, which it much resembles.   The two sexes resemble each other in markings, but the females are lighter and browner and the males darker and grayer.   The cephalothorax has a narrow white middle line, widened opposite the dorsal eyes, and a shorter white line just below the eyes on the sides (fig. 119).   The edge of the cephalothorax is also white.   On the abdomen the front middle spot is not so

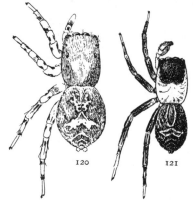

Figs. 120, 121.   Saitis pulex. — 120, female.
121, male.   Both enlarged six times.

distinct as in *pulex*, but in place of it are two white spots. Behind these is a large transverse light marking, sometimes broken into two spots. The legs are dark or light gray, without any distinct markings. The male palpi are smaller than in *pulex*, though the males are larger. *Palustris* lives on plants and makes nests among the leaves.

Saitis pulex. — This is one of the smallest of the family. It is about a sixth of an inch long, sometimes even smaller. The colors are various shades of gray like the ground, and when still it is hard to find, but it is an active spider and exposes itself by jumping in open places. The cephalothorax is half longer than wide, longer and narrower than in Habrocestum and Attus. The abdomen is usually shorter than the cephalothorax and wider (figs. 120, 121). The

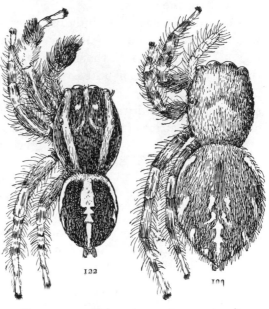

FIGS. 122, 123. Habrocestum auratum. — 122, male. 123, female. Both enlarged eight times.

cephalothorax has a large light-colored triangle in the middle, covering the head between the eyes in front and ending in a point behind. In alcohol this spot disappears, especially in the males, and the head appears black between the eyes and light behind and at the sides. The front half of the abdomen has a light middle stripe, lightest at the edges and darker gray in the middle. Behind this is a transverse white spot nearly the whole width of the abdomen and behind it several smaller light markings.   In the male these markings are brighter and the surrounding dark color blacker than in the females.   The legs are marked with indefinite spots of dark gray on a lighter ground, the contrast stronger in the males.   The hairs all over the body are short and fine and the spines on the legs distinct, especially in the males.

Habrocestum auratum. — In life this spider is covered with bluish white hairs that give it a light gray color and obscure the markings.   The markings of the male are so much stronger that those of both sexes can be best understood by describing the male first (fig. 122).   The cephalothorax has a white middle stripe for a short distance back from the front eyes and two distinct white stripes from the lateral front eyes back the whole

length.   In the middle of the head are two small white spots and just behind them between the posterior eyes two curved white lines.   The latter marks show indistinctly in the females.   Down at the sides of the cephalothorax are white stripes meeting in front under the eyes.   The abdomen has a white line extending entirely around it and a middle stripe of varying width.

FIGS. 124, 125.   Third and first legs of male Habrocestum auratum to show differences between this species and the next. — 124, third leg.   125, first leg.

The female (fig. 123) has only faint indications of the markings of the cephalothorax, usually a little lighter color in the middle and at the sides below the eyes.   The white stripe around the abdomen is broken into three pairs of oblique white markings and the middle stripe into several spots or pairs of

spots.   There is nothing distinctive in the markings of the
under side or of the legs except the ornaments of the male.

The front legs of the male
(fig. 125) in this species are
much ornamented.   The femur
has long black hairs on the
under side.   The patella has
long black hairs beneath, a
spot of short black hairs on the inner
side, and a crest of long white hairs mixed
with shorter black on the upper side.
The tibia is covered with long black
hairs except at the tip, where they are
white.   There is nothing peculiar about
the third leg (fig. 124).   The form and
general appearance can best be understood
from the figures.

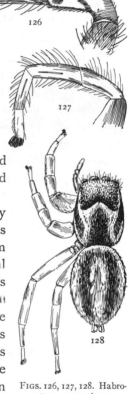

FIGS. 126, 127, 128. Habrocestum peregrinum. —
128, female enlarged
six times. 126, third
leg. 127, first leg.

At the mating time the males, as they
approach the females, hold the front legs
extended sidewise and lifted a little from
the ground, with the tibia nearly horizontal
and the tarsus turned downward.   In this
position they advance slowly, at the same
time running rapidly sidewise from one
side to the other and at short intervals
jerking the abdomen and the front legs
slightly upward.   They go almost close
enough to touch the female and then
quickly retreat.

Habrocestum peregrinum. — This is about
the same size as *auratum* and looks very
much like it.   The female, at any rate in alcohol, has a more
distinct light mark in the middle of the cephalothorax, curving

under the eyes and pointing forward in the middle (fig. 128). The abdomen has light markings in the middle similar to those of *auratum*, but those at the sides are less distinct.

The male has the white stripes in the middle and around the abdomen like *auratum*. The cephalothorax has the same white lines at the sides under the eyes and at the posterior end. It does not have a middle white stripe on the head between the eyes or two white spots just behind it, as *auratum* has, but the

marking behind the eyes is more distinct, as it is in the female. The front legs of the male (fig. 127) are not ornamented with long hairs like *auratum*, but the third legs have a very peculiar shape, the patella being wide and flat, with a dark spot in the middle of the front side (fig. 126). The shape of this joint is best shown by the figure. When approaching the female he holds up the front legs and draws in the third pair so that the ornamented patellæ show from in front.

Habrocestum splendens. — A little larger than the other species, with the female distinctly marked with black and white and the male with brilliant red and iridescent scales. The females are about a quarter of an inch long, sometimes longer, and the males are a little smaller. The cephalothorax of the female is covered with brown scales mixed with black hairs. Across the middle, just behind the dorsal eyes, is a light band that curves behind the eyes and extends forward in the middle. The abdomen has a white band in front, one on each side, and one in the middle, the rest being deep black. The shape of these markings varies and the black parts are often broken into two rows of spots. The cephalothorax of the male is covered with dark iridescent scales, with blue, green, and purple

FIG. 129. Habrocestum splendens. — Male enlarged eight times.

reflections. The abdomen is covered with bright red shiny
scales mixed with fine black hairs. It is lighter in front and
at the sides, and in the middle shows indis-
tinctly through the scales dark markings like
those of the female (fig. 129). The legs are
dark like the cephalothorax.

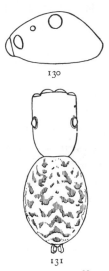

130

131

FIGS. 130, 131. Neon
nellii. — 131, female
enlarged sixteen
times. 130, side of
cephalothorax, show-
ing position of eyes.

Mr. Peckham says that when the male
approaches the female he lifts his abdomen
into an almost vertical position so that the
red color shows from in front.   Then he
rises on the tips of his feet and, with the
front legs off the ground and pointing forward, he dances back and
forth sidewise in front of
her, gradually drawing
nearer.   At inter-
vals he stops and
turns his back to
her, then faces her
and dances again.

Neon nellii.—This
is one of the small-
est spiders of the family, only a tenth
of an inch in length.   The general
color is dark gray, darkest toward the head.
The cephalothorax is high, the highest part
being a little behind the middle, from which
it curves downward to the front eyes and
slopes abruptly backward (fig. 130).   The
eyes are large and prominent, the front row
nearly straight and as wide as the widest part
of the cephalothorax.   The posterior eyes
are nearly as large as the front middle pair and are in the

FIG. 132. Zygoballus bettini. — Female enlarged
eight times.

middle of the cephalothorax. The abdomen is a little longer and wider than the cephalothorax (fig. 131). The cephalothorax is smoky gray, darker toward the front and darker in males than females. The abdomen is gray, with yellowish markings in a herringbone pattern through the middle. Common under stones and leaves at all seasons.

FIG. 133. Phidippus multiformis. — Female enlarged six times.

Zygoballus bettini. — This is a very beautifully colored spider, having in life spots of white hairs and shining scales of the color of copper and bronze. The cephalothorax of both sexes is high and wide in the middle and slopes down steeply from the posterior eyes under the front of the abdomen (fig. 132). The top of the cephalothorax between the eyes is nearly square. The posterior eyes are almost the full width of the cephalothorax apart, and the front row of eyes is nearly as long. The cephalothorax is dark brown covered with iridescent scales. The legs are pale, except the dark femora of the first pair and dark spots on the ends of the joints of the fourth pair. In the male all the legs are a little darker than in the female and without the spots on the fourth leg. The abdomen of the female is light brown, marked with white in a row of irregular spots. In the male the abdomen is brown, covered with shining scales and with a white band around the front and two white spots on each side. The mandibles of the male are much elongated and bent apart at the ends to make room for the long claw. At the inner angle is a large tooth, and there is another one of complicated shape on the middle of the under side.

Phidippus multiformis. — This is a very common spider on plants throughout the summer. It matures in July, and the males and females are so little alike as to be taken for different species. The males (fig. 134) are black, with white and orange markings on the abdomen, while the females are brown mixed with black, white, and yellow scales and small white spots.

The usual length is about a third of an inch in both sexes. The cephalothorax is nearly as broad as long, and the abdomen of the female as wide as the thorax and a little longer.

The general color of the adult female is yellowish brown, with black and white markings (fig. 133). Around the front of the abdomen is a white band, and on the back are two indistinct longitudinal black stripes in which are four pairs of white spots. The general brown color

FIG. 134. Phidippus multiformis. — Male enlarged six times.

is produced by a mixture of scales and hairs of various colors. The females are most brightly colored just before reaching maturity, and then there is a large proportion of yellow and orange scales in their covering and the black stripes and white spots are more distinct. The hairs and scales are of various shapes, the most common being that of slightly flattened hairs. The yellow and orange scales are wider and less pointed, and

the white spots have short and wide scales.   Under the abdomen the color is light gray, with two parallel darker stripes.
The legs are pale in the middle of the joints and dark toward
the ends and covered with gray and black hairs.   The palpi are
light yellow.

In alcohol the orange color disappears almost entirely, the
black and white markings become less distinct, and all the
colors browner.   The colors of the male (fig. 134) are entirely
different.   The cephalothorax and legs to the end of the tibia
are black.   The palpi are black, with a stripe of white scales on
the upper side.   Around the front end of the abdomen is a
white stripe; the sides are bright orange red and the middle
black.   Between the orange and black are three pairs of white
spots.   They make a bag of white silk
among leaves, in which in the early summer a male and female may sometimes
be found together and in which the female
later makes a cocoon of eggs.   The young
hatch soon and become half grown before
winter.

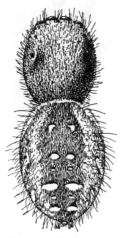

FIG. 135.   Phidippus my-
staceus,   enlarged   six
times.

Phidippus mystaceus. — A stout species
half an inch long, gray and hairy, in alcohol
turning brown.   The abdomen is light
gray at the sides and dark in the middle,
with four pairs of white spots, the third
pair largest (fig. 135).   The cephalothorax
is round and nearly as wide as long.   The
front row of eyes is little longer than half
the greatest width of the cephalothorax.
The cephalothorax is flat on top for almost its whole length
and in front about twice the diameter of the largest eyes in
height.   The mandibles are large and bright metallic green in
front (fig. 118).   The legs are stout and short, the fourth pair

extending little beyond the spinnerets. The first and fourth
pairs are of the same length, but the first are twice as thick as
the fourth. The legs are without markings and darker toward
the head. The abdomen is longer than the cephalothorax and
as wide or wider. There is little difference
between the sexes, the males being only a little
darker colored and larger in front. Usually
found under stones in a thick silk nest.

Phidippus tripunctatus. — Black, with three
bright white spots on the back of the abdomen (fig. 136). Large females are half an
inch long and the males a little smaller.
Though the general color is black, it is modified, especially in fresh specimens, by white
hairs on parts of the body. The joints of the
legs are grayish in the middle and black
toward the ends. There are white hairs on
the front of the head and upper side of the
palpi and a white band around the front of
the abdomen, plainest in the males. The

Fig. 136. Phidippus tri-
punctatus, enlarged six
times.

three large white spots on the abdomen correspond to the
second and third pairs in *mystaceus* (fig. 135) and *multiformis*
(fig. 133), and the other pairs, though generally present, are
small and inconspicuous. On the under side of the abdomen
are usually two gray stripes. This is a common spider all over
the country. It lives under stones and sticks and passes the
winter half grown in a thick silk bag.

Plexippus puerperus. — Very variable in size, from a third to
half an inch in length. The females (fig. 137) are pale, light
yellow, or almost white, with a few black spots, while the
males (fig. 138) have the cephalothorax and legs brown, sometimes almost black. In both sexes the mandibles are large
and the cephalothorax high and flat on the top as far back as

the hinder eyes. The front middle eyes nearly touch each other. The lateral eyes are half their diameter higher than the front ones. The middle eyes are nearer the lateral than the dorsal. In the males the front eyes are nearly their diameter above the mandibles, and below them is a white band and a line of white hairs from the middle of the head down to the base of the first legs.

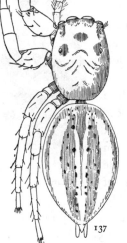

139

FIG. 137.   Plexippus puerperus. — Female enlarged
six times.

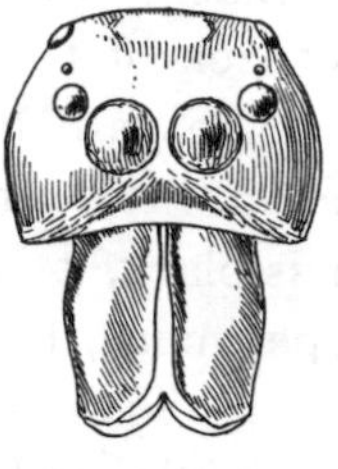

The legs are rather slender in both sexes and long in the males. The fourth pair are longest in females, and in males the first and fourth are the same length. The markings of the abdomen are much alike in both sexes, with two light stripes, more definite in the males, bordered by a few small black spots irregularly arranged. The stem of the abdomen is long, and the abdomen and thorax appear farther apart than in many species. In the females the cephalothorax is pale, with a few gray

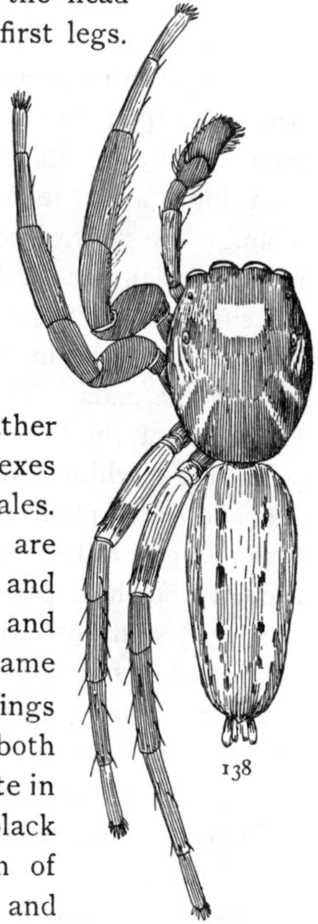

138

FIGS. 138, 139.   Plexippus puerperus. — 138, male enlarged six
times.   139, front of head of
male.

spots from the middle toward the sides. In the males the legs
are dark brown except the inner half of the femur of the third
and fourth, which is light like the abdomen. The male cephalothorax is dark and has a square white spot between the eyes,
two white lines pointing up from the third and fourth legs each
side, and two short white lines under the dorsal eyes. The
under side of the thorax and legs is dark or light like the upper

side. The under side
of the abdomen is
usually darker in the
middle and sometimes has a few black
spots each side. This
is a common spider
in the southern states
and has been found as
far south as Brazil.

Dendryphantes militaris. — This spider
resembles in many
ways the next species, *Dendryphantes
militaris*, but is one
half larger and has
a shorter and wider

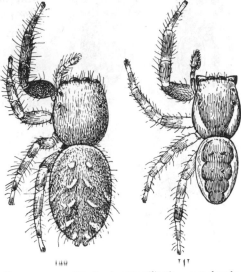

FIGS. 140, 141. Dendryphantes militaris. — 140, female.
141, male. Both enlarged six times.

cephalothorax. The general color is brown, covered with gray
and black hairs. The abdomen of the female is brown, with
white at the front end and four pairs of oblique white marks in
the middle and four at the sides (fig. 140). In the male the
cephalothorax has a white band on each side under the eyes
and a white band around the abdomen, with a dark middle area
(fig. 141). The dark parts of the legs and cephalothorax are
darker than the same parts in the female. The palpi are

slender in both sexes, and in the male the palpal organs are
small for so large a spider. The mandibles of the male
are widened at the end and have a strong projection with two
teeth on the inner corners.

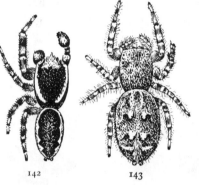

Dendryphantes æstivalis. —
One of the most common
Attidæ, on all kinds of bushes
and small trees, and one of
the most variable in size and
color. Large females are
from a fifth to a quarter of
an inch long, and the males
are smaller. The females are
of two varieties, which run
into each other. The light variety (fig.
144) has the light parts white or light
yellow and the dark parts dark brown
covered with white hairs and scales.
The cephalothorax is dark brown, thinly
covered with scales, so that the dark
color shows between them in places.
The legs are light yellow and translucent, indistinctly ringed with brown at
the base and, near the tip of each joint,
all covered with greenish white hairs.
The palpi are light and without rings
except on the femur and patella. The
abdomen is brighter yellow than the
thorax, with four pairs of purplish brown
spots, the second pair largest, connected with a paler brown middle marking. The abdomen has beneath a purple brown
stripe in the middle and oblique brown marks at the sides.
Sternum, maxillæ, and mandibles light brown. The dark

142

143

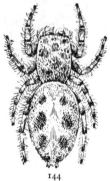

144

FIGS. 142, 143, 144. Dendryphantes æstivalis. — 142,
male. 143, dark variety of
female. 144, light variety
of female. All enlarged
six times.

variety (fig. 143) is generally smaller and covered with longer
hairs and scales.   The legs and palpi are more distinctly ringed
with brown.   The dark spots on the abdomen are larger and
more closely connected, so that
the markings appear as light
spots on a dark ground.

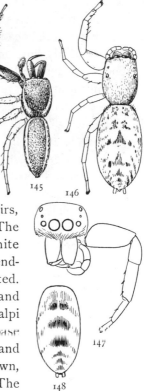

In alcohol they become bright
red and afterward fade to a dull
red color that remains for a long
time, both varieties in this con-
dition looking much alike.

The males (fig. 142) differ, at
first sight, extremely from the
females.   The legs are ringed as
in the female and the brown parts
are wider and less obscured by white hairs,
while the white parts are whiter.   The
cephalothorax is dark brown, with a white
stripe on each side under the eyes bend-
ing toward each other but not connected.
The front of the head is also white and
covered with long white hairs.   The palpi
have the femur dark brown at the base
and white at the end.   The patella and
tibia are brown, and the tarsus is brown,
with white hairs on the upper side.   The
abdomen is white in front and
around the sides.   The middle
is dark brown, with a few yellow
and greenish scales.   The brown

FIGS. 145, 146, 147, 148. Icius palmarum.
— 145, male. 146, female. Both enlarged six times. 147, front of head of
male. 148, abdomen of female to show
a variety of marking.

area is often notched at the sides in four points and sometimes
indistinctly divided into four pairs of spots, as in the female.
The male palpi are large for the size of the spider, and the
palpal organ extends back beyond the tibia.

Icius palmarum. — This is very common on trees and bushes, and may be mistaken for *Dendryphantes æstivalis*, which it much resembles. It differs from *æstivalis* in both sexes in being a little smaller and more slender and in the females lighter colored. In the males the head is wider, the front legs longer and darker colored than in *æstivalis*, and the mandibles longer and more nearly horizontal.

The living female has the legs and palpi transparent white, sometimes a little darker at the ends of the joints. The whole body is covered with light gray or white scales mixed with fine black hairs. The abdomen has a row of darker triangular spots in the middle and oblique rows of small spots at the sides. In alcohol the legs become yellow and the rest of the body red, as in *æstivalis*, afterward fading to a dirty yellow. The markings of the abdomen become more distinct and in some individuals form four large dark brown spots.

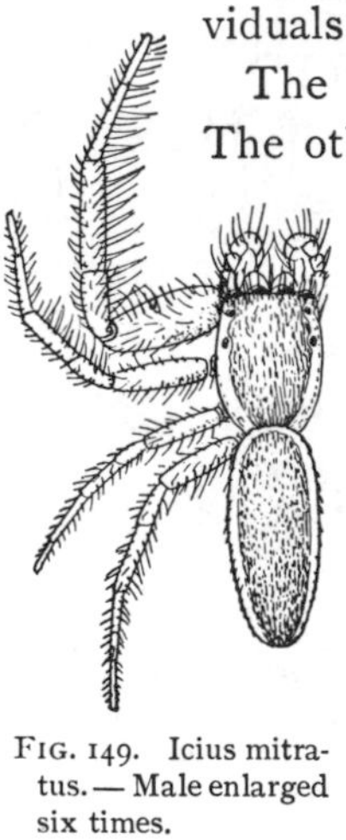

FIG. 149. Icius mitratus. — Male enlarged six times.

The males have the front legs very dark brown. The other legs are transparent white. The cephalothorax and abdomen are dark reddish brown mixed with shining greenish white scales and sometimes copper red around the eyes. On each side is a white stripe the whole length of the body, the two meeting in front below the eyes. The mandibles, maxillæ, and palpi are dark brown. Some males show indistinctly dorsal markings of the abdomen like the female. The mandibles of the male are longer than those of the female and more or less turned forward according to their length. In some the mandibles are only a little longer than those of the female, and in these the patella and tibia of the front legs are not much longer than the femur. In others, usually larger spiders, the mandibles are nearly as

long as the cephalothorax and extend forward horizontally, the
maxillæ are longer, and the first pair of legs have the patella and
tibia one and a half times as long as the femur. The female is
longer in proportion to its
width than in *æstivalis* and
has the front legs stouter.
The epigynum has two small
anterior openings directed forward instead of toward each
other, as in *æstivalis*. This
and the next species live on
low bushes all summer.

Icius mitratus. — This species
closely resembles *Icius palma-*
rum, differing mainly in color.
The legs are all white in both
sexes, and the mandibles of the

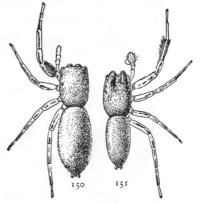

FIGS. 150, 151. Icius elegans. — 150, female.
151, male. Both enlarged six times.

male are white and not long and horizontal, as in *palmarum*.
The females resemble *palmarum* so closely that it is difficult
to tell them apart. The cephalothorax is a trifle wider, and
the abdomen narrower, and the front legs longer than in
palmarum. The general color is whiter, and the spots on the
abdomen are more distinct, as in fig. 148. The male has the
legs white or a little greenish, with long white hairs, those on
the front legs longer than the diameter of the legs. The rest
of the body is white, except a light brown stripe in the middle
of the cephalothorax and abdomen, covered with light yellow
hairs, through which three or four dark spots show indistinctly
on the abdomen (fig. 149). When fighting with other males,
or when approaching the female, the hairy front legs are
straightened and extended sidewise.

Icius elegans. — A little bronze green spider, from a sixth to
a quarter of an inch long. The cephalothorax is two-thirds

as wide as long, with the sides nearly straight and parallel in the female but widened behind the middle in the male. The abdomen of the female is oval and nearly twice as long as wide. The color is bronze green, changing in some lights to copper red. The legs are yellow, with longitudinal dark stripes, except the front femora, which are dark brown. The males are much more brightly colored. The legs are orange, darker toward the ends, with fine dark longitudinal stripes. The ends of the front tibiæ are dark brown and have long brown hairs on the inner and upper side. The palpi are orange, darker toward the end. The sides and hinder part of the cephalothorax are orange, and there is a white line over the coxæ. The upper part of the cephalothorax and abdomen is covered with greenish yellow scales. On the front of the head are two tufts of long hairs, yellow mixed with black, pointing forward and a little inward between the middle and lateral eyes. On the hinder end of the abdomen is an iridescent purple spot. The abdomen is green on the under side, and the sternum and coxæ are orange. In alcohol all the colors become dull.

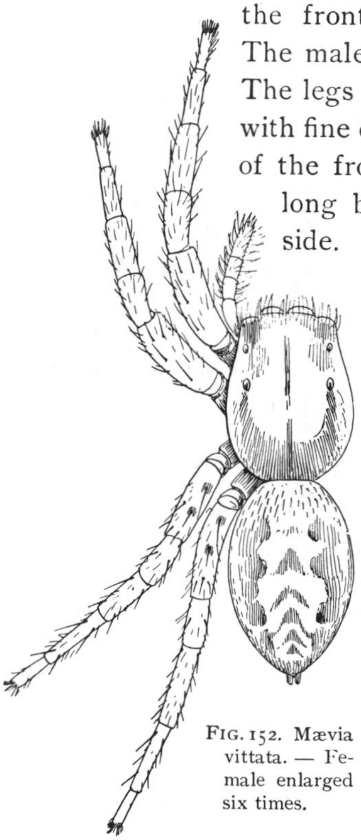

FIG. 152. Mævia vittata. — Female enlarged six times.

The mandibles are slender, and the claw short and strongly curved inward toward the point. In the male the mandibles are a little longer and hollowed a little on the inner side. The male has the first pair of legs much longer and larger than the others. In the female the fourth legs are longest.

Mævia vittata. — This is a brightly colored spider about a third of an inch long and with unusually long legs for this family, — the fourth pair longest in the females and the first and fourth of equal length in the males. The female (fig. 152) has the legs and palpi translucent yellow or greenish white. They are marked with indistinct light gray rings and black spots at the base of the hairs and spines. The cephalothorax is dark brown between the eyes and translucent like the legs in the thoracic part. There is a fine black line in the middle and one on each side and a few gray marks radiating from the dorsal groove. The whole top of the cephalothorax is covered with greenish yellow scales mixed with gray hairs. The eyes are black, and sometimes there is a red stripe under the eyes at the sides. The abdomen is covered

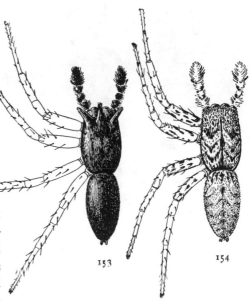

FIGS. 153, 154. Mævia vittata. — Males enlarged six times. 153, dark variety with long hairs on front of head. 154, light variety colored like the female.

with scales which in the middle and at the sides are gray and mixed with black hairs. There are two longitudinal bands of light red and indistinct angular marks of the same color in the middle of the hinder half. On the under side the colors are light gray and yellow, with spots of darker gray on the abdomen.

The males are of two very different colors. One kind (fig. 154) resembles the female. The red bands on the abdomen are broken up into rows of spots connected with the middle angular markings. The gray and black spots on the legs and cephalothorax are larger, and there are several black marks on the front of the abdomen. The palpi are bright orange yellow, with the tibial hook black and a black spot on the inner side of each joint. The size of the black spots varies in different individuals, and so this passes into the other variety (fig. 153), in which the cephalo-thorax and abdomen are entirely black and the palpi black, except a few orange hairs on the outer

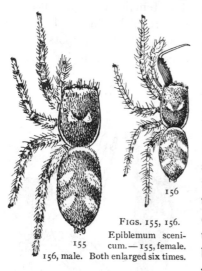

FIGS. 155, 156.
Epiblemum sceni-
155   cum. — 155, female.
156, male. Both enlarged six times.

side. The black cephalothorax and abdomen are covered with dark greenish shining scales. The legs in this variety are transparent white except the hairs, and on the front of the head are three tufts of long hairs which are wanting in the light-colored males.

Epiblemum scenicum. — This is the common gray and white spider that lives on houses and fences (fig. 155). It is about quarter of an inch long, the cephalothorax half longer than wide, and the abdomen a little wider and longer. The front of the head around and above the eyes is white. There is a white stripe on each side of the cephalothorax, and in the middle two white spots, one each side of the dorsal groove. On the abdomen there is a white stripe across the anterior end, and two oblique marks on each side. The legs are gray, with white rings not

very distinctly marked, and the palpi white. On some individuals the white marks are more definite than on others, the
gray ground having but few white scales mixed with it. In
others yellow and white scales are
largely mixed with the gray, and so
the contrast with the white spots is
less. The males (fig. 156) differ but
little in size, color, or markings from
the females, but the male mandibles
are much larger and extend horizontally in front of the head, sometimes
two-thirds as long as the cephalothorax. This is a common European,
as well as American, spider. It is
occasionally found on the ground or
on plants, but commonly on and
about houses.

Marptusa familiaris. — This is another
common species on fences and the outside of houses (fig. 157). When full
grown it is half an inch long. The
whole body is much flattened, and
both the cephalothorax and abdomen
are widened in the middle. The
cephalothorax is rounded at the sides
and three-quarters as wide as long,
and the abdomen is half as wide as
it is long. The legs are long and
stout, the fourth pair one-half longer
than the abodmen.

FIG. 157. Marptusa familiaris. —
Female enlarged six times.

The general color is gray, with long
gray and white hairs. The cephalothorax has a dark brown
band along the edge on each side, which is larger and darker in

the males.   The abdomen has in the middle a yellowish white
marking covering half its width, the front half straight and the
hinder half notched at the sides.   The legs are darker at the
ends of the joints and light in the middle.   The under
side of the abdomen has a dark middle stripe.

Hyctia pikei. — A slender species a quarter to a third
of an inch in length, with the abdomen twice as long
as the cephalothorax, and in general appearance like
a seed or piece of straw (fig. 158).   The whole body
is covered with silvery white hairs mixed with a few
longer black ones.   The markings of the back in
the male are a dark middle stripe on the abdomen, partly divided by notches into four spots
and a fine middle line and two less distinct side
lines on the cephalothorax.   In the female the
stripe on the abdomen is less definite and is
broken up into spots, and in young spiders the
whole body is pale yellow or greenish.   The
front legs are as long as the abdomen in both
sexes, colored brown, and with the middle joints
thickened.   They are not much used in walking, being extended straight forward and raised
enough to clear the ground while the spider
walks with the other six.   The other legs are
pale and slender.

The elongated shape of this spider distinguishes it from all the other common Attidæ.
The markings and the position of the legs, two
pairs pointing forward and two backward,
increase the long appearance.   The basal joints of the fourth
legs are brought close together, and those of the first pair
almost as close.   The labium and maxillæ are a little longer
than usual and are partly covered by the first legs.

Fig. 158. Hyctia
pikei, enlarged
eight times.

I have found this spider common on sand grass, where nothing else grows, and the young lying lengthwise on the leaves could hardly be seen. They mature in the middle of the summer. When the male approaches the female he raises the front legs at an angle of sixty degrees with each other, raises the abdomen a little, and advances by short runs, twitching the front legs and abdomen every few moments.

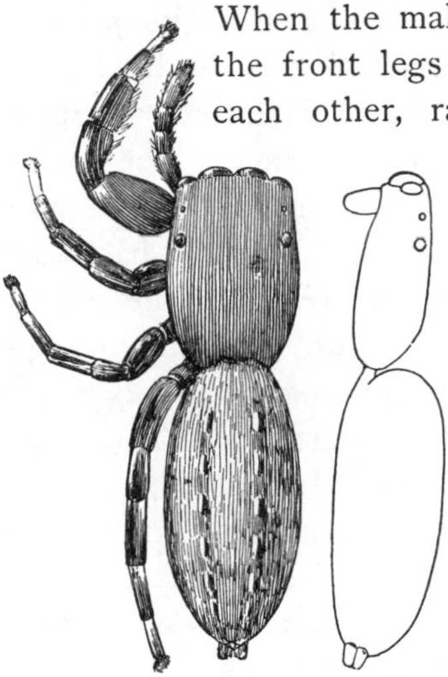

Cyrba tæniola. — A small flat spider, nearly black, the females quarter of an inch long, and the males a sixth of an inch (fig. 159). The cephalothorax is one-half longer than wide, very low and flat, with the sides parallel for half its length. The front middle eyes are large and close together, the lateral eyes half as large and a little separated from them. The

FIGS. 159, 160. Cyrba tæniola. — 159, female enlarged eight times. 160, profile to show flatness of the back.

first legs are twice as thick as the others and have the femora flattened, but in the female the fourth legs are longest. The abdomen is as wide as the cephalothorax and a little longer. The hairs all over the body are short. The cephalothorax is black, smooth, and without markings. The abdomen is

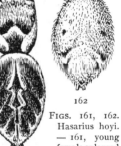

162

FIGS. 161, 162. Hasarius hoyi. — 161, young female enlarged six times. 162, abdomen of adult female to show difference in markings.

dark gray, with two rows of white spots often indistinct and perhaps sometimes absent. The legs have the femora and patella and tibia of first and second pairs black or dark brown and the other joints light and black at the ends. The under side is black. The sternum is very short, so that the basal joints of the front legs touch each other.

Hasarius hoyi. — This species may be known by its peculiar colors, — the dark portions brown or black and the light parts white and orange brown (figs. 161, 162). These colors are, as usual, brighter and the markings more distinct in the males. In front around the eyes the cephalothorax is covered with white hairs. At the sides a white band extends backward under the eyes, turning inward but not reaching the middle line. There is a light band, part white and part orange, around the abdomen and several angular marks in the middle, two of them in the hinder half, sometimes united into a large spot. In alcohol, and less plainly seen when alive, is a light band under the hairs, extending across the middle of the cephalothorax and forward on the sides under the eyes.

In females all these markings are less distinct, but traces of them can be found in most individuals. The colors are more brownish, and the markings of the abdomen smaller and more uniform in shape. The markings of the legs are dark on the middle joints and light at the base and on the tarsi, with strong contrasts in color in the males and little in the females. The length of this species is about a quarter of an inch for large females. The males are smaller.

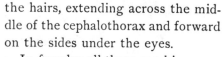

163   164

FIGS. 163, 164. Synemosyna formica. — 163, female enlarged eight times. 164, side of female.

Synemosyna formica. — A small spider so much like an ant as to be often mistaken for one (fig. 163). It is about quarter of an inch long and very slender. The cephalothorax is narrowed behind and the abdomen in front, and each has a deep depression in the middle. The stem of the abdomen is flat, and widened behind so that it is nearly as wide as the ends of the thorax and abdomen, which it connects. The front middle eyes are large and cover two-thirds of the width of the front of the head, and the rest of the eyes are small. The legs are all slender, the hind pair longest. The general color is black, with yellowish or orange-white markings. There is a triangular white spot in front of the dorsal groove, and one on each side widening downward under the posterior eyes. On the abdomen there is a white stripe extending downward from the dorsal depression on each side and uniting in a large white patch underneath (fig. 164). In pale individuals the whole front half of the abdomen is light yellow or orange brown. The second legs are entirely white, the others partly black. The male has the head higher and is darker colored and more slender.

FIG. 165. Lyssomanes viridis, enlarged six times.

This spider not only resembles an ant in form and color but moves like an ant. It does not jump like most Attidæ, though It can do so, but walks and runs irregularly about and lifts its first legs high like the antennæ of ants.

Lyssomanes viridis. — A bright green spider common in the southern states. The arrangement of the eyes differs from that usual in the Attidæ by the front lateral eyes being higher and closer together, so that they are over and behind the front middle pair (fig. 165). The cephalothorax is narrow in front, — not much more than half as wide as it is across the middle. The abdomen is narrower than the thorax and more than twice as long as wide. The female is a third of an inch in length, and the male quarter of an inch. The legs are long and slender, the first pair longest and thickest, in the male half an inch in length and in the female a little shorter.   In the female the mandibles are vertical and about as long as the height of the head.   In the male they are as long as the cephalothorax, curved apart, and extended almost horizontally in front of the head. The color is light transparent green, sometimes without any markings.   Usually there are four pairs of small black spots on the abdomen, and there are black spots around the eyes, except around the front pair, where there is a little orange color.   They live on low bushes and mature early in the summer.

THE LYCOSIDÆ

THE Lycosidæ are among the commonest spiders, or, at any rate, those most often seen. Most of them live near the ground and move actively about without attempting to conceal themselves. Their colors are black and white or the colors of the ground, stones, and dead leaves, sometimes nearly uniform all over the body, in other kinds arranged in a distinct pattern, with strong contrasts between the light and dark parts. In some species the markings are brighter and more characteristic on the under side than on the back. The legs are long, the fourth pair longest. The spines on the legs are long and often darker colored than the skin, and when the spider is active they stand out from the legs and make them appear larger. The first and second legs are more covered with fine short hairs and have the spines shorter and less easily seen than the third and fourth. The feet have three claws, the under one small and covered by the surrounding hairs. The eyes have a peculiar arrangement, the front row being small and nearly straight, the middle pair of the upper row just above them and much larger, while the lateral eyes of this row are carried back and upward on the sides of the head so that the eyes are really in three rows of four, two, and two (fig. 170). In those species with low heads, like Dolomedes, the upper row of eyes is less curved and smaller, and the whole arrangement resembles that in Tibellus and others of the Thomisidæ. The body is usually long and the head high, the abdomen about as long and as wide as the cephalothorax and as thick as it is wide.

Our largest spiders belong to this family. The females carry their eggs in round cocoons attached to their spinnerets, and the young for a short time after coming out are carried about on the back of the mother. Dolomedes and Ocyale carry their cocoons in the mandibles and spin a loose web in bushes, where the young live for a time after leaving the cocoon. The young of most species pass the winter half grown and mature the next summer. Most of the little spiders seen spinning their threads on the tops of plants and fences in the Indian summer are young Lycosidæ.

Most of these spiders belong to two genera, Lycosa and Pardosa, the first including the larger species, with the eyes covering only a small part of the front of the head and the front row about the same length as the second; the other, Pardosa, consisting of comparatively small species, with the four upper eyes very large and covering the whole top of the head and the front row much shorter than the second.

THE GENUS LYCOSA

The genus Lycosa includes spiders that differ greatly in the proportions of different parts of their bodies. In general, they are large and stout and their legs short compared to those of Pardosa and Dolomedes, the front legs being not much longer than the body. In the short and stout species, like *pratensis* (fig. 170), the eyes cover only a small part of the head, while in the longer legged and more slender species, like *communis* (fig. 181), they are larger and spread farther apart. The head is highest behind and rounded downward in front, but less so in those species with large eyes. The spines of the legs are comparatively small and on the two front pairs concealed by the surrounding hairs. The fine flattened hairs on the front feet sometimes form a thick brush on the under side, extending up from the claws as far as the tibia. The colors are all shades of brown and gray.

Lycosa nidicola. — When full grown three-quarters of an inch long; the legs short, the longest an inch in length. The color is dull yellow or greenish brown. On the cephalothorax there is a narrow yellow stripe in the middle and one on each side (fig. 166), and on the front of the abdomen the usual pointed stripe, dark at the edges and bordered by lighter bands. On the hinder half of the abdomen are indistinct cross marks. The legs are without markings, and the spines short and hardly visible. The under side of the abdomen (fig. 167) is light in the middle and darker at the sides and marked with small brown spots. The males and young are lighter and more plainly marked than the adult females. This spider lives under stones and other shelters in the woods in a shallow nest, lined with silk, where the female may be found with her cocoon of eggs early in the summer.

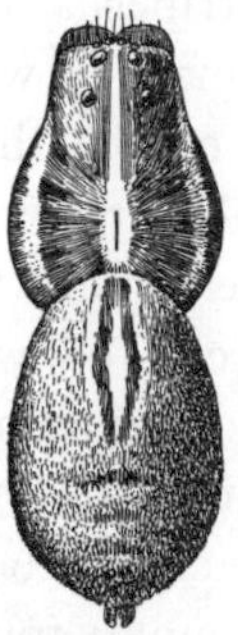

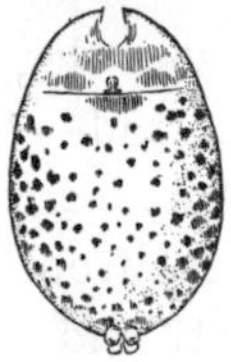

FIGS. 166, 167. Lycosa nidicola. — 166, female enlarged twice. 167, under side of abdomen.

169

170

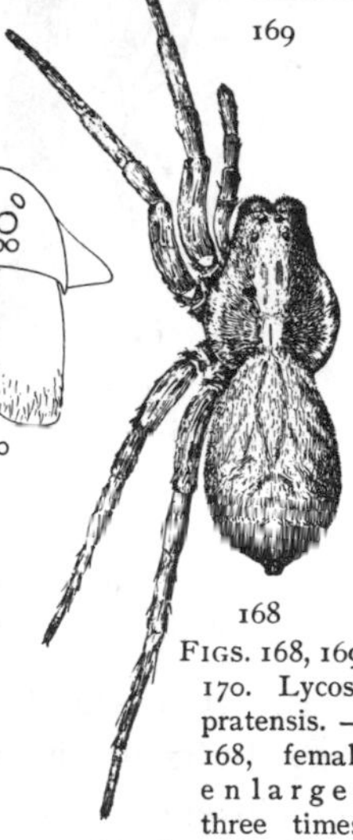

168

FIGS. 168, 169, 170. Lycosa pratensis. — 168, female enlarged three times. 169, side of cephalothorax. 170, front of head and mandibles.

Lycosa pratensis. — A small species, four-fifths to half an inch long, yellowish brown, with indistinct light and dark markings. The cephalothorax has a middle light band as wide as the eyes, narrowed a little in front of the dorsal groove and broken in the middle by two brown spots (fig. 168). The sides of the cephalothorax near the edge are faintly lighter than the rest. The abdomen has a pointed middle stripe, dark at the edges, extending back half its length, and behind this four or five dark cross stripes. The legs are darker toward the ends; the femora are marked with two broken dark bands, and the patella and tibia of the third and fourth legs have faint dark rings. The spines are small and, on the two front pairs of legs, hardly visible among the other hairs. The under side is light colored, with the ends of the legs darker. The epigynum is short and wide. The males differ little from the females. This does not seem to be a very active spider and is commonly found under stones.

Lycosa polita. — This is a short-legged species resembling in size and color *Lycosa pratensis.* The hairs are very short and often entirely absent from the cephalothorax, which is smooth and shining. The eyes are very close together, especially the two of the middle row, which is much shorter than the front row (fig. 171). The cephalothorax and legs are often light brown without any markings, but in some individuals there are irregular dark marks along the sides of the thorax and broken rings on the legs. The abdomen is gray, light in the middle, with dark transverse marks behind and closely placed dark spots at the sides, much as in *Tegenaria medicinalis* and Amaurobius. The abdomen is light underneath, with a darker middle line and irregular oblique rows of spots at the sides.

FIG. 171. Lycosa polita, enlarged three times.

Lycosa nidifex. — This spider lives in sandy regions, — the females in holes ten or twelve inches deep, the adult males on the surface of the ground. The males (fig. 174) are half or five-eighths of an inch long and spread two inches. They are colored like the sand, — a little redder sometimes in the middle spots and on the femora, and gray at the sides. There is a spot in the middle of the abdomen edged with black and

FIG. 172. Mouth of hole of Lycosa nidifex in sand, and footprints of the spider where it ran out from the hole and back again. One-third the real size.

a black band on each side of the head divided in front, the branches extending to the lateral eyes of both rows. The ends of the palpi and the spinnerets are black. The mandibles are black, except in the middle, where they are covered with bright yellow hairs. On the under side (fig. 175) the two front pairs of legs, sternum, and mouth parts are black, the hinder

legs and abdomen light sand color, like the back.   The female
(fig. 173) is larger,—three-quarters of an inch or more in length.
The color is more gray or slate color, darker in front and
lighter behind, as in the male.   The cephalothorax has a
light gray band in the middle, and the abdomen
a middle dark band broken at the sides by three
or four pairs of light spots.   The front two pairs
of legs are thicker than the others and more
closely covered with hair in both sexes.

In August the males wander about on
the sand and are easily caught.   Though
their color is much like the sand, the
marks of the back and legs make them
more easily seen than *L. cinerea* (fig. 177)
and other sand spiders.   The females live
in holes three-quarters of an inch wide
and ten inches or more deep.   The sand
is held together by silk, which is very
thin below but thicker toward the opening.   Sometimes bits of sticks and straw
are fastened around the hole, but as often
it is entirely clean and not concealed in

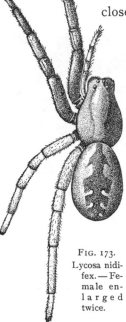

FIG. 173.
Lycosa nidi-
fex.— Fe-
male en-
larged
twice.

any way.   The females keep near their
holes and drop into them at the least
fright.   As one walks across the neighborhood no spiders are to be seen, only
open holes.   After a short time they
come to the surface, at first slowly, but sometimes, as they see
the place clear, with a sudden jump, and stand over the hole
ready to drop back into it.   The color of the females is more
gray or slate color than that of the males.   The markings of
the abdomen are larger and more distinct, but the black on the
thorax and front legs is less marked than in the males.

Lycosa carolinensis. — This is one of the largest spiders living in the northern states, and it resembles in size and color the famous Tarantula of southern Europe (fig. 175). The female is sometimes over an inch in length, with the fourth legs an inch and a half long, so that it spreads over three inches. The males have the legs as long but more slen- der, and the body is smaller, measuring three-quarters of an inch. The color is gray mixed with brown, like the fur of a mouse, the males lighter than the females.

On the under side the whole body is black, including the first and second joints of the legs and the maxillæ. The legs are light gray, with dark bands at the ends of the joints. The man- dibles are brown, with orange- yellow hairs on the front. There is sometimes a little yellow on the ends of the first and second legs and palpi of the male.

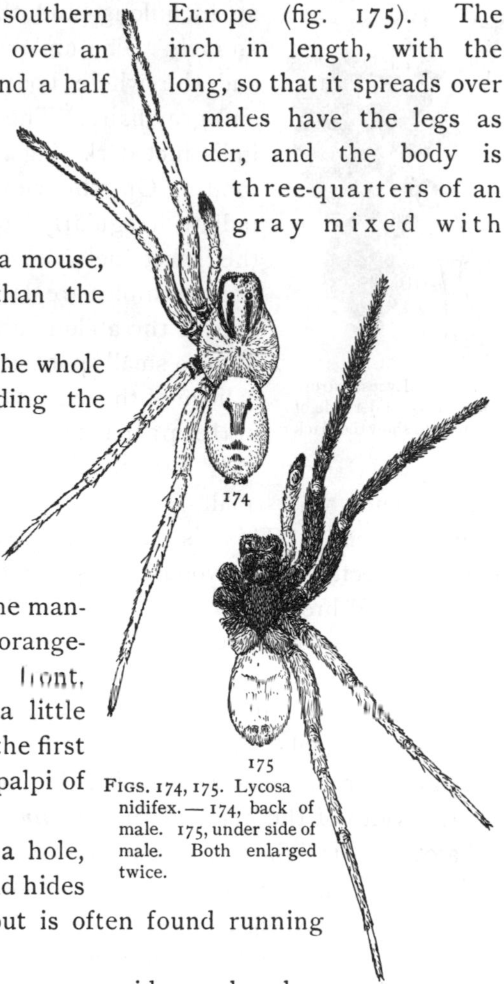

The female makes a hole, but not a deep one, and hides in it with her eggs, but is often found running about on the ground.

FIGS. 174, 175. Lycosa nidifex. — 174, back of male. 175, under side of male. Both enlarged twice.

Lycosa cinerea. — A common spider on beaches and sandy fields all over this country and in Europe (fig. 177) The general color is dirty white covered with small black and

gray marks, so that, when it lies flat on the sand, it
can hardly be distinguished from it.   The body is half
an inch long, and the fourth legs nearly
an inch.   The under side is white or gray,
and the whole body covered with white
and gray hairs.   The legs are marked with
indistinct dark rings, two or three to each
joint.   On the cephalothorax the spots
radiate irregularly from the dorsal groove;
the space between the eyes is dark, and
the mandibles are dark brown.   The markings of the abdomen are broken
up into small spots, so that there

FIG. 176.   Lycosa carolinensis. — Under side of
female to show the black
markings.

is little of the usual figures.   The
male palpi are
long and slender
and the ends very small.

Lycosa kochii. — This is a
common species in the woods,
and is colored brown and gray,
like dead leaves (fig. 179).   It
is half an inch long when full
grown, and the fourth legs three-
quarters of an inch.   The upper eyes

178

177

are larger than in *pratensis* and *nidicola*, and cover
half the width of the head, as in *communis*.   The
cephalothorax is light gray in the middle and dark
at the sides and around the front of the head.
The legs are gray, lighter toward the body and
darker toward the ends, marked with indistinct
rings, two or three to each joint.   The abdomen
is gray, with broken darker gray markings forming indistinctly a row of transverse marks in the

FIGS. 177, 178.   Ly-
cosa cinerea. — 177,
female enlarged
four times. 178,
maxillæ.

middle. The sides are darkest toward the front end, where there are two black spots. The under side is lighter than the back. The epigynum (fig. 180) differs from that of the related species, having the middle lobe narrow in front and wide and triangular at the end.

Lycosa communis. — This is a common spider in pastures, running in grass or hiding under stones. It varies in color from light gray to almost black, but the markings are almost always the same and distinct. On the thorax there is a middle stripe extending forward to the eyes, and a narrower one between the eyes to the front of the head (fig. 181). At the sides are light stripes nearly as wide as the middle one extending under the eyes to the front of the head. On the abdomen the front pointed stripe is large. The light stripes at the side of it are wide and distinct, uniting on the hinder half of the abdomen into a middle stripe, broken sometimes into a row of four or five spots. In dark individuals this light marking is yellow and more

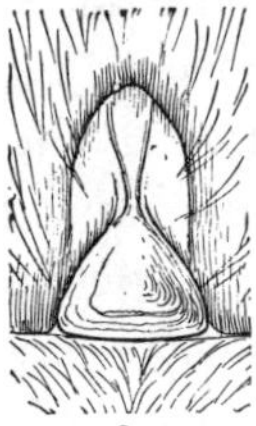

179

180

FIGS. 179, 180. Lycosa kochii. 179, female enlarged twice. 180, epigynum.

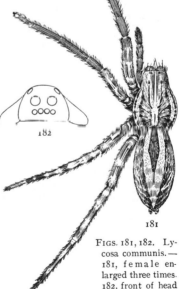

182

181

FIGS. 181, 182. Lycosa communis. — 181, female enlarged three times. 182, front of head showing eyes.

strongly defined than in lighter ones.   On the thorax, especially in light colored-spiders, there are usually two or three light marks radiating from the dorsal groove.   The legs, except the ends of the first and second, are marked with rings at the ends and middle of the joints, indistinct in light spiders and brighter in dark ones.

The length is two-fifths to half an inch.   The legs are long, the fourth pair three-quarters of an inch in length.   The second row of eyes is a little wider than the first, and the second eyes are large and their diameter apart (fig. 182). On the under side of the abdomen are two dark stripes meeting at the spinnerets so as to form a horseshoe-shaped figure, but in some very dark individuals the whole under side of the abdomen behind the epigynum is dark colored. There is little difference between the sexes. The females carry eggs in June and July.

FIG. 183. Lycosa scutulata. — Female enlarged twice.

Lycosa scutulata. — This is a large and well-marked species, over half an inch in length and with hind legs over an inch long (fig. 183). The legs are yellowish gray without markings. The cephalothorax is dark gray, with a light middle stripe and one on each side extending under the eyes to the front of the head.   There is also a narrow light line on the edge of the thorax at the sides.   In the middle of the abdomen is a dark stripe, with five or six pairs of light spots, those of the front pair being only partly inclosed by the stripe.   At the sides of the middle stripe are narrower light bands, and beyond these fine light and dark oblique lines.   On the under side the whole body is light gray.

In the males the front legs are a little longer and much darker colored than the others.   The male palpi are slender,

and the tarsi small for so large a spider. The second row of
eyes is a little wider than the front row.

Lycosa ocreata. — The female may easily be mistaken for young
L. kochii (fig. 179) or *communis* (fig. 181), but the male is conspicuous on account of the dark
head and front legs and especially the thick covering of
black hairs on the tibiæ of the
first pair. The cephalothorax
has a distinct light middle
stripe, narrower and straighter
in the male (figs. 184, 185).
The middle of the abdomen is
yellow, with the pointed stripe
only a little darker and marked
with black spots around the edges. At
the sides the abdomen is brown, broken
in spots, and in the middle of the hinder
half are three or four cross marks. The
legs are yellowish and ringed with gray
in the females. In the males the femora
and the sides of the thorax are much
darker brown, and the tibiæ of the front
pair dark and thickly covered with hairs.
The male palpi have the patella and tibia
thickened and about as wide as long.

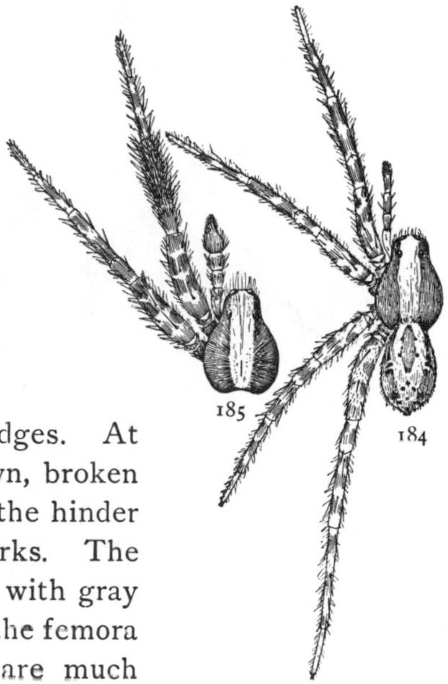

FIGS. 184, 185. Lycosa ocreata.
— 184, female enlarged eight
times. 185, cephalothorax
and front legs of male.

The front legs are plainly thicker than the second in both
sexes. The second row of eyes is wider than the first. The
length of either sex is a little over quarter of an inch. The legs
are slender and thinly covered with long fine hairs. The longest
leg is about half an inch.

THE GENUS PARDOSA

Pardosa con-
small spiders, all
slender.   The

187

sists of comparatively
of them long legged and
head is high in front, and
the four upper eyes large
and spread over the whole front
of the head (fig. 200).   The
front row of eyes is plainly
shorter than the second
row.   The colors are generally dark, often
black, and with
white markings.
The spines of the
legs are long, even
on the front pairs,
and the whole body
is often covered
with long hairs.   To
show the compara-
tive size of the dif-

188

186

ferent species of this genus, all
the figures are made on the
same scale, four times the
real size.

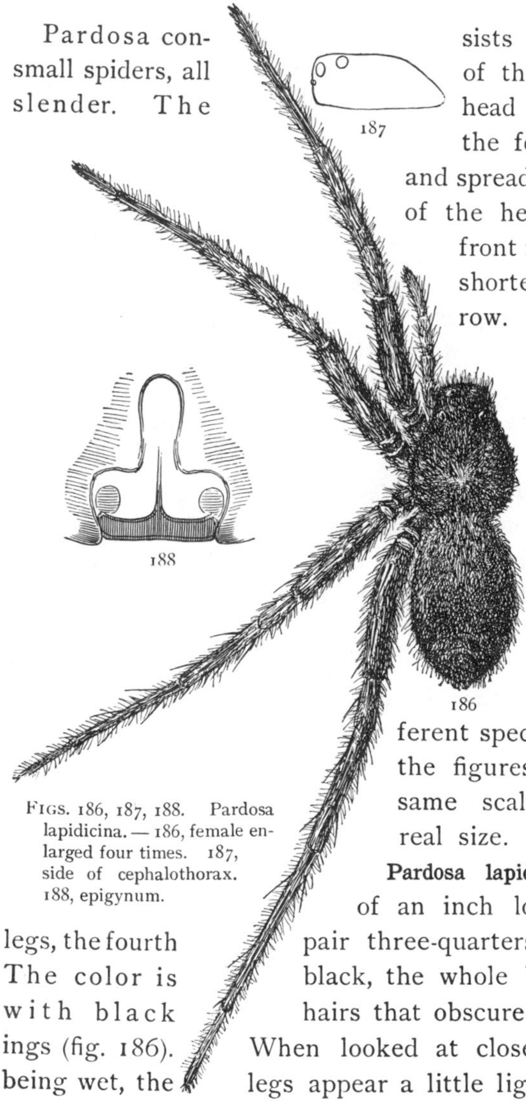

FIGS. 186, 187, 188.   Pardosa
lapidicina. — 186, female enlarged four times.   187,
side of cephalothorax.
188, epigynum.

Pardosa lapidicina. — Four-fifths
of an inch long and with long

legs, the fourth
The color is
with black
ings (fig. 186).
being wet, the

pair three-quarters of an inch long.
black, the whole body being covered
hairs that obscure the few light mark-
When looked at closely, especially after
legs appear a little lighter colored toward

the ends, and the femora faintly marked with light rings. In the middle of the cephalothorax there is a large light spot, widest just in front of the dorsal groove, and at the sides are rows of irregular light spots. On the abdomen are three or four pairs of light spots near together in the front half, and behind are two rows of spots meeting over the spinnerets. On the under side the color is a lighter gray than on the back. The color, as in all spiders, varies according to age, the young and freshly molted having a deeper black color, while older ones are gray. The epigynum is shown in the figure (fig. 188), and is quite constant in shape. It distinguishes this species from *greenlandica* (fig. 189), for which it is most likely to be mistaken. The male differs little from the female. This spider lives among gray stones in the hottest and driest places from Connecticut to Labrador.

189

Pardosa albomaculata or **greenlandica**. — This species resembles *lapidicina* (fig. 186), but is a little larger and not quite as long legged. It has longer hairs and is marked with bright white spots on a black ground. There are two rows of white spots on the abdomen, and others along the sides of the cephalothorax and on the legs (fig. 189). Wet in alcohol it shows similar irregular markings on the abdomen as *lapidicina*, but the light spots

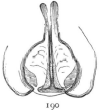

190

FIGS. 189, 190. Pardosa greenlandica. — 189, female enlarged four times. 190, epigynum.

on the thorax are smaller, the middle one extending forward only to the dorsal groove. The epigynum (fig. 190) is large and distinct. Its outline has been compared to that of a decanter, narrow in front and rounded out at the sides behind.

There is a long narrow middle lobe, generally widened at the end, but varying much in shape. At the front end of the epigynum are two small depressions. It resembles the epigynum of *glacialis* (fig. 192), but is always longer and narrower and has the middle lobe straighter and more distinct. White Mountains, on bare stones. Rocky Mountains, Canada, and Greenland.

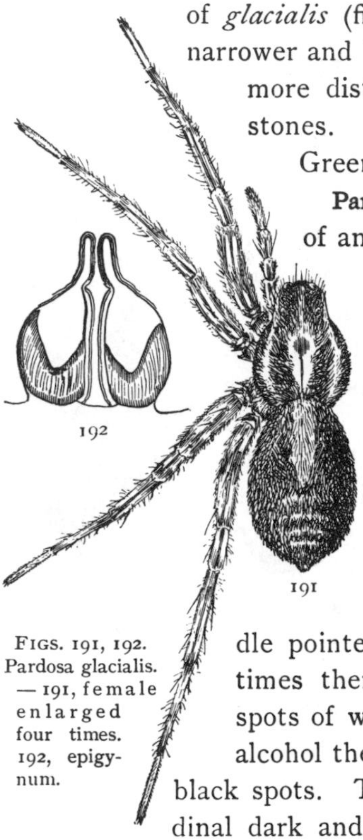

Pardosa glacialis or **brunnea.**— One-third of an inch long. Color dark brown with some light markings. In the middle of the cephalothorax is a light stripe, widening and fading out toward the eyes and divided by a dark middle line, widest in front and extending back as far as the dorsal groove (fig. 191). On each side is a light stripe extending under the eyes to the front of the head. The abdomen has the middle pointed stripe light colored, and sometimes there are four or five pairs of small spots of white hairs on the hinder half. In alcohol there are obscure cross markings and black spots. The legs are marked with longitudinal dark and light lines. On the under side there is usually a light middle stripe on the front of the sternum, and the middle of the abdomen is lighter than the rest. The whole body is hairy; there are long black hairs on the front of the head, and the spines are long and colored like the legs. The epigynum (fig. 192) has a narrow middle lobe transparent at the end so that it is difficult to see, and dark brown pieces at the sides, with the outer ends turned forward. The shape

192

191

FIGS. 191, 192. Pardosa glacialis. — 191, female enlarged four times. 192, epigynum.

can best be understood from the figure. The epigynum varies, but distinguishes this species plainly from *greenlandica* (fig. 190), with which it is likely to be associated. The male palpi are large and black at the ends, the tarsus oval and pointed, and the tibia short and as thick as

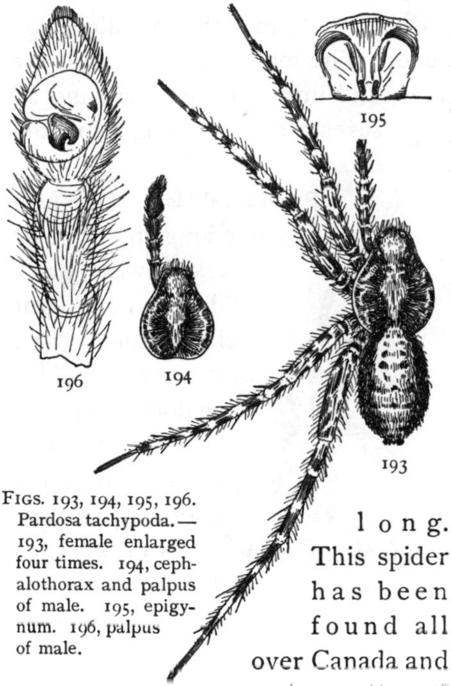

FIGS. 193, 194, 195, 196. Pardosa tachypoda. — 193, female enlarged four times. 194, cephalothorax and palpus of male. 195, epigynum. 196, palpus of male.

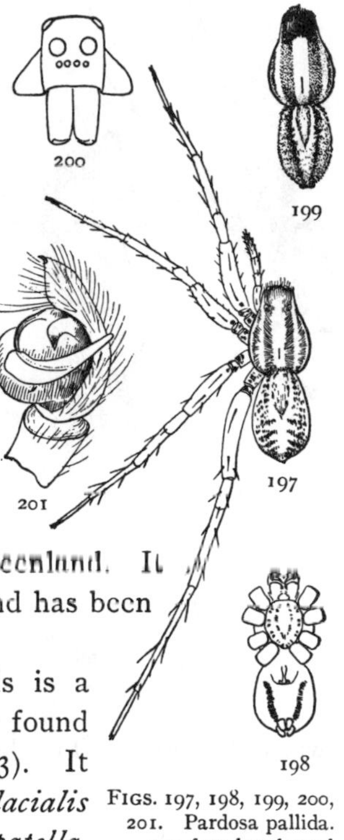

l o n g. This spider has been found all over Canada and as far north as Greenland. It is common in the White Mountains and has been found as far south as Connecticut.

Pardosa tachypoda or **montana**. — This is a Canadian and White Mountain spider found as far south as Massachusetts (fig. 193). It is smaller than either *greenlandica* or *glacialis* and larger than *nigropalpis* and *albopatella*. The colors are more like the last two species, but the legs are darker and more distinctly ringed. The light markings of

FIGS. 197, 198, 199, 200, 201. Pardosa pallida. — 197, female enlarged four times. 198, under side of female. 199, back of male. 200, front of head. 201, end of palpus of male.

the cephalothorax and abdomen are less distinct and more broken and irregular. The epigynum (fig. 195) has a character-istic shape different from any of the allied species, the two anterior depressions being wide apart and the middle ridge narrow and rounded at the end. The male palpi (fig. 196) are rather slender, as in *lapidicina*, and uniformly colored, and all the differences between the sexes are less strongly marked than in *nigropalpis* and *albo-patella*.

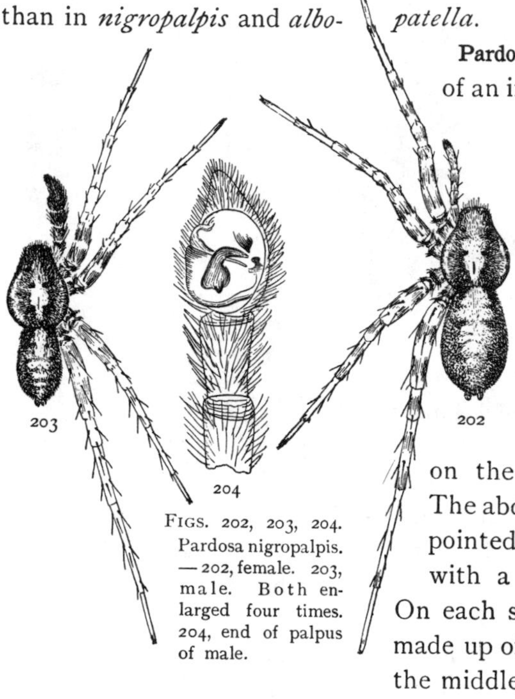

Pardosa pallida. — One-fifth of an inch long and brightly marked with black and brown on a light yellow ground (figs. 197, 199). T h e cephalothorax is nar-rower than in most species. The ceph-alothorax h a s t w o wide gray stripes and a fine black line on the edge at each side. The abdomen has the middle pointed stripe light brown with a broken black edge. On each side is a black band, made up of spots closer toward the middle and more scattered toward the sides. The legs are light yellow, with a few black spots near the body. The spines of the legs are long but not dark colored. On the under side there are dark spots on the sternum near the base of each leg, and sometimes two rows of spots or two bands nearer the middle. On the under side of the abdomen are two black stripes, sometimes connected

FIGS. 202, 203, 204. Pardosa nigropalpis. — 202, female. 203, male. Both en-larged four times. 204, end of palpus of male.

behind. In the males (fig. 199) the colors are darker and the dark markings larger. The ends of the palpi are large and covered with black hairs.

In one freshly molted young male there was hardly any trace of the spots on the sternum. The male palpi were dark gray with black hairs, except the tarsus, which was light colored, with a dark spot in the middle and a few black hairs. The markings of the abdomen were very indistinct, and the light color brownish, while the thorax and legs are slightly green. The first femora were black toward the end.

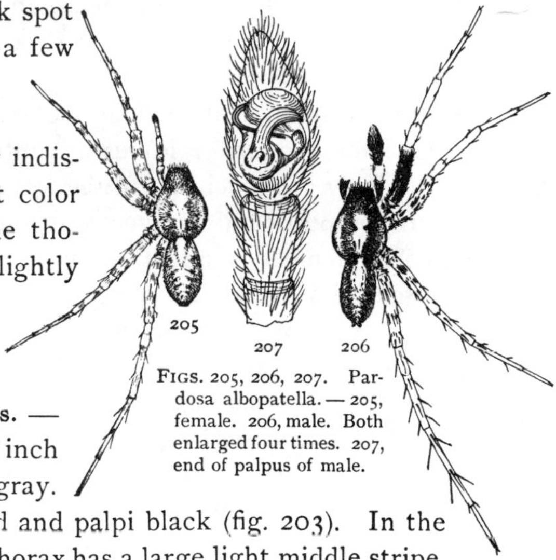

Pardosa nigropalpis. — About quarter of an inch long. Black and gray.

FIGS. 205, 206, 207. Pardosa albopatella. — 205, female. 206, male. Both enlarged four times. 207, end of palpus of male.

The male with head and palpi black (fig. 203). In the female the cephalothorax has a large light middle stripe, widest between the eyes and the dorsal groove, and a narrow light stripe on each side (fig. 202). The abdomen is light in the middle for its whole length in an irregular stripe partly divided by faint cross lines of gray. The sides are darker and spotted with black. The legs are faintly marked with darker rings. In the male the contrast between the light and dark markings is greater, the markings of the cephalothorax are smaller and brighter, and the head and palpi are black and covered with black hairs.

Pardosa albopatella. — Smaller than *P. nigropalpis*, but resembling it in shape and color (figs. 205, 206). The middle stripe of the cephalothorax is narrower. The middle stripe of the abdomen is narrower and brighter at the front end. The femora are distinctly marked with four rings, and the other joints less plainly. In the male the ends of the legs are pale, without rings, and the rings of the femora are broken into spots except on the front legs, where the femora are black. The palpi (fig. 206) have the femora black and the patella white. The tibia is dark, and the tarsus is dark at the base and white toward the tip.

Pirata piraticus. — A small and active spider living in short grass in summer and under leaves in winter. The colors and shape of the body are much like *Lycosa pratensis* (fig. 168), but the legs are proportionally larger and longer, and the colors brighter. The length is about a quarter of an inch. The front and second rows of eyes are of the same length, those of the second row large and their diameter apart (fig. 209). The eyes of the upper row are nearly as large as those of the second, and twice as far apart. The color is pale yellow, with gray or black markings. The cephalothorax has a narrow light line in the middle and one on each side (fig. 208). In the middle of the front of the abdomen is a light stripe with dark edges, which tapers into a line or row of spots behind the middle. At the sides of this are light stripes that unite behind, and outside of these are dark markings becoming smaller behind. The legs have conspicuous dark spines, especially the hinder pair, and are faintly marked with rings or sometimes are without markings.

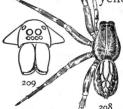

209

FIGS. 208, 209. Pirata piraticus. — 208, female enlarged three times. 209, front of head.

208

Dolomedes and Ocyale differ in many respects from the other Lycosidæ. They are more flattened, have the head lower, and the eyes all more nearly of the same size. The front row of eyes are small and near together.   The upper row is about twice as long and strongly curved, and the eyes are nearly equal in size and twice as large as those of the front row (figs. 214, 216).   In Dolomedes the lower eyes are ⟍   about half as high as the top of the head.   In Ocyale they ⟍ are lower and farther apart, and the head resembles still more Tibellus of the Thomisidæ.   Both Ocyale and Dolomedes resemble this family in their flattened body and wide thorax.

Dolomedes sexpunctatus. — Dark greenish gray or, in young spiders, yellow, with a silvery white line each side the whole length of the body, meeting in front under the eyes and reaching back to the spinnerets (fig. 210).   In the middle of the cephalothorax is a narrow light line.   On the hinder half of the abdomen are four pairs of small white spots, and sometimes another pair near the front end. On the under side the general color is lighter, and there are six dark spots on the sternum (fig. 211).   The cephalothorax is three-quarters as wide as long, but looks narrower on account of the white stripes. The abdomen is proportionally longer than in *tenebrosus* (fig. 213).   The full-grown

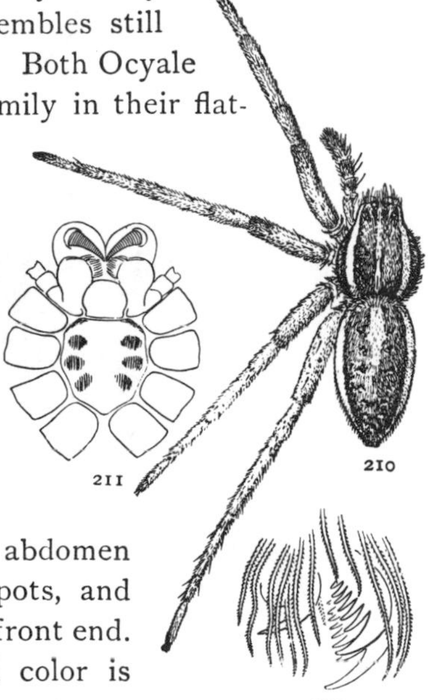

FIGS. 210, 211, 212. Dolomedes sexpunctatus. — 210, female enlarged twice. 211, under side of cephalothorax. 212, one of the feet, showing three claws.

female is six-tenths of an inch long, with a spread of an inch and three-quarters.   In winter and spring the half-grown young are very common everywhere.   It lives near water and runs easily on it, each foot making a depression on the surface without becoming wet.

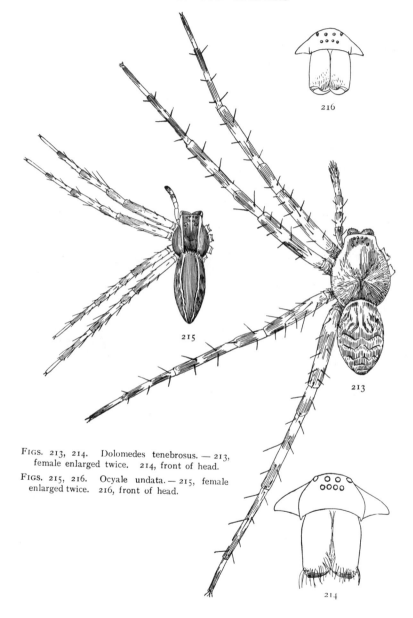

FIGS. 213, 214.   Dolomedes tenebrosus. — 213,
female enlarged twice.   214, front of head.

FIGS. 215, 216.   Ocyale undata. — 215, female
enlarged twice.   216, front of head.

Dolomedes tenebrosus. — This is one of our largest spiders, spreading its legs over four inches. The color is light and dark gray. The legs are indistinctly marked with light and dark rings and have long dark spines (fig. 213). The thorax is dark in the middle and lighter toward the eyes. On each side are light bands that extend around under the eyes and meet in front. The abdomen has three pairs of transverse dark stripes, each with a light border on the hinder edge. The cephalothorax is four-tenths of an inch long and three-tenths wide, half as wide in front, and nearly straight on the front edge. It is rounded in the middle, but not very high, and just behind the eyes is nearly flat. The under side of the thorax and legs is light colored, without markings, the abdomen a little darker. The abdomen is as

FIG. 217. Nest of the young of Ocyale undata in a wild-rose bush. One-third the real size.

long as the thorax, widest across the middle, and a little pointed behind. The male has longer legs and is more slender and strongly marked; under the fourth femora near the end is a bunch of stiff hairs. The male palpi are long, with large tarsi and palpal organs and a long hook on the outer side of the tarsus. They live near water, on the ground or low bushes.

The female carries her cocoon in her mandibles and makes a large bunch of silk in the bushes, in which the young live for some time after hatching.

Ocyale undata. — When full grown over half an inch long, the thorax quarter of an inch, and the first and fourth legs an inch long. The thorax is almost as wide as long, and the head not much more than half as wide (fig. 215). The abdomen is long and narrower than the thorax and a little pointed behind. The color is a light brownish yellow, with a wide darker and browner band on the middle of both thorax and abdomen. This band

is bordered by a white line a little curved in and out toward the tail. In younger spiders the color is lighter and yellower; the middle stripe has the edges more undulating, and in very young ones it is serrated or even broken up into spots. The legs, which are plain in adults, are sometimes marked with rings in the young. The front end of the stripe is sometimes divided into two. These spiders live on bushes, without any web, until they have young. In the latter part of summer the females carry their flat cocoons under them, holding on with the mandibles. When the young are about to hatch the female builds a mass of web (fig. 217) three or four inches through, in which she leaves the cocoon, and the young come out and live for a time together in the web.

FIGS. 218, 219. Oxyopes salticus. — 218, female enlarged six times. 219, front of head.

Oxyopes salticus. — The eyes are in three rows, the front one of two small eyes, the second of four eyes, and the upper of two. The head is wide and less separated from the thorax than in Lycosa and very high in front. The cephalothorax is two-thirds as wide as long and rounded both in front and behind (fig. 218). The abdomen of the male is smaller than the cephalothorax, but that of the female is wider and longer. It is widest in the middle, rounded in front, and pointed behind. The legs are slender, the first pair longest, but all nearly of the same length and with very long spines. The colors and markings are very variable. The legs are white or pale yellow, with black spines. The light parts of the body are the same color, with brown and black markings. There are usually four brown stripes on the cephalothorax from the eyes backward, and two black lines in front from the lower eyes down the front of the mandibles (fig. 219). The most constant mark of the abdomen is a pointed middle spot extending as far as the middle of the back. This is generally surrounded by light color, and at the sides are narrow oblique brown marks. There are sometimes fine black lines on the under sides of the femora and a wide black middle stripe under the abdomen. The males are sometimes colored like the female,

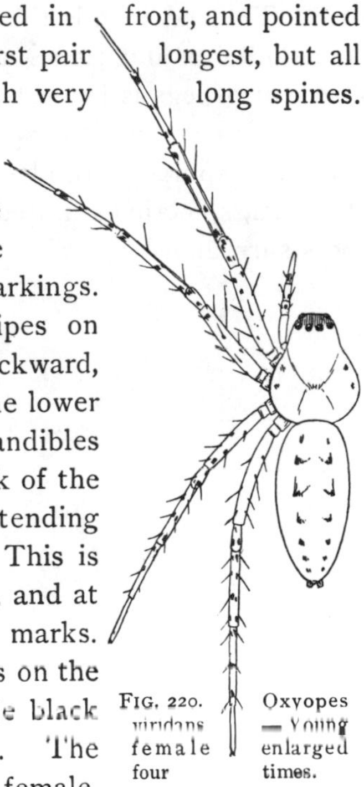

FIG. 220. Oxyopes viridans female — Young enlarged four times.

and vary from this to black abdomen and palpi, with the rest of the body pale. A very common species in the southern states in the early summer, running on low bushes. There is another Oxyopes about the same size that has been found a few times as far north as New England.

Oxyopes (Peucetia) viridans.— This is a common and conspicuous spider in the South. It is a bright transparent green, with red spots and black spines. It grows to a length of three-quarters of an inch, but is found in great numbers early in the summer, when it is only a quarter of this size (fig. 220). The head is narrower than in *O. salticus*, and the lateral eyes so high that they appear to belong to the upper rather than the middle row. The abdomen is the same width as the back part of the cephalothorax and tapers a little toward the spinnerets. The first pair of legs is longest and the second next. The general color is green, with the space between the eyes red, red spots and black spines on the legs, and two rows of red spots on the abdomen, sometimes united into a stripe, with pairs of white spots surrounded by red.

THE AGALENIDÆ

THE larger Agalenidæ are the makers of the flat wide cobwebs that are so common on the grass and in the corners

FIG. 221. Web of Agalena nævia in long grass, seen from above. One-third the real size.

of barns and cellars. They resemble some of the Drassidæ, especially Agrœca and Anyphæna (pp. 1–14). The head is large and marked off by shallow grooves from the thorax, and is often contracted behind the eyes, so that it is narrower there than in front. The mandibles are large and, in the females, much swelled at the base in front. The arrangement of the eyes differs little from that in the Drassidæ. The upper spinnerets are longer than the others and have the terminal joint

FIG. 222. Web of Agalena nævia in short grass on the side of a hill, seen from the side. The spider stands in its usual place at the mouth of its tube. Half the real size.

narrowed toward the end, with the spinning tubes on the inner side. The feet have three claws, like the Lycosidæ, and do not have the brush of hairs common in the Drassidæ. The males and females differ little in size, but the males have longer legs and smaller abdomen and large and complicated palpi.

Agalena nævia. — This spider is known everywhere by its web, which it makes on grass, among stones and weeds, and in houses (figs. 221, 222). It varies greatly in size and color. Large females may be three-quarters of an inch long, with legs measuring an inch and a quarter, while others may be full grown at half that size. In color some are pale yellow with gray markings, and others reddish brown with the markings almost black. Whatever the color, they are thickly covered with fine gray hairs. The cephalothorax has two longitudinal gray stripes and a black line along the edge on each side (fig. 223). The head is high and a little darker in front. Both rows of eyes are strongly curved, with the middle eyes highest, so that the middle eyes of the lower row and the lateral of the upper row form a nearly straight line (fig. 224). The mandibles are stout, not much swelled in front, and covered with hair. The abdomen is gray or black at the sides and lighter brown in the middle, with two rows of white or light-colored spots. The upper spinnerets are more than twice as long as the others, and the terminal joint much longer than the basal. The legs are large and long, the fourth pair almost

224

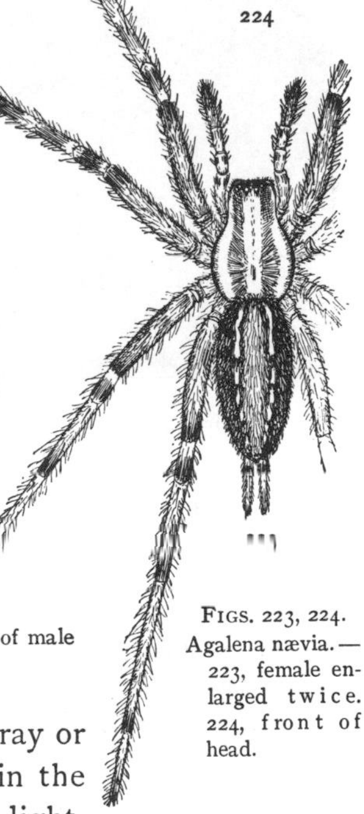

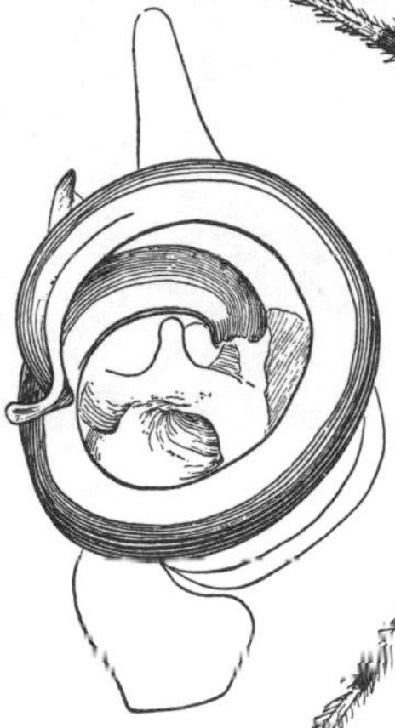

225

FIG. 225. End of palpus of male Agalena nævia.

FIGS. 223, 224. Agalena nævia. — 223, female enlarged twice. 224, front of head.

twice as long as the body. The legs are marked with dark rings at the ends of the joints and lighter rings in the middle of femur and tibia. On the under side the coxæ are light colored and the sternum dark, and there is a broad dark middle band on the abdomen from the hinder legs to the spinnerets. The males are as large as the females, with longer legs and smaller abdomen. The male palpi have a very large black tube coiled one and a half turns under the tarsus (fig. 225). The web (fig. 222) is flat and shaped according to

FIG. 226. Newly made edge of web of Agalena nævia, showing arrangement of the threads.

the surrounding objects to which it is fastened, with a tube at one side in which the spider hides. The eggs are laid in August and September in a flat cocoon, attached by one side in some sheltered place and covered with silk, often mixed with dirt. Most of the adult spiders die before winter, and females are often found dead on or near their cocoons. The young hatch in the winter and leave the cocoon early in the spring, and soon begin to build their webs among the short grass. The webs become more distinct when covered with dew, but, though too transparent to be seen at other times, they remain in the same places throughout the summer and are repaired

and enlarged as the spider grows. If, however, the web
should be destroyed, the spider is able in one day to make
a new one as large as the old, but thin and transparent. The
web contains many long threads crossing it from one side to

FIG. 227. Web of Agalena nævia in a plant of golden-rod two feet above the ground,
showing upper threads. One-fourth the real size.

the other and nearly parallel, and these are crossed in all
directions by finer threads (fig. 226). The long threads are spun
from the lower spinnerets, the upper pair being held up over
the back, out of the way. The fine threads are spun from the
upper spinnerets, which are swung from side to side as the

spider moves along.   There is nothing adhesive about the web.
It serves merely as a clearing where insects may alight to rest
and the spider may have a good
chance to run after them.   Where
the web is made under plants or
rocks a great number of threads are
carried upward from it, which may
help in stopping insects (fig. 227), as
they do in the webs of Linyphia.
(See p. 135.)

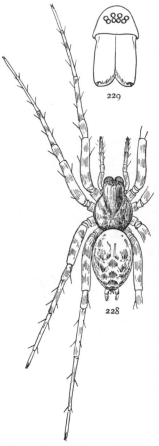

FIGS. 228, 229.   Tegenaria derhamii. — 228, female enlarged four
times.   229, front of head.

Tegenaria derhamii. — This is a common species in barns and cellars,
and has probably been imported from
Europe, where it is even more common.   The head is high and wide,
as in *T. medicinalis*.   The mandibles
are less swelled in front and the
eyes are closer together than in that
species, and cover more than half
the width of the head (fig. 229).   The
cephalothorax is shorter and wider
across the hinder half and the abdomen shorter than in *medicinalis*, and
the legs are longer and more hairy.
The colors are lighter and the hairs
of the whole body longer.   The
female is two-fifths of an inch long.
The cephalothorax is pale, with two
gray stripes.   The abdomen is marked
with a series of gray spots, formed of
a middle row more or less connected with two side rows; the
front of the abdomen often pale, with the markings faint
(fig. 228).   The legs are long, the first and fourth pairs nearly

twice the length of the body. They are marked with faint gray rings at the ends and two in the middle of each joint. The palpi are long and slender in both sexes, and those of the male have the patella and tibia of about the same length and each nearly twice as long as wide. There are no processes on the patella, but two small teeth on the tibia near its end. The tarsus is small and narrow, not as long as the patella and tibia.

FIG. 230. Web of Tegenaria derhamii in corner of cellar.

The webs are made in all parts of cellars and unswept buildings, sometimes forming a shelf in the corner, not as large or as flat as those of *A. nævia*, but with a similar tube on the most sheltered side (fig. 230). The webs more often spread under beams and floors, fastened up by threads at the sides and edges, and, as they gather dust, hang down by its weight and become

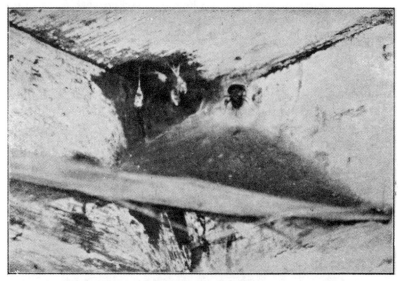

FIG. 231.   Web of Tegenaria derhamii with spider in mouth of tube.
Old cocoons hanging at the left.

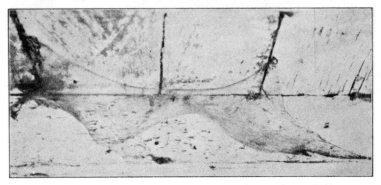

FIG. 232.   Web of Tegenaria derhamii curving downward on each side.

torn and tangled. Old webs are repaired and extended until they become as thick as cloth with silk and dirt. The tube is generally smaller and less funnel shaped where it enters the web than that of Agalena. The web is not as flat as that of Agalena, curving usually down from the tube and up in front of it, often turning up abruptly at the edge. Sometimes it is fastened up in the middle of the front edge and curves downward each side (fig. 232).

Fig. 231 shows a web of the most common form in the corner of a cellar, with the spider standing at the mouth of the tube, and the remains of egg cocoons hung up at the left. This web was at least a year old, and the front edge had just been extended with clear and transparent silk, while the middle was black with coal dust.

Fig. 232 is another web in the same cellar, with the front edge fastened up to the boards above. It is drawn lightest in the middle and curves down on each side.

Tegenaria (Cælotes) medicinalis. — A large gray spider living in the woods, among rocks, in hollow trees, and under loose bark. It is half an inch long, with the legs of the female not much longer (fig. 233). The head is large and wide,

FIGS. 233, 234. Tegenaria medicinalis. — 233, adult female enlarged four times. 234, cephalothorax of young female to show spots.

and the eyes cover a little more than half its width. It is a little constricted in front of the legs and raised above the thorax as far back as the dorsal groove. The abdomen of the females is large and oval, widest across the hinder half. The spinnerets are small, but plainly two-jointed, and the upper pair longest.   The general color is light yellow brown, covered with gray hairs, the cephalothorax browner, and the abdomen grayer, than the legs.   The cephalothorax has two indistinct gray stripes.   The abdomen is marked with a series of gray spots of irregular shape, smallest toward the front and larger and darker toward the end.   The legs are faintly ringed with gray, more distinctly in the young.

The males are as large as the females, with smaller abdomen and longer legs.   The palpi have the patella and tibia short, not much longer than wide (fig. 235).   The patella has a short

FIG. 235.   Palpus of male Tegenaria medicinalis.

process on the outer side near the end.   The tibia is of complicated shape, as shown in the figure.   The tarsus is twice as long as the tibia and patella together, with a long narrow tip.   The palpal organ is large and complicated, with a long fine tube that can be seen from above, where it curves around the base of the tarsus.

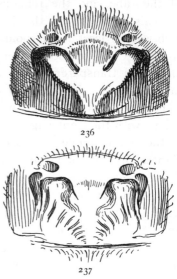

FIGS. 236, 237.   Two forms of epigynum of Tegenaria medicinalis.

The epigynum varies in appearance according to the thickness and color of different parts.   The two figures show common varieties (figs. 236, 237). This species and *longitarsus* are both easily mistaken for *Amaurobius sylvestris* and *ferox*, which are of the same size and color and live in the same situations. Amaurobius does not have the long upper spinnerets like Tegenaria, the eyes are lower on the front of the head, and there are larger light-colored markings on the front of the abdomen. The young of *Tegenaria medicinalis*

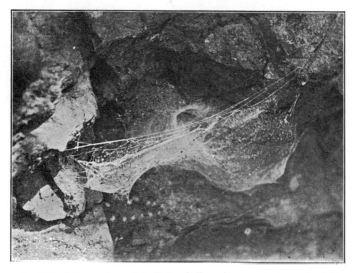

FIG. 238. Web of Tegenaria medicinalis in a hollow of a rock, the front edge held up by threads running across the hollow, and the mouth of the tube showing behind it.

are pale, with light gray markings, and the cephalothorax is marked with spots radiating from the dorsal groove (fig. 234). The web of this spider is not flat like that of Agalena, but curved in various shapes according to the place where it is built. If there is an open level place near the nest, the web spreads across it, but usually curves upward at the edges and is fastened to surrounding stones and weeds. Where the spider lives in the cracks of a wall or rock, the net spreads along the surface of the rock, held away from it a short distance by threads fastened to projecting points on the stone (figs. 239, 240). This species is sometimes mistaken for the longer legged and more hairy *Tegenaria derhamii* (fig. 228), that makes similar webs in barns and cellars.

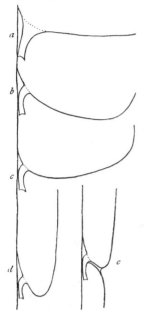

Fig. 239. Sections of webs of Tegenaria and Agalena. — *a*, Agalena nævia; *b*, common form of Tegenaria derhamii, with the edge lower than the tube; *c*, Tegenaria, with the edge higher than the tube; *d*, Tegenaria, with the edge carried up along the face of a rock; *e*, Tegenaria, with the edge carried down as well as up.

Tegenaria (Cælotes) longitarsus. — Smaller than *medicinalis;* about two-fifths of an inch in length. The head is very wide, and the mandibles of the female more swelled in front than in *medicinalis,* and the eyes are smaller and cover less than half the width of the head (figs. 244, 245). The cephalothorax is darker colored in front and does not have the two longitudinal stripes seen in *medicinalis* (fig. 241). The legs are only faintly marked with gray in the middle of the joints. The abdomen is marked with gray, in a series of dark and light spots, as in other species, and of more regular shape than in *medicinalis.* The epigynum is light colored, with a middle bar covered with hair and slightly forked at the hinder end (fig. 242). The male differs in the usual way from female and has the palpi shorter than *medicinalis.* The tarsus has a projection at the base that covers the tibia. The patella has a short process on the outer side that points directly forward (fig. 243).

Tegenaria (Cicurina) complicata. — A small spider, resembling the young of the larger species of Tegenaria, found usually under dead leaves in woods (fig. 246). It is a fifth to a quarter of an inch long, with the longest legs one and one-half times as long as the body. The spines of the third and fourth legs are long and stout, and there are long fine hairs on all the legs and the abdomen. The color is pale yellowish brown, lighter on the abdomen, which has faint gray markings. The sexes are much

FIG. 240. Web of Tegenaria medicinalis, with the front edge carried up along the face of a rock. See diagram (fig. 239, *d*).

alike, and both vary in size. The palpi of the males are very large and conspicuous (figs. 248, 249). The patella is short and wide, and the tibia is narrower at the end and wide toward the base, where it has a short process on the outer side. On the under side of the tibia is a long thin appendage of irregular shape that is nearly as long as the tarsus. The tarsus itself is long

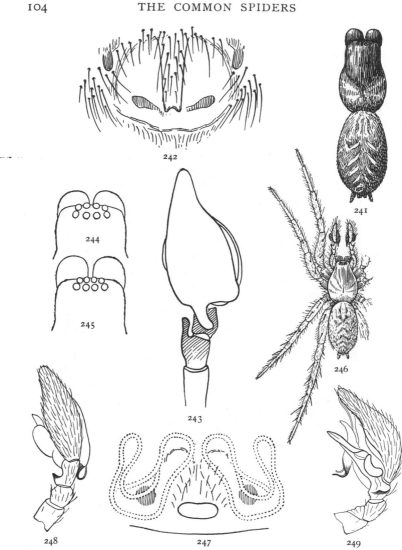

FIGS. 241, 242, 243, 244, 245.   Tegenaria longitarsus. — 241, back of female.   242, epigynum.
   243, palpus of male seen from above.   244, head of Tegenaria medicinalis.   245, head
   of Tegenaria longitarsus.
FIGS. 246, 247, 248, 249.   Tegenaria complicata. — 246, female enlarged four times.
   247, epigynum.   248, 249, male palpus.

and narrow, and the palpal organ large and complicated, with a long fine tube that extends from the base along the outer side and back to the hard appendages in the middle. The epigynum (fig. 247) has a small, transverse, oval opening at the hinder end, in front of which the coils of long tubes can be seen through the skin.

In New England Agalenidæ Pl. VII, fig. 2 is the epigynum of this species and not of *Cælotes longitarsus*.

Hahnia bimaculata. — The Hahnias resemble Tegenaria, but are much smaller and have the spinnerets extended in a line across the under side of the abdomen (fig. 251). *Hahnia bimaculata* is about one-eighth of an inch long, with the abdomen large and oval, widest behind, as it is in Cælotes (fig. 250). The cephalothorax is bright orange brown, and the legs and abdomen pale yellowish with gray markings. The legs are ringed with gray, the longer joints having two rings, and the abdomen has a pattern of light yellow and gray spots. The spinnerets are all long and in a nearly straight line, half as long as the width of the abdomen. The outer or upper pair are half as long

250   251

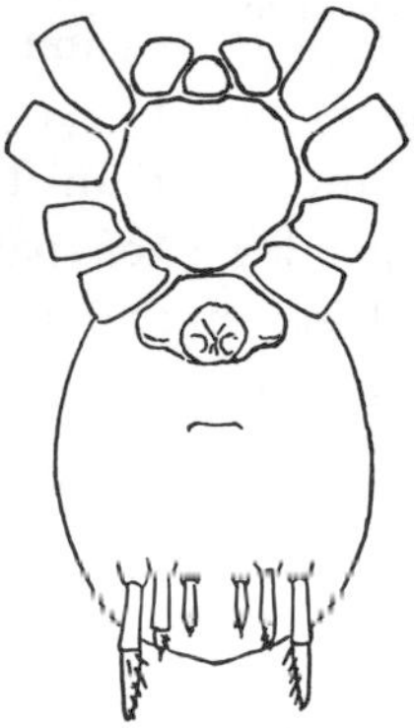

FIGS. 250, 251. Hahnia bimaculata. — 250, female enlarged twelve times. 251, under side showing the peculiar arrangement of the spinnerets.

as the abdomen, and the two joints are nearly of equal length. The tracheal opening is in the middle of the abdomen, nearer the epigynum than the spinnerets. The sternum is as wide as long, widest opposite the second legs. The maxillæ are straight in front and have a slight projection at the outer corners, where there are two or three stiff hairs.   In some other species there is a longer process at these corners.

This spider is common in winter under stones and under leaves.   In summer it makes webs close to the ground, among short and thin grass and moss.

Hahnia cinerea. — About a twelfth of an inch long ; much smaller than *bimaculata* (fig. 251). The color is dark gray, the cephalothorax and legs brownish, and the legs a little lighter at the ends of the joints.   The abdomen has a row of angular light spots in the middle.   The spinnerets are in not quite as straight a line as in *bimaculata*, the outer pair being a little higher and farther behind the next.   The tracheal opening is not as far forward as in *bimaculata*, being nearer the spinnerets than the epigynum.   The male palpi have the appendages of patella and tibia longer than in *bimaculata*, and softer and more curved.   They are found under stones and leaves.

Fig. 252. Hahnia cinerea, enlarged sixteen times.

THE THERIDIDÆ

THE Therididæ are the builders of the loose and apparently irregular webs in the upper corners of rooms, in fences and among rocks, and between the leaves and branches of low trees

FIG. 253.   Webs of Theridium in a fog, on the tops of burnt bushes.   Half the real size. These webs are too fine to be noticed in dry weather.

and bushes. They are generally small, soft, and light-colored spiders, with the abdomen large and round and the legs slender and usually without spines. The eyes are all about the same size and in two rows across the front of the head, with the lateral eyes of the two rows near together and often touching each other. The mandibles are weak and without teeth at the end. The maxillæ are pointed at the end and turned

Fig. 254.   Webs of Theridium in a fog, on the tops of golden-rod.
One-third the real size.

inward toward each other. Most of the Therididæ live always in their webs, hanging by their feet, back downward. The webs have in some part a more closely woven place under which the spider stands, sometimes in the middle of the web, sometimes in a corner out of sight. Where the spider's usual standing place is without other shelter, it is often concealed by pieces of leaves or sand carried into the web by the spider, and sometimes

made into a tent. The outer part of the web is usually
loosely made in large meshes, but is sometimes in a distinct
sheet spreading from the nest and held out by threads in all
directions.   The cocoons are round and soft and hang in the
web, several being made in the same season by one spider.

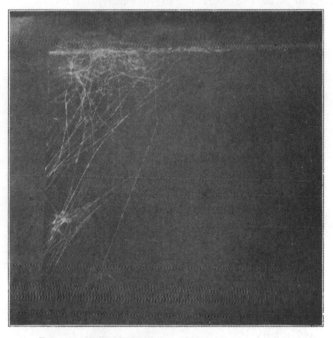

Fig. 255.   Web of Theridium tepidariorum in a dark corner.
Half the real size.

Several of this family, like Spintharus and Euryopis, have
the abdomen smaller and flatter than usual and the fourth legs
longer, so that they are better fitted for walking.   They are
found on plants, and little is known about their webs.

THE GENUS THERIDIUM

The Theridiums are small soft-bodied spiders, making large and loose webs without any large flat sheet of silk, but only a slightly closer portion where the spider stands, or a nest or tent connected with the web. *Theridium tepidariorum* (fig. 258) and *rupicola* (fig. 261) live in houses or among rocks, making large loose webs, in which the spider often stands without any covering. They have the abdomen high in front and

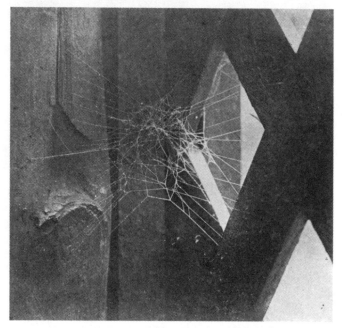

FIG. 256. Web of young Theridium tepidariorum in a corner of a trellis. A little less than the real size. The spider stood in the close part near the middle.

tapering a little toward the spinnerets. *Theridium globosum* (fig. 262) has the abdomen of the same shape. The other species are all small and have the abdomen round and brightly

colored.   They live in more open places on plants, where they
make nests in which they are partly hidden, and carry their
webs over the neighboring leaves and twigs (figs. 253, 254).

FIG. 257.   Web of young Theridium tepidariorum in a crack of a rock.   Half the real size.
The spider stood in the middle under the closely woven part.

Theridium tepidariorum. — This is one of the most common
house spiders, and is often found in its webs among rocks, but
seldom on plants.   The females (fig. 258) measure sometimes
over a quarter of an inch in length, but may mature much
smaller.   The legs of the first pair are nearly three times the

length of the body.   The male (fig. 259) is shorter and has
longer legs.   The color varies from dirty white to almost black.
The cephalothorax is yellow brown, and the legs light yellow,
with brown or gray rings at the ends and the middle of the
joints.   In the males the legs are orange brown, darker at the
ends of the joints.   The abdomen is high in front and narrows

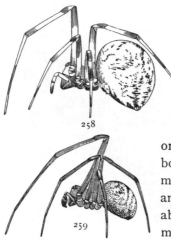

258

toward the spinnerets.   In dark
and well-marked specimens the
abdomen has, on the hinder part,
six transverse black marks curved
upward, thicker in the middle, and
partly connected by black spots
at the ends (fig. 260).   These
marks are most sharply defined
on the hinder edge, where they are
bordered by silver white.   The upper
mark often forms a conspicuous black
and white spot in the center of the
abdomen.   In light individuals all the
markings are smaller and less definite.

259

260

FIGS. 258, 259, 260.
Theridium tepida-
riorum. — 258, fe-
male.   259, male.
260, abdomen of
female seen from
behind.

It makes a large web in the corners
of rooms, under furniture, and in the
angles of fences and between stones
(fig. 255).   It usually stands in the
most sheltered part of the web, where
a part of it is more closely woven than
the rest, but not enough so to conceal the spider.   It occasionally makes the web in an open place where there is no shelter
above, and then it sometimes carries a piece of leaf into the
web and hides under it, as is the usual habit with some allied
species.   The webs of the young are usually more regular in
form than those of adults (figs. 256, 257).   A male and female
often occupy the same web for a long time.   The eggs are

laid in brownish pear-shaped cocoons, several of which are made in the same season by one spider and hang in the web. This species is found all over the world.

Theridium rupicola. — This resembles closely *tepidariorum* and is easily mistaken for the young of that species. It does not grow larger than an eighth of an inch long. The colors are like *tepidariorum*, usually dark gray with black spots, the back of the abdomen sometimes almost white. The legs are distinctly ringed with light and dark. In the middle of the abdomen is a pointed hump, the front part generally black and the hinder part white (fig. 261).

Fig. 261. Theridium rupicola, enlarged eight times.

It lives under stones and among rocks, in webs like those of *tepidariorum*, often containing grains of sand which look as if placed there by the spider, as sand falling into such a web would go through without sticking to the threads.

Theridium globosum. — This is another species with a high abdomen like *tepidariorum*. It is about a twelfth of an inch long and almost as high (fig. 262). The abdomen is a little flattened behind and pointed toward the spinnerets. The hinder part is white, with a large black spot in the middle, below which is sometimes a smaller black spot. Sometimes there is a bright white line around the light area. The front upper part of the abdomen is yellowish gray, and the

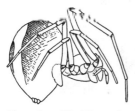

Fig. 262. Theridium globosum, enlarged eight times.

under part brown. The cephalothorax is orange brown, except a black spot between the eyes. The legs are orange brown.

Theridium differens. — Female about one-eighth of an inch long, and the male smaller.   The abdomen is round, and the middle stripe often very brightly colored, with white or yellow at the edges and red in the middle (fig. 264).   The rest of the

Fig. 263.   Web of Theridium differens in the top of a young pine tree.   Half the real size.

abdomen is reddish brown, darkest next to the white edge of the stripe.   There are no distinct marks on the under side. In males the stripe on the abdomen is obscure, and the whole abdomen dark reddish brown (fig. 265).   Sometimes, especially in young spiders, the abdomen is entirely yellow, with indistinct brown markings. The cephalothorax is orange brown, often darker in the middle, but with no distinct stripe. The legs and palpi are yellow in females and orange brown in males, slightly darker at the ends of the joints. The epigynum has no open-ings in sight. They are on the inner side in the transverse fold across the abdomen. The palpal organ (fig. 266) has two appendages at the end, one hard and roughened and the other soft. The web is on low plants of all kinds, usually two or three feet from the ground (fig. 263). There is sometimes a small tent, often hardly deep enough to cover the spider, from which the web spreads two or three inches, according to the shape of the plant. The cocoons of eggs are white and nearly as large as the spider, and are attached in the nest.

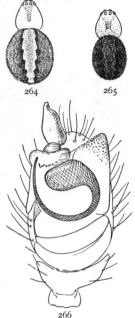

Theridium murarium. — Length about one-eighth of an inch, with the abdomen nearly spherical. The general color is gray. The legs are pale, with dark bands at the end and middle of each joint. The cephalothorax is pale, with a dark line in the middle and one on each side, the middle line sometimes divided into two near the eyes (fig. 267). On the abdomen

FIGS. 264, 265, 266. Theridium differens. — 264, female en-larged eight times. 265, male enlarged eight times. 266, end of palpus of male.

there is an undulated middle stripe, white at the edges and the front end, and reddish in the middle. On both sides of this stripe the abdomen is nearly black and becomes gradually lighter toward the sides. The sternum is pale, with a black edge and black stripe in the middle. The under side of the abdomen is gray, with a long black spot in the middle and a smaller one over the epigynum. There is little difference in size or color between the sexes. The epigynum (fig. 269) has two round holes, wide apart, near the thickened edge. The palpal organ (fig. 268) is shorter and simpler than it is in *differens*.

Theridium spirale. — This is a round-bodied spider of the same size as *differens* and *murarium*. The cephalothorax is orange brown above and below, with an indistinct dark stripe as wide in front as the eyes and narrowed behind. The abdomen has a middle stripe like *differens*, nearly as wide in front as it is in the middle (fig. 271). The rest of the abdomen is gray, darkest toward the stripe. The legs are pale, sometimes with faint gray rings at the ends and middle of each joint. The middle stripe of the abdomen is sometimes reddish as in *murarium*, but oftener gray, with a dark spot near the front end. The males (fig. 270)

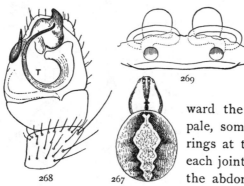

FIGS. 267, 268, 269. Theridium murarium. — 267, female enlarged eight times. 268, end of palpus of male. 269, epigynum.

have the same color and markings as the female and are sometimes more distinctly marked. The male palpi (fig. 272) are very large, and the palpal organ has a long tube coiled on the under and outer side. The openings of the epigynum (fig. 273) are about their diameter apart.

Theridium frondeum. — White, light yellow, or greenish white, with black markings that are very variable (fig. 274). Usually the cephalothorax has two fine black lines running back from the eyes and uniting behind the dorsal groove, and black edges. The legs are usually darkened with brown at the ends of the joints. The abdomen is large and round, and has on the back a light undulated band bordered by brownish translucent spaces, with two black spots just over the spinnerets. Sometimes there are black spots in the translucent spaces, especially toward the hinder end, and these may be united into two long black stripes. In some individuals of either sex the black on the cephalothorax forms a wide band in the

FIGS. 270, 271, 272, 273. Theridium spirale. — 270, male. 271, female. Both enlarged eight times. 272, end of palpus of male. 273, epigynum.

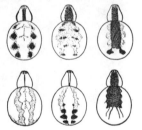

FIG. 274. Theridium frondeum. — Varieties of marking, enlarged four times.

middle, almost covering the back, and a black stripe of similar width extends backwards on the abdomen for half its length. These black-striped individuals have all the other variations of color and markings. The males have all the colors and spots brighter and the legs longer than the females. The mandibles of the male are longer than those of the female and have at the base, in front, a low conical point.

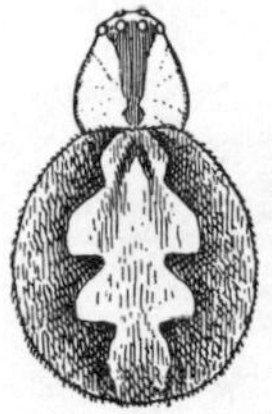

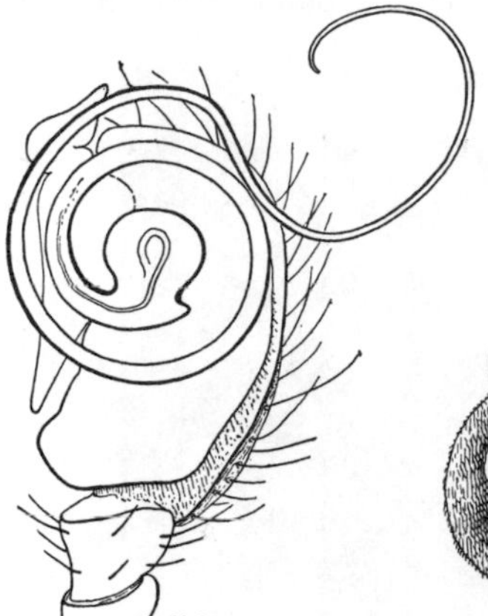

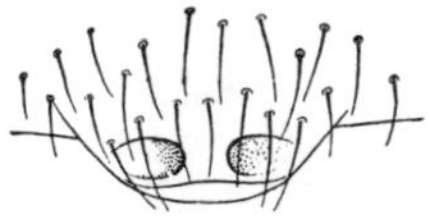

This species is found from the White Mountains to Alabama. In New England it matures in July and is found on bushes all summer.

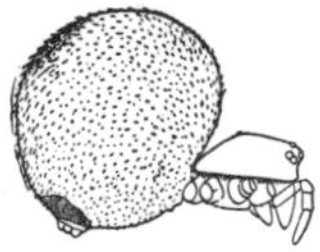

FIG. 275. Theridium unimaculatum, enlarged eight times.

Theridium unimaculatum. — This little species differs in color and markings from all the others, and may almost always be distinguished by the white abdomen, with a black spot in the

FIG. 276.   Web of Steatoda borealis on the face of a conglomerate rock in the cavity from which a pebble has dropped out.   Half the real size.

center of the back.   The females are a twelfth of an inch long and the males smaller.   The cephalothorax is orange yellow, with a black spot around the eyes, extending back in a point as far as the dorsal groove, and there is also a fine black line

along the edges. The legs are orange, lighter in the female
and darker in the male, with the first and second pairs in the
male much stouter. The sternum is orange, with black edges.
This spider makes a web, like the other small species, among
small leaves and winters under dead leaves on the ground.

THE GENUS STEATODA

Steatoda has the legs shorter and stouter than Theridium.
The abdomen is oval and often a little flattened on the back.
It is smooth and shining, the hairs being fine and scattered so
as to be hardly visible. The thorax is thick and hard, and in
some species marked with hard
projections and depressions. The
head is generally narrow, and the
front middle eyes are in several
species larger than the others and
farther forward and wider apart.
In other species all the eyes are
about the same size. The webs
consist of a flat sheet supported
and held down by threads.

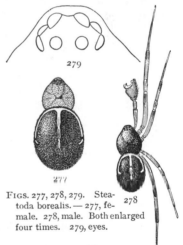

FIGS. 277, 278, 279. Steatoda borealis. — 277, female. 278, male. Both enlarged four times. 279, eyes.

Steatoda borealis. — This is a dark
reddish-brown spider, quarter of
an inch long, living among stones
or in the corners of fences and
window frames, generally well
concealed by its web or nest. The cephalothorax is orange
brown and covered with short stiff brown hairs. The head is
one-third as wide as the thorax and a little higher, the eyes near
together, with the front middle pair projecting forward beyond
the mandibles (fig. 279). The legs are brown, with faint darker
rings, and are thickly covered with hairs. The abdomen is dark

chocolate brown, sometimes without any light marks on the upper side, but usually there is a light line running around the front half and another in the middle, extending back half the length of the abdomen and usually broken into several spots. The four depressed spots on the abdomen are distinctly marked. On the under side there is a light stripe on each side, meeting behind the spinnerets. The sexes are much alike in size and color, but the palpi of the male (fig. 278) are longer than the cephalothorax, and the terminal joint is very large and complicated. The web consists of a flat sheet, held out by threads in all directions, but is often so crowded into a corner that its structure is hard to understand (fig. 276).

Steatoda guttata. — Only one-tenth of an inch long. The cephalothorax is high, with scattered hairs, at the base of each of which is a horny ridge. The cephalothorax is dark brown, with the legs lighter and more yellow. The abdomen is nearly spherical and hard at the front end, where there is a ring around its attachment to the thorax. Sometimes the abdomen is bright yellow or orange, without markings on the back, but oftener it is partly brown, with two or three pairs of silvery white spots (fig. 280). The males and females are alike in size and color, and the palpi of the males are very large, as in *borealis*. They live under stones at all seasons and mature in April and May.

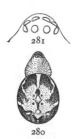

FIGS. 280, 281. Steatoda guttata. — 280, female enlarged eight times. 281, head and eyes.

Steatoda marmorata. — About a quarter of an inch long. The cephalothorax and legs yellowish brown. Cephalothorax smooth, with a few hairs. Legs covered with fine hair. The abdomen is usually nearly covered by an oblong dark spot darkened at the edges, where it is bordered by silvery white (fig. 283). The middle is lighter, with a central dark stripe. In some individuals the dark markings are broken up into four pairs of black spots

partly connected with a middle line (fig. 282). The head is
wider and the eyes smaller and farther apart than in the other
species, and the front middle eyes are
the smallest. The head is wider in
males (fig. 284) than in females, and
the mandibles larger. It lives under
stones and leaves at all seasons and
occasionally on bushes.

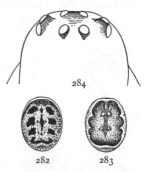

Steatoda corollata. — This, when full
grown, is a little larger than *marmorata* and darker colored, and the legs
are shorter and stouter. The cephalothorax is dark brown, and the legs
lighter brown, with dark rings at the
ends of the joints. The abdomen is
yellowish at the sides and has four or

FIGS. 282, 283, 284. Steatoda
marmorata. — 282, 283, markings of the abdomen of the
female enlarged twice. 284,
head of the male.

five irregular yellow spots, or pairs of spots, along the middle
of a dark brown oval patch which nearly covers the middle of
the back. In young specimens the abdomen is lighter, with

several pairs of dark spots. The eyes
are all nearly the same size, the front
middle pair slightly larger and farther
forward than the others. It lives under
stones, like the other species.

Steatoda triangulosa. — The female is a
fifth of an inch to a quarter of an inch
long. The legs are longer and more
slender than in the other species, the
first pair twice as long as the body.
The cephalothorax is orange brown,
slightly rough in females and with short

FIG. 285. Steatoda corollata.
— Back of a small female
enlarged four times.
FIG. 286. Steatoda triangulosa. — Back of female enlarged four times.

ridges at the base of the hairs in males. The front middle eyes
are not larger than the others and are not as far forward as in

borealis. The legs are light yellow, with slightly darker rings at the ends of the joints. There are thickened brown spots at the base of the hairs all over the body. The abdomen is light

yellow, with two irregular brown stripes partly broken into spots and sometimes connected together (fig. 286). The palpi of the male are as long as the femur of the second legs and are small at the end. This spider lives in

FIG. 287. Asagena americana. — Back of female enlarged eight times.

houses, around window frames and similar places, like *bore-alis.* The egg cocoons are white and hang in the web.

Asagena americana. — This resembles Steatoda, but the abdomen is longer and flatter, and the whole appearance more like some of the Drassidæ. Like Steatoda, it is usually found with its web under stones. It is about a sixth of an inch long. The cephalothorax is dark reddish brown, slightly rough in the females and with sharp points along the sides in the males. The legs are yellow brown and in the males have two rows of small teeth under each femur. They are stout, as in *Steatoda*

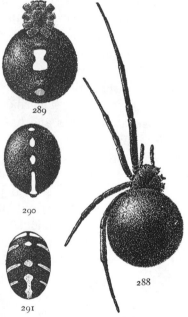

289

290

288

291

FIGS. 288, 289, 290, 291. Latrodectus mactans. — 288, female enlarged twice. 289, under side of abdomen. 290, back of abdomen of young female, with four red spots. 291, markings of abdomen of male.

marmorata, and differ little in length. The abdomen is oval and dark brown in color, with two white spots across the middle (fig. 287). The front of the head is rounded and a third as wide as the thorax. The eyes are close together and all about the same size. The males have the cephalothorax larger and rougher, but in size and color resemble the females.

Latrodectus mactans. — This is the largest spider of the family. It is sometimes half an inch long, with the abdomen round and the whole body black, except a bright red spot underneath and one or more red spots over the spinnerets and along the middle of the back (figs. 289, 290). The spots turn yellow or white in alcohol. The cephalothorax is about as wide as long, and the grooves between the head and thorax are deep. The lateral eyes are farther apart than usual in this family. The legs of the male are much larger than those of the female,

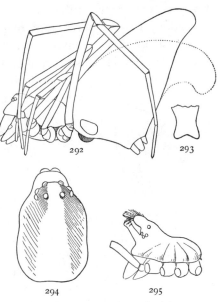

FIGS. 292, 293, 294, 295. Argyrodes trigonum. — 292, side of female enlarged eight times, the dotted line showing the abdomen bent downward. 293, tip of abdomen seen from above. 294, top of cephalothorax. 295, cephalothorax of male.

and each joint is orange brown in the middle and black at the ends. The abdomen of the male has a row of red and white spots in the middle line, as some females do, and across the front end, and along the sides four pairs of stripes, red in the middle and white at the edges (fig. 291). The young of both sexes are colored somewhat like the male and, when very small, have very little black on them. The males vary much in size, some being only a quarter as large as the female. This spider makes its nest among loose stones, on plants, or in houses. Around its hiding place it spins a large funnel-shaped tent that widens into a flat or curved sheet of web, closer in texture toward the tube and more open toward the edges, spreading two or three feet over plants and stones. It is found all over the United States, as far north as Massachusetts and New Hampshire and south through Florida, the West

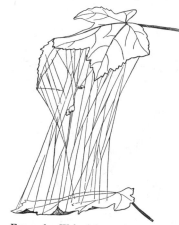

Indies, and South America, as far as Chile. It is everywhere feared as poisonous and dangerous, probably on account of its large size and conspicuous colors, as there is no good reason for considering it more poisonous than other spiders.*

Argyrodes trigonum. — A little yellow triangular spider, with a high, pointed abdomen (fig. 292). Large females measure an eighth of an inch from the head to the spinnerets and nearly as much from

FIG. 296. Web of Argyrodes trigonum between two maple leaves. In the middle of the web are two egg cocoons and above them the spider.

the spinnerets to the tip of the abdomen. Seen from above, the end of the abdomen is a little flattened and notched in the middle (fig. 293). In the female the part of the head around the eyes is slightly raised and the lower part of the front of the head carried forward a little beyond it (fig. 294). In the males there are two horns on the head, one between the eyes and one below them (fig. 295). The color is light yellow, sometimes with a metallic luster, as though gilded. On the back of the cephalothorax are three light brown stripes, and sometimes there are dark spots at the sides of the abdomen and over the spinnerets. The legs

*It is now known that this spider, commonly called the black widow, is extremely poisonous; its bite has been known to cause death.

are slender, without markings, the front pair longer than the others. The point of the abdomen is movable and is sometimes curved downward when the spider is disturbed in the web, as shown by the dotted line in fig. 292. They make webs like those of Theridium, between branches of shrubs (fig. 296) and also among the upper threads of the webs of larger spiders.

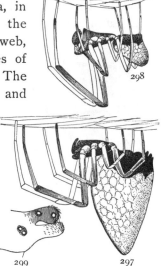

They have been found in the webs of Agalena, Theridium, and Linyphia, in the looser parts, out of reach of the maker of the web. Hanging in the web, they look like straws or the scales of pine buds that have fallen into it. The cocoons of eggs hang in the web and have a peculiar shape (fig. 296), the upper part conical and the lower part contracted into a narrow neck. The species is common in New England and is found all over the country as far south as Florida.

Argyrodes nephilæ. — This is about as large as *Argyrodes trigonum*, with the hump silver white and the under side of the body black or dark brown (fig. 297). The hump ends in a blunt round point.

Figs. 297, 298, 299. Argyrodes nephilæ. — 297, female. 298, male. Both enlarged eight times. 299, head of male.

The front of the head is more nearly vertical than in *trigonum*, and the upper part projects forward, carrying with it the front middle eyes. In the male there are two horns in front of the eyes, the upper one carrying the middle eyes of both rows (fig. 299). The cephalothorax is black or dark brown above and below. The abdomen is black on the under side, including the spinnerets, and there is a black middle stripe extending back to the tip of the hump. The basal joints of all the legs are white. The third and fourth legs are light colored, with a little brown at the ends of the joints. The second legs are darker, and the first pair are almost black, except at the ends. The males are colored like the females, but have the abdomen not much larger than the cephalothorax (fig. 298), and the hump rounded. This is a southern species and is said to live among the outer threads of webs of large Epeiridæ. It does, however, make webs of its own, and I have seen the adults of both sexes at Charleston, S.C., in these webs away from any other spiders.

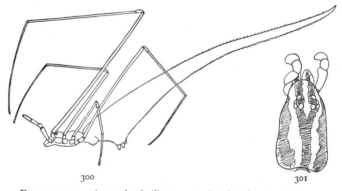

300   301

FIGS. 300, 301.   Argyrodes fictilium. — 300, female enlarged eight times.
301, top of the cephalothorax.

Argyrodes fictilium. — In this species the pointed hump on the abdomen is much more elongated than in *trigonum*, in some spiders to eight or nine times the length of the cephalothorax (fig. 300). The tip is rounded in young specimens and sharp pointed in the larger ones. The front of the head is more inclined than that of *trigonum* (fig. 301). The colors are light yellow and silvery white, with three darker lines on the cephalothorax and a faint middle line on the abdomen. The legs are very slender and long in proportion to the long abdomen. Found rarely from New England to Alabama.

Spintharus flavidus. — A sixth to a quarter of an inch long. The cephalothorax is nearly circular, and the head small and narrow like that of Argyrodes, with the hinder middle eyes very far apart. The abdomen is widest across the front third, where it is two-thirds as wide as it is long, and from here it tapers to a blunt point over the spinnerets (fig. 302). On the back the abdomen is flat and marked with white stripes each side, and between them a large pattern in black and red, lighter toward the middle, where there are two or three pairs of white spots. The legs are slender like those of Argyrodes, the first and fourth pairs the same length and twice as long as the second pair. The

FIG. 303. Euryopis funebris, enlarged four times.

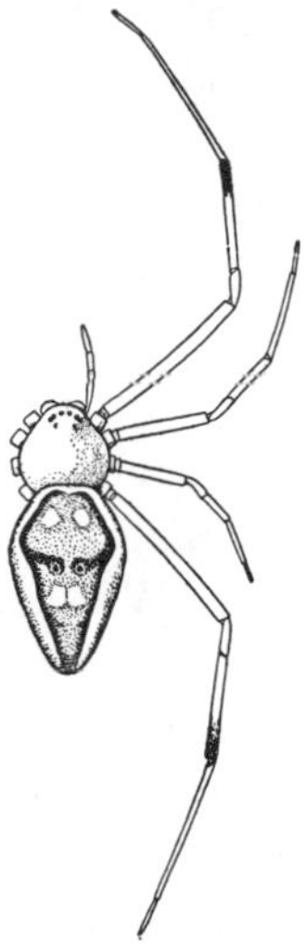

FIG. 302. Spintharus flavidus, enlarged four times.

tibiæ of the first and second legs are bright orange color, and the rest, like the cephalothorax, pale yellow. The male has longer legs and more slender abdomen. They live on low plants, and the web is unknown. They have been found from Massachusetts to Alabama.

Euryopis funebris. — A little dark-colored spider, with a flat abdomen pointed behind and bordered with a silver-white stripe. It is almost an eighth of an inch long. The cephalothorax is small and as wide as it is long, with the sides rounded. The head is half as wide as the thorax,

FIG. 304. Theridula sphaerula, enlarged four times.

a little raised and extended forward over the mandibles (fig. 303). The front middle eyes are largest and are farther apart and farther forward than the others. The abdomen is flat and nearly as wide in the middle as it is long, and tapers to a point behind. The general color is black or dark gray. The cephalothorax is yellowish under the abdomen and black in front. The abdomen has a bright silvery stripe around the hinder half, and inside this the color is black, broken by light spots in the middle. The legs and palpi are light yellow, with dark rings on the ends of the joints. The fourth legs are longest. It is shaken from bushes in summer, or from dead leaves on the ground in winter, and its web is unknown. It is found from the White Mountains to Alabama.

Fig. 305.   Pholcus phalangioides. — A young female in a natural position hanging in its web.

Theridula sphærula. — This is a very distinct and easily recognized species, although it is less than a tenth of an inch long (fig. 304). The cephalothorax is yellow, with a wide black stripe in the middle. The abdomen is high and round and wider than it is long ; it is yellowish gray, with a greenish white spot in the middle and a black spot on a slight elevation at each side. There is also a black spot around the spinnerets. The legs are light yellow. In the male the light parts of the cephalothorax and legs are orange color, and the markings of the abdomen less distinct than in the female. It lives on bushes all over the country.

Pholcus phalangioides. — This is a large pale spider, with legs so long that it is often confounded with Phalangium, under the nickname of "daddy longlegs." The body is quarter of an inch long, and the longest legs two inches. The abdomen is

about three times as long as wide and nearly straight at the
sides unless full of eggs.   The cephalothorax is nearly round
and flat behind.   Around the eyes the head is raised and in
the males separated at the sides from the rest of the head.
The middle pair of eyes are not higher than the tops of the
lower lateral eyes.   The mandibles are nearly as high as the
front of the head, and in the males they have a small conical
tooth near the base.   The color is pale brown, covered with
fine gray hairs, and the whole body and legs are translucent.

The head is a little darker
around the eyes, and there
is a large gray patch in the
middle of the cephalothorax.
The abdomen is marked only
by a translucent middle line
over the dorsal vessel.   This
is a house spider, common
in America and Europe, and
probably imported.   It lives
in cellars where there is but
little light and makes large,
loose, flat webs, horizontal
where there is a convenient
place, or irregular to fit into
surrounding objects (fig. 308).
The spider hangs in the web
with the abdomen directed
upward, and when alarmed
swings itself around rapidly
so that it can hardly be seen.

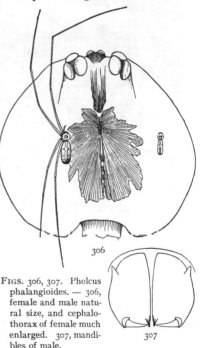

FIGS. 306, 307. Pholcus
phalangioides. — 306,
female and male natu-
ral size, and cephalo-
thorax of female much
enlarged. 307, mandi-
bles of male.

The egg cocoon is so thin that it does not conceal the eggs
and is carried about in the spider's mandibles until the young
hatch out.

Pholcus cornutus. — A small species from the southern states, with a body about a tenth of an inch long and the legs from half to three-quarters of an inch.   The abdomen is humped on the back and short on the under side, so that seen from the side it is nearly triangular (fig. 309).   The cephalothorax is as wide as long and nearly circular.   The head is small and marked by

FIG. 308.   Web of Pholcus phalangioides between two shelves in a cellar.

a shallow groove on each side.   In front it is higher than wide and inclined a little forward toward the mandibles.   The eyes (fig. 310) are raised a little from the head, three large eyes almost touching each other in a group on each side, and a small pair between them just above the lower eyes of the larger groups.   The mandibles are three-quarters as high as the head, with a small tooth on the inner corners and, in the males, a long curved horn projecting forward near the base of each mandible (fig. 311). The legs are very slender and transparent, slightly colored brown, with darker rings at the ends of the femur and tibia. There is a dark mark around the eyes and head, forming behind them a middle line that widens toward the hinder end of the cephalothorax. The abdomen is gray, marked on the upper side with three or four pairs of darker spots and behind with lighter spots, somewhat like *Theridium tepidariorum*.

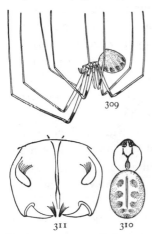

FIGS. 309, 310, 311. Pholcus cornutus. — 309, side of female enlarged four times. 310, back of female. 311, front of mandibles of male, showing the curved horns.

Scytodes thoracica. — This is a very peculiar spider, probably imported from Europe, and found in cellars and closets. It is about quarter of an inch long when full grown. The cephalothorax and abdomen are both round and nearly of the same size. The cephalothorax is low and narrow in front and slopes upward to the highest point opposite the third legs (fig. 313), and from there falls abruptly behind. The eyes are six in number, in three pairs, the middle pair lowest and the lateral pairs wide apart at the sides of the head (fig. 312). The front of the head below the eyes projects forward beyond the mandibles. The legs are slender and tapering, the tarsus and metatarsus not more than

FIGS. 312, 313. Scytodes thoracica. — 312, female enlarged eight times. 313, side of cephalothorax.

half as thick as the tibia. The color is pale yellow or white, with black or gray spots, in a regular pattern on the cephalothorax and abdomen, and in rings on the legs.

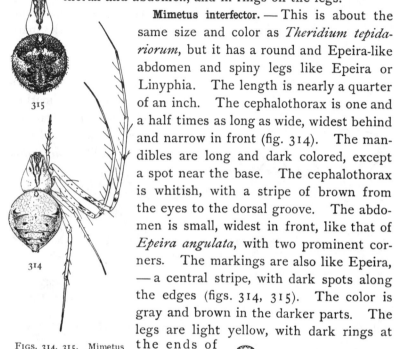

Mimetus interfector. — This is about the same size and color as *Theridium tepidariorum*, but it has a round and Epeira-like abdomen and spiny legs like Epeira or Linyphia. The length is nearly a quarter of an inch. The cephalothorax is one and a half times as long as wide, widest behind and narrow in front (fig. 314). The mandibles are long and dark colored, except a spot near the base. The cephalothorax is whitish, with a stripe of brown from the eyes to the dorsal groove. The abdomen is small, widest in front, like that of *Epeira angulata*, with two prominent corners. The markings are also like Epeira, — a central stripe, with dark spots along the edges (figs. 314, 315). The color is gray and brown in the darker parts. The legs are light yellow, with dark rings at the ends of the joints. It lives on bushes and

FIGS. 314, 315. Mimetus interfector, enlarged four times, showing markings of two different individuals.

occasionally on houses and fences, where it has been found in webs among those of *Theridium tepidariorum*.

FIGS. 316, 317. Ero thoracica. — 316, back of female enlarged eight times. 317, side of female.

Ero thoracica. — This spider resembles the young of *Theridium tepidariorum*, but the colors are brighter, and the hairs longer and coarser. It is an eighth to a sixth of an inch long. The cephalothorax is nearly as high in the middle as it is long and slopes at a sharp angle under the front of the abdomen (fig. 317). The head is lower than the middle of the thorax, and the front middle eyes project beyond the mandibles. The abdomen is as high as long and has a pair of humps on the highest part. The cephalothorax is light yellow, with a dark irregular stripe on each side and a middle line crossed by a crescent-shaped mark on the highest part. The abdomen is white, with brown spots of various shapes. The front half of each hump is dark brown, and a dark line extends from there down the sides (fig. 316). At the back of the abdomen are several transverse stripes, which are sometimes reddish. Stiff brown hairs are scattered all over the abdomen. The legs are ringed with brown and yellow, and have coarse brown hairs and long spines on the tibia and tarsus, which is unusual in this family. It is found under stones and in winter under leaves in woods. It lives also in Europe.

THE LINYPHIADÆ

The Linyphiadæ consist of a great number of species of small spiders living, for the most part, in shady woods, among the lower branches of plants, under leaves, and in caves and cellars. They differ from the Therididæ generally in having the body more elongated, the legs stouter and with more spines, the mandibles larger and stronger and furnished with teeth around the claw, and the maxillæ straighter and not inclined inward toward the labium. There are two groups among them, — Linyphia and its allies, which are comparatively large and some of which live in the open woods, with large cobwebs, and Erigone and its allies, which are all very small spiders, living mostly in short grass, dead leaves, and moss. The latter usually have narrower bodies and stouter legs, resembling the Drassidæ. Their colors are generally plain and dull, and the females are difficult to distinguish from each other, while the males often have peculiar modifications of the head and proportionally very large and complicated palpi.

The webs usually have a large flat sheet, supported by threads above and below, under which the spider lives. Some species have the sheet of web curved upward or downward. *Linyphia marginata* forms a dome-shaped web four or five inches in diameter.

THE GENUS LINYPHIA

These spiders vary in size like the species of Theridium, from a quarter of an inch to a tenth of an inch long. In appearance they differ greatly from Theridium; the cephalothorax is longer and higher in front, the legs are long and slender, with distinct spines, and the abdomen is sometimes a little flattened on the back as in Steatoda, but oftener high in front and a little pointed toward the spinnerets. The sexes differ little in size,

FIG. 318. Web of Linyphia marginata. Half the real size.

but often in color and markings. The palpal organs and the terminal joints of the palpi of the males are very large and complicated, and in the smaller species form the best means of distinguishing them. There are a great number of minute species of Microneta, Bathyphantes, and other allied genera, but only the larger and more common are here described.

Linyphia marginata. — This is one of the most common web spiders in shady woods all through the summer. It is a sixth of an inch long, with slender legs, the longest of which are usually half an inch. The cephalothorax is two-thirds as wide as long, the middle of it brown and the edges light. The abdomen is flat on top and widest and thickest behind, the colors light yellow and purplish brown (fig. 319). In the middle there is a dark stripe, consisting usually of three parts united by a narrow line, and behind this is another dark spot. At the sides are several dark stripes, the front ones lengthwise and the hinder vertical, all connected with the dark color of the under side. The legs are light yellow without markings, and the hairs and spines fine and not easily seen. In the males all the colors are darker and the abdomen narrower, with only a few light marks at the sides. This spider has no nest, but lives all the time in the middle of its web. It matures in June, and the young brood are common in their small webs in August and September.

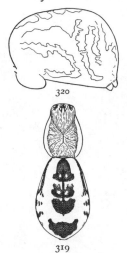

FIGS. 319, 320. Linyphia marginata. — 319, female enlarged eight times, showing markings of the back. 320, side of abdomen.

The web of *L. marginata* (fig. 318) is in the form of a dome four or five inches in diameter, hung between rocks and plants, seldom much concealed by leaves. The threads are fine, and the web so transparent that it easily escapes notice unless the sun shines upon it. The meshes are larger than in *L. phrygiana* and other flat web-making species. The depth and width of the dome depend somewhat on the shape of the opening

in which it is made, and the number and length of the sup-
porting threads vary according to the surroundings. The
spider stands apparently all the time under the top of the
dome. Insects flying near touch the threads above the dome
and, their flight being broken, drop down among closer threads
and, finally, to the dome itself, where they are caught by the
spider and taken through the meshes. Remains of insects and
other rubbish are cut loose from the web and dropped. The

Fig. 321. Beginning of a web of Linyphia marginata.

webs seem to be used for a long time, but if they are injured
a new one is soon made, either in the night or day, and the
remains of several old webs are often seen hanging flat and
torn below a new one. The dome is begun at the top and
extended downward by inclined threads, an inch or two long,
which are crossed by shorter threads in all directions (fig. 321).
The spider works very rapidly, but I have never seen a dome
finished, the spider always working a few minutes and then
resting a long time.

Linyphia communis. — A little smaller than *marginata*, with legs a little shorter.   The colors are the same light yellow and purplish brown, but the markings are distinctly different.   The cephalothorax is uniform light brownish yellow.   The middle

FIG. 322.   Web of Linyphia communis between the branches of a spruce tree.
Half the real size.

stripe of the abdomen extends the whole length of the upper side and connects with several narrow brown stripes that extend down the sides (fig. 323).   The abdomen is more regularly oval and less enlarged behind than in *marginata*, but the upper part extends back farther over the spinnerets.   The under side is dark brown. The male is smaller than the female, with the head higher and the abdomen narrower. The palpi of the male are unusually small for the genus (fig. 324). The web of *communis* (fig. 322) consists of a horizontal sheet, convex below and supported by threads above. Below this, about an inch distant, is another sheet of web. Insects flying between the upper threads fall down to the sheet below and are taken through by the spider, as they are in the dome of *marginata*.

Linyphia mandibulata. — A little larger than *L. communis* and *marginata*, with the head longer and more distinct from the thorax, and the abdomen larger and flattened on the top (figs. 326, 327). The length is about

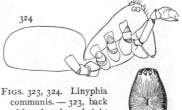

324

FIGS. 323, 324. Linyphia communis. — 323, back of female enlarged eight times. 324, profile of male.

323

a sixth of an inch. The cephalothorax is dark orange brown, and the legs a lighter shade of the same color. The length of the legs is about as in *communis*, shorter than *marginata* and *phrygiana*. The abdomen is dark brown, often almost black, with several white spots, usually two across the front end and several others around the sides (fig. 326), sometimes forming a complete light stripe around the middle. In the males the abdomen is narrow, and the only markings are usually the two spots on the front end. The cephalothorax of the male is long and narrow ; the head is extended forward, and the mandibles inclined backward toward the maxillæ. The mandibles are more than half as long as the cephalothorax and widened at the ends, with four teeth on the inner corner (fig. 329). On the inner side of the mandibles, near the middle, is a large blunt tooth.

The webs are flat and near the ground, on short grass and leaves and across little hollows in the sod (fig. 325). The webs

are not as large as those of *phrygiana*, and the spider has no
nest, but stands always in the web and drops suddenly when
alarmed.   It lives all over the eastern part of the country and
resembles closely the *Linyphia pusilla* of Europe.

Linyphia coccinea. — About a sixth of an inch long and bright
red and orange color.   The size and length of legs are about

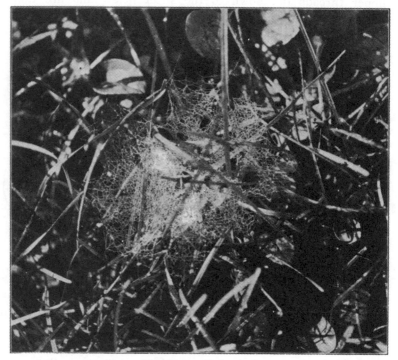

FIG. 325.   Web of young Linyphia mandibulata in short grass near the ground.
About the real size.

the same as in *communis*.   The legs are light orange, the
cephalothorax a deeper shade of the same color, and the abdomen light red.   The palpi have the ends black, and the legs
are sometimes streaked with black.   The hinder middle eyes are

twice as large as the others and twice as far apart as the front middle pair. The space between and around the middle eyes is black. The top of the abdomen is a little flattened and extended back in a blunt black point over the spinnerets (fig. 330). The male (fig. 331) differs little from the female except in the more slender abdomen and longer legs. The male palpi are

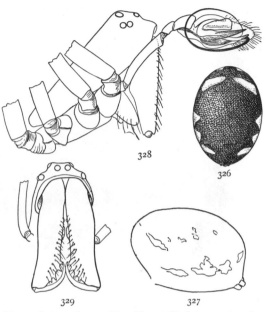

FIGS. 326, 327, 328, 329. Linyphia mandibulata. — 326, markings of abdomen of female enlarged eight times. 327, side of abdomen. 328, cephalothorax and palpus of male. 329, mandibles of male.

as long as those of the female and only a little thickened at the end. The blackened point on the end of the abdomen is less

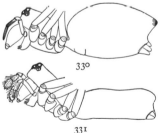

FIGS. 330, 331. Linyphia coccinea.— 330, female. 331, male enlarged twelve times.

distinct in the male than the female. The web is a little concave, not as deep as that of *marginata* and with smaller meshes. It is made among low plants. This is a common species in the South.

Linyphia phrygiana. — This is one of the most common species and lives both in the woods and around houses. It is larger than *marginata* and *communis*, measuring a fifth of an inch in length. The cephalothorax is light yellow, with a black line in the middle, forked at the front end, and another at the sides near the edge of the thorax. The legs are light yellow, with a dark ring at the end of each joint and at the middle of each tibia and metatarsus. The legs are also marked with dark spots, especially

FIG. 332. Web of Linyphia phrygiana in a barberry bush. The spider stood under the upper part of the inclined sheet close to the stem.

on the femora, and the spines are black and conspicuous. The abdomen is yellowish, with brown spots at the sides and beneath, and along the middle of the back is a dark brown or red herringbone stripe (fig. 333). The head of the male is higher than that of the female and has a crest of stiff hairs. The male palpi (fig. 334) have a long spur on the patella and have the end small, like *communis.* The web (fig. 332) is a large flat sheet, sometimes over a foot across. A corner of it usually runs under a stone or other hiding place, and here the spider stands, often making a little tent in connection with the web.

Linyphia (Stemonyphantes) trilineata. — About a quarter of an inch long, with a large oval abdomen and comparatively short legs. The color is light yellowish gray, the cephalothorax with three dark lines, and the abdomen with three rows of dark spots partly connected in lines. The legs are marked with dark rings on the ends and middle of the joints, more distinctly on the under than on the upper side. The sternum is light in the middle and black around the

333   334
FIGS. 333, 334. Linyphia phrygiana. — 333, markings of abdomen enlarged eight times. 334, palpus of male.

edge, and the abdomen has irregular black spots at the sides and beneath. The male has longer legs and wider thorax and smaller abdomen. It lives under stones and logs and winters under leaves in the woods. It is common both in this country and Europe.

FIG. 335. Linyphia trilineata. — Markings of abdomen enlarged eight times.

Linyphia (Bathyphantes) nebulosa. — Length a sixth of an inch. Color light brownish yellow, with gray markings (fig. 338). Some are almost white, and others are dark, with the black spots covering a large part of the body. The cephalothorax is dark on the edges and has a dark middle stripe, forked toward the eyes. The abdomen has six or seven pairs of irregular dark spots, more or less connected with a dark middle line. The under side of abdomen and sternum have black spots which, in dark individuals, run together, making these parts entirely black. The legs have dark rings on the ends and

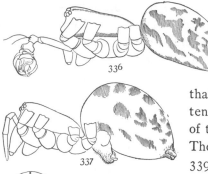

336

337

FIGS. 336, 337, 338. Linyphia nebulosa. — 336,
male. 337, female en-
larged twelve times.
338, markings of back
of abdomen.

338

middle of the femora
and tibiæ. The spines
are long and darker than
the skin. The epigy-
num is folded twice, so
that only part of it is seen extending out from the under side
of the abdomen (figs. 340, 341).
The palpus of the male (fig.
339) has large and complicated
appendages at the end. In
general shape it is rounder than
in the next species, and the
angle at the base of the tarsus
is less prominent. This spider
is common in cellars and other damp and shady
places about houses. It is common in Europe and is perhaps
imported. The web is flat,
like that of *L. phrygiana*, and
often large for the size of the
spider, sometimes covering a
pail or box a foot wide.

Linyphia (Bathyphantes) minuta.
— One-eighth of an inch long,
a little smaller than *nebulosa*.
The cephalothorax is yel-
lowish brown, darker at
the edges, but without any
middle line. The dark
markings of the abdomen
nearly cover it, so that it
appears dark gray with
light markings instead of

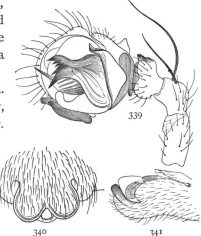

339

340   341

FIGS. 339, 340, 341. Linyphia nebulosa. — 339,
palpus of male. 340, epigynum from below.
341, epigynum from the right side.

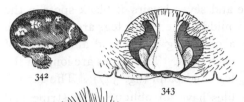

342

343

344

FIGS. 342, 343, 344. Linyphia minuta. — 342, side of abdomen of female. 343, epigynum. 344, end of palpus of male.

light with dark markings, as in *nebulosa*. The legs are light brownish yellow, with dark rings on the ends and middle of the femora and tibiæ. The epigynum is folded twice, as in *nebulosa* (fig. 343). The male palpi (fig. 344) have a general resemblance to those of *nebulosa*, but there are some distinct differences. The tarsal hook is very large and has a longer and narrower point than *nebulosa*. The tarsus has on the outer side near the base a conical point roughened with short ridges. This is more prominent in this species than in *nebulosa*. It lives in cellars and similar places often in company with *nebulosa*.

Linyphia (Drapetisca) socialis. — This very distinct species is marked with gray and white and is often found on the bark of trees without any web. It is a tenth to an eighth of an inch in length. The cephalothorax is white with black edges, a black spot in front under the eyes, and a black mark in the middle, from which indistinct lines radiate toward the edge. The abdomen is widest just behind the middle (fig. 345). It is white, mottled with gray, and has a

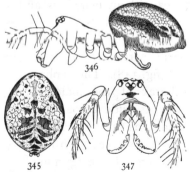

345   347

FIGS. 345, 346, 347. Linyphia socialis. — 345, markings of back of abdomen enlarged eight times. 346, side of female. 347, front of female showing eyes, mandibles, and palpi.

black stripe on each side and several pairs of black spots in the middle, connected with a middle line.   The legs are white, with

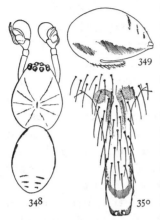

a gray ring at the end and middle of each joint.   The spines are long on the legs and palpi (fig. 347).   The mandibles have an oblique dark stripe and several long hairs in front and a row of teeth in front of the claw.   The epigynum (fig. 346) is large and extends obliquely backward away from the abdomen and curves inward again at the end.   It lives all over the northern part of this country and Europe, under leaves and sometimes on trees, where it is occasionally found on the bark without any web.

FIGS. 348, 349, 350.   Linyphia insignis. — 348, female enlarged twelve times.   349, side of abdomen of female.   350, epigynum.

Linyphia (Helophora) insignis. — An eighth of an inch long, as long as *socialis*, but more slender.   The cephalothorax and legs are light yellow, and the abdomen gray or white, sometimes without markings and sometimes with gray stripes at the sides and two or three pairs of gray marks across the hinder half (fig. 348).   The cephalothorax of the male is twice as wide across the middle as at the head.   The legs are without markings.   The epigynum (fig. 350) is long and straight, extending backward close to the abdomen for half its length.   The tibia

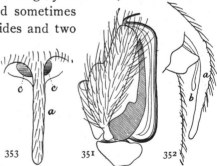

FIGS. 351, 352, 353.   Linyphia concolor. — 351, end of palpus of male.   352, side of epigynum.   353, epigynum from below.

of the palpal organ has a short, pointed process, extending
directly outward from the side (fig. 348). They live in flat
webs among low plants.

Linyphia (Diplostyla) concolor. — About a twelfth of an inch
long, a little smaller than *nigrina*, with long slender legs, and
the abdomen slightly pointed toward the spinnerets and not
much larger than the cephalothorax. The color is light yellow

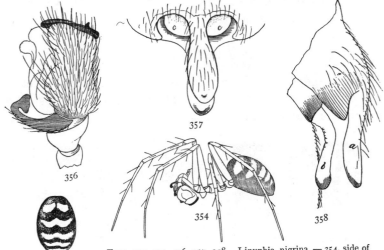

FIGS. 354, 355, 356, 357, 358. Linyphia nigrina. — 354, side of
male. 355, markings of back of female. 356, end of palpus
of male. 357, 358, epigynum.

brown, the abdomen gray without any markings. The epigynum (figs. 352, 353) has a long, slender, flexible process on the
outer edge that extends backward to the middle of the abdomen, and under it is another shorter one not easily seen. The
tarsus of the male palpus (fig. 351) is longer and more tapering
than that of *nigrina*. Adults of both sexes are common under
leaves in winter all over the northern part of the country.

Linyphia (Diplostyla) nigrina. — A tenth of an inch long.
Cephalothorax and legs light yellow brown. Abdomen dark

gray or black, with five or six transverse light markings, usually in the male and often in the female broken into pairs of
spots (fig. 355). The abdomen is high in front and a little
pointed behind (fig. 354). The epigynum (figs. 356, 357) has
two flexible processes, one over the other, extending backward,
the tip of the inner one extending beyond the outer. The
tarsus of the male palpus (fig. 356) is short and truncated, with
its tube twisted in a circle around the end. It lives under
leaves in winter.

THE GENUS ERIGONE

The Erigones are all very small spiders, and for this reason
few of them will be described. They live, for the most part,
near the ground in grass, moss, and dead leaves, with small

FIG. 359.   Web of Erigone dentigera among stems of grass close to the ground.
About the real size.

webs like those of Linyphia, and are seldom seen unless carefully searched for. There is one season of the year, however,
when the Erigones appear in immense numbers. This is
during the fine weather that comes after the first frosts in

October and November, when they, in company with the young of many larger kinds of spiders, come to the tops of posts and fences and, turning their spinnerets upward, allow threads to be drawn out by ascending currents of air, until

sometimes the spiders are lifted off their feet and carried long distances. Though not so easily seen, the same performance is going on at the tops of grass and bushes, and at times the whole country is covered with threads of silk, and the threads in the air tangle together into flakes, which at length

FIG. 360.   Erigone dentigera trying to fly.   Enlarged eight times.   From a photograph on Boston Common.

fall, sometimes from great heights.   This appearance is called in England "gossamer" and in Germany the "flying summer" and the "old woman's summer."   Why the spiders spin the thread and what use it is to them to be blown about are unknown.   At the time of the autumn flights great numbers of these spiders may be seen on fences and doorsteps in city streets wherever there is a neighboring park or grass plat, and the spiders probably live the rest of the year among this grass near the ground.

Erigone longipalpis and **dentigera**. — These spiders are a tenth of an inch to a twentieth of an inch long and generally dark brown in color, with the cephalothorax smooth and shining.

In some, especially the larger males, the cephalothorax is bright orange and the legs partly of the same color. The females vary considerably in size, but are otherwise much alike.

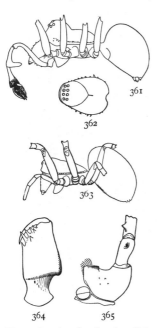

The peculiarities are in the males. The head is about half the length of the cephalothorax and abruptly raised and rounded on the top (fig. 361). Along the sides of the thorax are small pointed teeth of various sizes in a single irregular row (fig. 362). The mandibles are very much thickened in the middle and have a row of teeth on the front outer side (fig. 364). The palpi of the males are sometimes as long as the whole body and of a complicated shape. The femur is curved upward and forward and has a row of little teeth on the under side. The patella and tibia are together about as long as the femur. The patella has at the end a straight tooth directed downward with a short point (fig. 361). The tibia is widened at the end, where it spreads around the base of the tarsus. The maxillæ are much thickened and the bases of the palpi spread wide apart (fig. 365). The palpi are usually carried doubled up in front of the head, with the curved ends of the femora just below the eyes and the palpal organs over the ends of the mandibles. The legs of Erigone are only moderately long, and they walk easily, like the small Drassidæ. They move slowly and are not easily frightened, so that at the time of flying they can be closely watched.

FIGS, 361, 362, 363, 364, 365. — Erigone dentigera. — 361, side of male. 362, back of cephalothorax of male enlarged sixteen times. 363, female. 364, mandible of male. 365, maxilla of male.

Erigone autumnalis. — This is one of the few species of Erigone that can be distinctly separated from the others. It lives in the same places and is found with *longipalpis* in the autumn flights. It is only a twentieth of an inch long, but can be distinguished by its light color and bright yellow head. The palpi of the males have the tibia shorter than the patella and the tooth on the patella turned more forward than in *longipalpis*, with a longer and sharper point tapering from the base to the tip (fig. 367).

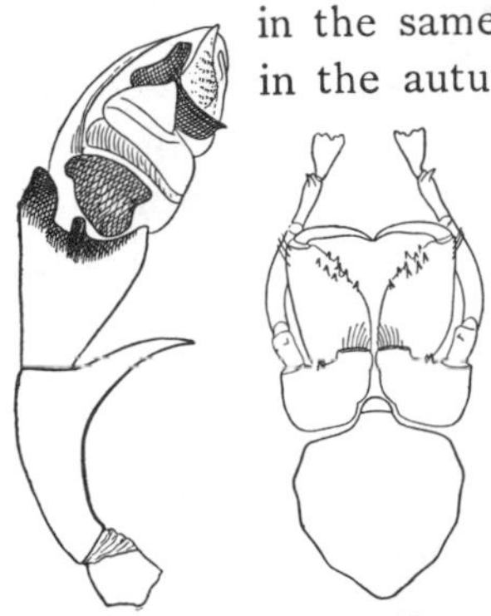

367　　　　366

FIGS. 366, 367. Erigone autumnalis. — 366, under side of cephalothorax of male. 367, palpus of male.

Ceratinella lætabilis. — This is about the same size as *fissiceps*, — a sixteenth of an inch long, — but much darker colored, and the males do not have horns or humps on the head. The cephalothorax and sternum are dark brown, and the legs dark orange. The thickened circle on the abdomen (fig. 368) is dark orange brown and the thinner parts gray. In the female the thick circle is usually wanting and the whole abdomen dark gray, with lighter spots around the muscular marks. There are also hardened spots around the stem of the abdomen and under the spinnerets in both sexes. The head is slightly elevated behind the eyes, a little more in the male than in the female. The male palpi (figs. 369, 370)

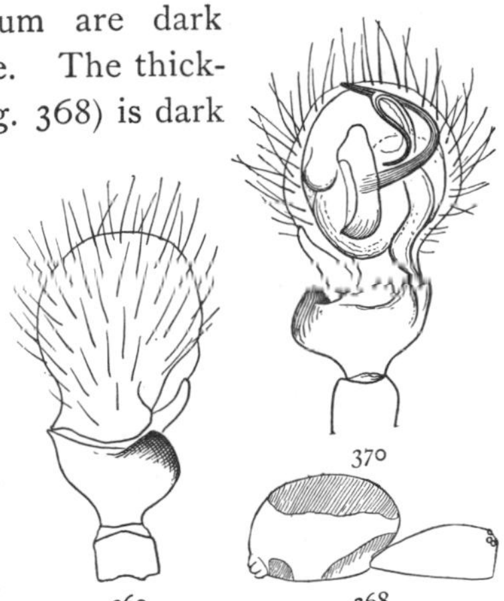

370

369　　　　368

FIGS. 368, 369, 370. Ceratinella lætabilis. — 368, outline of side of female enlarged sixteen times. 369, 370, end of male palpus.

are shorter and stouter than those of *fissiceps*. It lives in dead leaves and moss, sometimes under stones, and is sometimes found flying in the autumn.

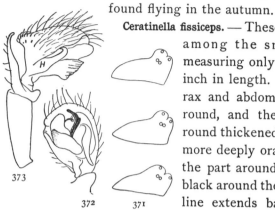

Ceratinella fissiceps. — These little spiders are among the smallest species, measuring only a sixteenth of an inch in length. The cephalothorax and abdomen are short and round, and the abdomen has a round thickened spot on the back, more deeply orange colored than the part around it. The head is black around the eyes, and a black line extends backward half the length of the cephalothorax. The head of the male extends forward over the mandibles, carrying with it the front middle eyes, and above it is a rounded hump with

FIGS. 371, 372, 373. Ceratinella fissiceps. — 371, varieties in the form of the head. 372, 373, palpus of male.

the hind middle eyes. The pairs of lateral eyes are opposite the crease between the humps (figs. 371). The female has at the same point a slight crease across the head and an elevation before and behind it. They are very common on low bushes in summer and under leaves in winter, and are occasionally seen in the autumn flights.

Cornicularia directa. — The males and females are of the

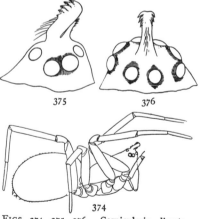

FIGS. 374, 375, 376. Cornicularia directa.— 374, male enlarged sixteen times. 375, head of male showing the double horn. 376, head of male from above.

same size and about a twelfth of an inch long. The cephalothorax is brown, varying in different individuals. The abdomen
is gray, with the muscular spots lighter than the rest. The
cephalothorax is long, narrowing gradually toward the head.
In the males there is a slender horn extending forward between
the eyes, a little thickened at the end and covered on the upper
side with stiff hairs in rows (fig. 376). Under this horn is a
smaller one about half as long and close against it (fig. 375).

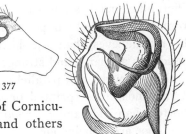

In females the horns
are absent, but the shape
of the head and arrange-
ment of the eyes are the
same, except that the
eyes are closer together.
377

There are several other species of Cornicularia, some with similar horns and others
with single horns on the heads of the
males. They are found under leaves in
winter, on plants and fences, and among
the flying spiders in autumn.

378

FIGS. 377, 378. Ceratinopsis
interpres. — 377, head of
male. 378, end of palpus
of male.

Ceratinopsis interpres. — Length about a
tenth of an inch. Color bright orange,
with a little black around the eyes and the
spinnerets. In the female the height of the head equals the
length of the mandibles, and in males it is greater. The size of
the sexes is about the same. The upper middle eyes are a little
larger and farther apart than the front middle pair, and between
them is a flattened space covered with stiff black hairs, longer
in the male than in the female (fig. 377). The male palpi have
the femur as thick as the femur of the first leg and the tibia
very short and wide, with a little recurved point on the front
edge. They live on low bushes in summer and under leaves
in winter.

THE EPEIRIDÆ

The Epeiridæ are the makers of the familiar round cobwebs. Like the Therididæ and the Linyphiadæ, they live always in their webs or nests back downward or, when in the round web, head downward. The cephalothorax is generally short, as in Therididæ, and low and wide in front, with the eyes near the front edge, the lateral pairs close together and farther from the middle eyes than the latter are from each other. The mandibles are large and strong. The maxillæ are short, often as short as wide, and parallel or a little divergent and rounded at the ends, never pointed or turned inward. The labium is shorter than wide and rounded or slightly pointed at the end. The legs are usually long and, more commonly than in the other cobweb spiders, stout and furnished with spines.

Most of the common species belong to the genus Epeira and its allies, having rounded abdomens and stout legs, some of them with humps and spines and peculiar angular forms of the abdomen. The colors are often bright, and those of the abdomen arranged in a triangular or leaf-shaped pattern. In Meta (p. 190) and Argyroepeira (p. 191) the abdomen is more elongated and the form and marking more like Linyphia. In Tetragnatha (p. 201) the whole body is long and slender, the abdomen several times as long as the cephalothorax, and the maxillæ and mandibles, especially in the males, much elongated. The colors are more uniform and the markings faint, usually light gray, yellow, or green, like the plants among which they live. The round webs of the Epeiridæ consist of a number of radiating lines, varying in different species from a dozen to seventy, crossed by two spirals, — an inner spiral that begins in the center and winds outward, and an outer spiral that begins at the edge of the web and winds inward. The inner spiral is made of smooth thread like the rays, and dust will not stick to it. The outer spiral is made of more elastic and sticky thread, which, when it is fresh, is covered with fine drops of a sticky liquid. In the finished web (figs. 379, 380) the outer

Fig. 379. Web of Epeira strix covered with dew hanging between the rails of a fence. One-third the real size.

spiral covers three-quarters or more of the diameter and the inner spiral a quarter or less, but in the unfinished web (fig. 381), before the sticky thread is put in, the inner spiral covers nearly the whole of it and is cut out, piece by piece, to make room for the outer spiral.

In beginning a web, after the radiating threads are finished, the spider fastens them more firmly at the center and corrects the distances between them by several short, irregular threads (fig. 379) and then begins the inner spiral with the turns, at first close together and then widening, in some species gradually, in others suddenly, until they are as far apart as the spider can

Fig. 380.   Finished web of Epeira sclopetaria with unusually small number of rays.   The spider hangs in the center, head downward, in its customary position.   The lower half of the web is wider than the upper half, as it usually is.   The cross threads with triangles at the ends are caused by two or more threads sticking together in the middle.

reach with the spinnerets on one and the front feet on the next, and so goes on nearly to the outside of the web, where it stops abruptly (fig. 381).   The spider usually rests a moment and then begins, sometimes at another part of the web, the outer sticky spiral. In the outermost parts of the web it usually forms several loops (fig. 381, *b* to *f*), filling in the corners until it approaches the inner spiral and finds room to pass completely

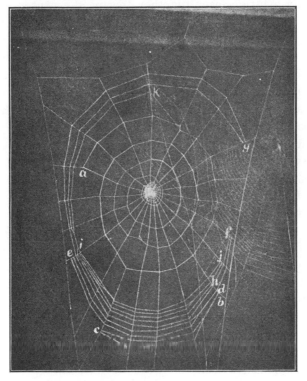

FIG. 381. Unfinished web of Epeira sclopetaria showing the completed inner spiral ending at *a*. The outer spiral began at *b*, went to *c*, and returned to *d*; turned and went to *e*, and then to *f*; and from there nearly around the web to *g*. From *g* it returned to the lower part of the web and made loops at *i* and *j*, and then started around the web until it was stopped at *k*.

around the web. As soon as the inner spiral is found in the way a part of it is cut out, and by the time the outer spiral is finished the inner is reduced to the small and close portion near the center.

While the temporary spirals are made as far apart as possible, the threads of the outer spiral are placed as close together as they can be without danger of their sticking to each other, and usually a little closer together toward the center of the web than they are at the outside. In fastening this thread to the rays of the web the spider first feels for the last thread with the first and second feet, and, having found it, turns the body slightly around and grasps the ray with the nearest foot of the fourth pair at a short distance from the point where the last thread crosses. After taking hold of the ray with the fourth foot, the spider turns down the abdomen so as to place the spinnerets against the ray and fastens the thread to it, at the same time holding the thread off with the other fourth foot to prevent its sticking to anything around it. The whole making of the web seems to be done entirely by feeling and is done as well in the dark as in daylight.

When the spider is active and the food supply good, a fresh web is made every day, the old one being torn down and thrown away. In tearing down a web (fig. 382) the spider walks out from the center on one of the rays and gathers in what web he can reach with the front feet, chews it into a ball, and drops it; then, having put in new rays in the cleared space, he goes to another part of the web and tears down another piece.

The variations between the webs of different species are chiefly in the central portion. In the webs of *hortorum* (p. 191), *gibberosa* (p. 177), and *placida* (p. 178), which spend most of their time in the web, the close part of the inner spiral is very large, circular, and finely finished, usually showing no trace of the wide temporary spirals. The number of rays is very large, and there is a wide clear space between the inner and outer spirals. In Argiope the inner spiral is very large and widens gradually until it almost touches the outer spiral.

It has a closely woven mat in the center and two zigzag bands of white silk extending up and down.

The webs of Tetragnatha, Meta, and Acrosoma have a hole in the middle, the irregular center being entirely removed.

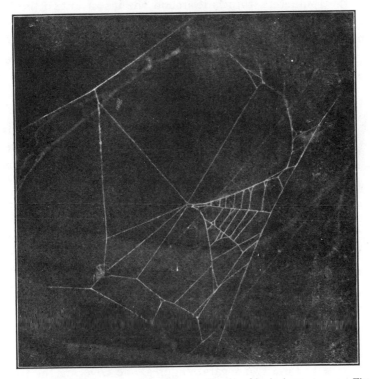

FIG. 382. Epeira sclopetaria tearing down an old web and beginning a new one. Five new rays have been made and a quarter of the old web remains at the right.

Insularis and *trifolium* live always in tent-shaped nests, with a thread, or several threads, leading to the center of the web. *Globosa, labyrinthea,* and Zilla have a similar thread from nest to web, and leave open a segment of the web through which it passes.

Insects flying through the web strike the sticky threads and, trying to free themselves, fall against others. The spider at the center of the web feels the movements of the insect and goes toward it by the nearest ray and, drawing out silk from the spinnerets, throws it around the insect until it is tied fast. Adult male Epeiridæ are seldom seen in webs of their own, but some of them do occasionally make webs. The male *E. sclopetaria*, for instance, sometimes makes a web nearly as large as that of the female and stands in it waiting for insects to be caught.

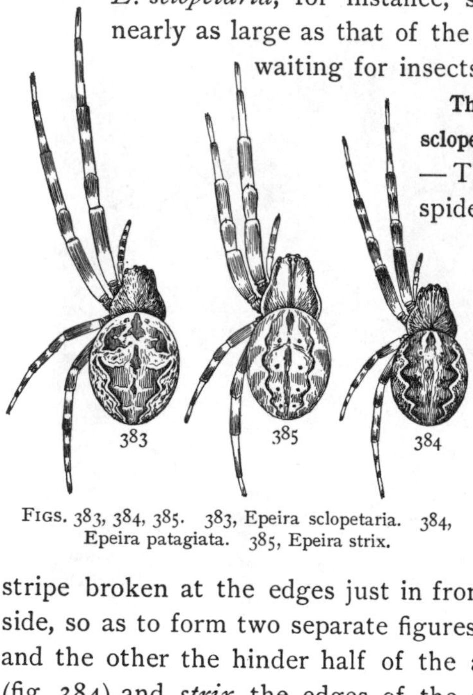

The Three House Epeiras: E. sclopetaria, patagiata, and strix. — These are the round-web spiders most commonly found about houses, barns, and fences. They are all about the same size, a third of an inch in length, and of various shades of brown, with a distinct scalloped middle stripe on the abdomen. *Sclopetaria* (fig. 383) has the middle

Figs. 383, 384, 385. 383, Epeira sclopetaria. 384, Epeira patagiata. 385, Epeira strix.

stripe broken at the edges just in front of the middle of each side, so as to form two separate figures, one covering the front and the other the hinder half of the abdomen. In *patagiata* (fig. 384) and *strix* the edges of the stripe are usually entire for their whole length. In *strix* (fig. 385) the middle stripe is narrower than in the others and usually lighter in color. The color of *sclopetaria* inclines to black, with the light marks yellow. *Patagiata* is oftener reddish brown, especially in alcohol, and the middle stripe is often dark and uniform in color, less broken by spots and transverse marks than in the others. The front legs of *sclopetaria* are longer than those of the other species, and the front legs of *strix* shorter and stouter. The cephalothorax of *strix* is more plainly marked than the others, with three longitudinal stripes. There is not much difference in the markings of the under side. The epigynum has two hard brown prominences at each side, with a soft finger-like appendage between. In *sclopetaria* and *strix* this finger is slender and tapers slightly toward the end. In *patagiata* it is wide at the end and flattened. In the palpi of the males there is a similar difference. Those of *sclopetaria* and *strix* are much alike, but that of *patagiata* has the forked hook at the base much thicker and more curved. *Patagiata* is a northern species, common in Canada and found occasionally as far south as Massachusetts and New York. It is also common in the north of Europe. *Sclopetaria* is also a European species, and is seldom found far from houses. It is more common north, but has been found as far south as Norfolk, Va. *Strix* is common all over the country, both around houses and in bushes.

The webs of these spiders have usually from twelve to twenty rays, and the inner spiral is small and carelessly finished (figs. 379, 380). The webs are made usually at nightfall, very young individuals beginning to spin soon after sunset, and larger ones beginning later, those that are full grown often waiting until dark, but some of them will occasionally spin their webs at any time of day. They stand in the web during the night, but seldom during the daytime, going then to their usual nests or hiding places, sometimes, especially with *Epeira strix*, a long distance from the web. As a rule, they have no special thread by which to enter or leave the web, but use any one of the rays which may be convenient, always injuring the web more or less; but occasionally, if

Epeira sclopetaria has a nest in a convenient situation, he will make the web near it and have a thread direct from the nest to the center of the web, as is the usual habit in some other species.   The eggs of *sclopetaria* are laid in the early summer

FIG. 386.   Egg cocoon of Epeira sclopetaria under the edge of a clapboard.
Natural size.

in large, round, white cocoons (fig. 386), fastened in sheltered places on the walls of houses and covered with a loose mass of silk threads.

The Angulate Epeiras. — *E. angulata* (fig. 389), *silvatica* (fig. 390), *nordmanni* (fig. 387), *cinerea* (fig. 391), and *corticaria* (fig. 392) all have the humps on the front of the abdomen, and in young spiders this is the widest part. *Angulata*, *silvatica*, and *cinerea* grow to a large size. *Cinerea* is light colored and lives in great numbers about houses and barns in northern New England.   *Angulata* and *silvatica* are found among trees and are dark colored like bark.   *Angulata* has a yellow stripe on the sternum and yellow spots under the abdomen between the spinnerets and epigynum. *Silvatica* has the sternum and under side of the abdomen brown, without any distinct markings. The male *angulata* has the thickened tibia of the second leg nearly as long as the tibia of the first leg. The male *silvatica* has the second tibia less thickened and a fourth shorter than the first tibia. The male *angulata* has a pair of long spines under the coxæ of the second legs, but in *silvatica* these spines are so small as to be hardly visible. *E. nordmanni* is a smaller species, about as large as *sclopetaria* and *strix*, with light gray colors and generally distinct marking both above and below. *E. corticaria* is not more than half as large as *silvatica* and might be mistaken for the young of that species, but the colors are lighter and the rings on the legs narrower and more numerous. The epigynum of *corti-*

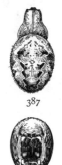

387

388

caria is nearly as large as that of *silvatica*, and the middle appendage is often wanting as if broken off.

Epeira nordmanni. — This is a little smaller and a little longer legged than *cinerea* and *angulata.* The abdomen is longer than in those species and has two similar humps in front (fig. 387). The female is not more than half an inch long. The colors are white and gray or black. The cephalothorax is light gray, darkest at the sides, but without stripes. The legs have a dark ring at the ends and a lighter one in the middle of each joint. The abdomen has a distinct middle stripe on the hinder half. In front there is an indistinct dark area extending to the top of the humps and, in the middle, inclosing a bright, long, white spot, with a round spot on each side sometimes united with it. The sternum is dark brown, without any stripe.

The under side of the abdomen has a middle dark area in which are four yellow spots, two just behind the respiratory openings and two farther back, halfway to the spinnerets.

Epeira angulata and **silvatica.** — These spiders, which are perhaps varieties of the same species, live usually among large trees and grow to over half an inch in length. The abdomen has two slight humps on the front. The colors are dark, like the bark of trees. The cephalothorax is dark brown, with traces of darker lines in the middle and at its sides. The legs are brown, with darker rings at the ends of the joints and less distinct rings in the middle. The abdomen has a bright yellow spot in front. The middle stripe is darker brown than the rest and has a scalloped edge marked by a dark and light line, which may be entire or broken into lines of spots. The under side of the abdomen is black or brown, with sometimes several yellow spots. The sternum is uniform brown in *silvatica* and has a yellow middle stripe in *angulata*. The males are colored like the females and are about half as large, with the legs longer, especially the front pairs. The tibia of the second legs is twice as thick as that of the first pair, a little bent, with the spines stouter and more numerous than in the female. In the male of the *angulata* variety the tibia of the second pair is nearly as long as that of the first, but in *silvatica* it is distinctly shorter. On the under side of the coxæ of the second legs is a conical spine, which is longest in the *angulata* variety. The epigynum is small for so large a spider and has a long slender finger in the middle. These spiders are found singly or in small

389

390

FIGS. 389, 390. — 389, Epeira angulata. 390, Epeira silvatica. Both enlarged twice.

numbers, usually in the woods, sometimes in webs hung
between trees high above the ground.

Epeira cinerea. — This large spider is common in the northern
part of New England, from Maine to New York, where it lives
in great numbers about barns and houses.
It grows to three-quarters of an inch in
length, with the abdomen proportionally
larger than *angulata* and with two small
humps on the front part (fig. 391). The
color is dirty white, with grayish markings
and long white hairs scattered all over the
body. The cephalothorax is a little darkened at the sides, but has no distinct stripes.
The legs have gray rings at the ends and
middle of each joint, which are hardly visible

FIG. 391. Epeira cinerea.—
Back of female enlarged
twice.

in some individuals and almost black in others. The markings
are like those of *angulata*, but paler and often indistinct. The
sternum is brown, and the under side of the abdomen has a

FIG. 392. Epeira corti-
caria.— Back of female
enlarged eight times.

central dark stripe bordered by curved yellow
markings. The epigynum is small, as in *angulata*, but the finger is flattened and turned up
at the end. The male is colored like the
female, with the hairs on the legs coarser
and darker. The tibia of the second legs of
the male is not thickened or modified as it
is in *angulata*. The webs resemble those
of *E. sclopetaria*, and the spider has similar
habits, standing in the web at night and
usually leaving it in the daytime; and it has
no special thread from the web to the nest.

Epeira corticaria. — This is a small species about quarter of an
inch in length, with the abdomen angular in front, where it is
as wide as long (fig. 392). The colors are generally lighter and

brighter than in *angulata* or *silvatica*. The cephalothorax has
the cephalic part brown and the sides pale. The legs are
marked with broken brown rings at the ends and middle of
each joint. The abdomen is brown of various shades, with
light markings on the front part that are often bright red or
yellow. There is a narrow light line across the
abdomen from the middle to each hump and
around the outer side
of it. In front of these
light lines the abdomen
is generally darker, ex-
cept a light spot, some-
times cross shaped, in
the middle. The hinder
half of the abdomen has
sometimes an indistinct
middle stripe. The
under side of the abdo-
men has the usual mid-
dle dark area, with a
curved yellow mark each
side of it. The finger
of the epigynum is usu-
ally absent, as if broken
off.

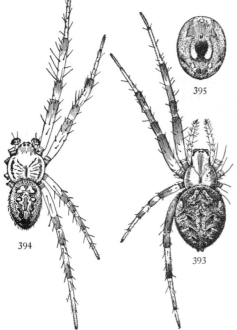

FIGS. 393, 394, 395.   Epeira trivittata, enlarged four
times. — 393, female.   394, male.   395, markings
of under side of abdomen.

Epeira trivittata and
domiciliorum. — These
spiders, which may be
considered varieties of
one species, are among the most common Epeiridæ, at least in
the northern part of the country, the smaller variety, *trivittata*,
quarter of an inch long, living in small bushes and marsh grass,
and the larger variety in trees and fences. The abdomen is

only a little longer than wide and is proportionally smaller than in *insularis* and *thaddeus*. The legs are long and slender, the first pair being nearly twice as long as the body. The color is most commonly light yellow, with brown markings. Sometimes the abdomen is thickly spotted with red, especially toward the latter part of the summer, and *domiciliorum* has usually gray and even black markings. The cephalothorax has three dark stripes not very sharply defined, and the legs have brown or gray rings at the ends of the joints. The back of the abdomen has a row of light spots in the middle, sometimes united into a stripe, and on each side of this a row of dark spots nearly surrounded by lighter color. The sternum is bright yellow in the middle, and the under side of the abdomen has a dark center and two or three pairs of yellow spots.

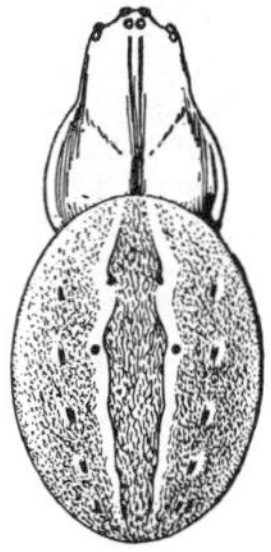

The males are usually smaller than the females, but resemble them in color and markings. On the under side of each femur is a single row of long spines. The tibia of the second legs is curved more in the small than in the large variety and has a row of strong spines on the inner side.

Fig. 396. Epeira pratensis, enlarged four times.

The webs are made usually just before dark, and the spider stands in them more in the night than during the daytime. Sometimes they make a thread from the center of the web to the nest, but this is not a regular habit, as it is with *insularis* (fig. 397).

Very young spiders make proportionally larger nests, often on the ends of grasses, where their round webs are destroyed every day by the wind. Some of them mature as early as June, and others, especially of the *domiciliorum* variety, as late as August.

Epeira pratensis. — This is the same size and color as *Epeira trivittata*, and lives, like that species, in grass and low bushes.

The cephalothorax and abdomen are both slightly longer than in *trivittata*, and the color is more uniform. The cephalothorax is dull yellow, with a middle and two lateral stripes, but these are often absent in light specimens. The legs are colored like the cephalothorax, sometimes a little darker at the ends of the joints. The abdomen has a middle dark stripe, at the sides of which are two narrow bright yellow lines, which are sometimes bordered with red. Outside of the middle stripes are six pairs of black spots partly surrounded by yellow. On the under side the sternum has a yellow stripe in the middle, and the abdomen two curved yellow marks, which may be broken into spots. In the male the body is longer and narrower than in the female and longer than the male *trivittata*, and the tibiæ of the second legs are a little thickened and curved as in *trivittata*.

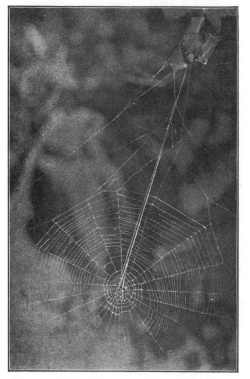

Fig. 397. Web of Epeira insularis, with nest above covered with leaves and several threads leading from the nest to the center of the web. One-third the real size.

Epeira insularis or **marmorea.** — The adult females are half to three-quarters of an inch long, the abdomen large and oval, and

bright yellow or orange color, with brown or purple markings
(fig. 398). The cephalothorax is dull yellow, with slightly
darker lines in the middle and at the sides. The femur and
patella of all the legs are bright orange, darker toward the ends.
The other joints are white, with brown ends. The light parts
of the abdomen are bright yellow marked with brown. In the
middle is a narrow deeply scalloped stripe, bordered by a wide
yellow line, outside of which are oblique yellow and brown
markings. In the middle of the stripe is a row of light spots,
each connected at the sides with two others, smaller and round,
forming a large figure at the anterior end. On the under side
the sternum is brown and bright yellow in the middle. The
abdomen is dark brown, with two semi-
circular yellow spots. The males (fig.
399) are about half as long as the
females. The tibiæ of the second legs
are thickened, and the spines on the
inner side short and stout. The coxæ
of the second legs have a
conical spine near the base.
This spider lives in bushes
three or four feet high. It
makes a tent of leaves (fig.
397), in which it usually
stands out of sight, holding
a thread which leads to the
center of the nest. Young
spiders make larger tents in
proportion to their size and
make them entirely of silk

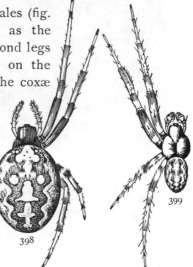

FIGS. 398, 399. Epeira insularis, enlarged
twice. — 398, female. 399, male.

(fig. 400). In Massachusetts and Connecticut it matures about
the first of September. It is found all over the country, and
is probably a variety of the European *Epeira marmorea*.

Epeira thaddeus. — A small species resembling the young of *insularis*, but with less distinct markings on the back. Full-grown females are about quarter of an inch in length, with the abdomen large and round (fig. 401). The colors are orange

FIG. 400. Web of young Epeira insularis, showing the nest above and the straight thread leading from the nest to the center of the web. Half the real size.

and light yellow like *insularis*. The two front pairs of legs have the femur, patella, and tibia orange, darker toward the ends. The third and fourth legs have the femur and patella orange. The other joints are white, with dark rings at the ends. The tibia of the fourth pair has a wide dark ring at the end.

The abdomen is white or light yellow on the upper side, and brown underneath, the edge of the dark color coming far enough up to be seen from above, around the sides and front (fig. 401). Under the middle of the abdomen is a yellow spot just behind the epigynum (fig. 401 a). In some individuals there is a trace of markings on the hinder part of the abdomen, and the under side is sometimes light, so that there is a dark ring around the middle of the abdomen. This spider makes a tent near the web and lives in it like *insularis*.

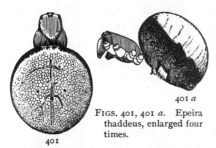

401 a

FIGS. 401, 401 a. Epeira thaddeus, enlarged four times.

401

Epeira trifolium. — This is one of the largest species of the family, measuring from half to three-quarters of an inch long, with a large round abdomen, usually of a purplish brown color, and legs strongly marked with black rings (fig. 403). The cephalothorax is white, with three wide black stripes. The legs are white, with a black ring at the end of each joint and in the middle of the fourth femur. The back of the abdomen varies in color from dark purplish brown to light gray or white, or

FIG. 402. Epeira trifolium in its nest in a plant of golden-rod. Natural size.

sometimes light yellow, and the same individual will change from light color to dark. The usual markings are four white spots and a middle row of smaller spots, with several oblique rows still smaller. All trace of the usual middle stripe is wanting except in very young individuals. The under side of the abdomen is dark brown, and the usual semicircular yellow marks are absent except in the young. The males (fig. 404) are not more than half as long as the females and slender and light colored. The markings are like those of the female, but less distinct. The tibiæ of the second legs are not thickened or modified in shape as they are in the male *insularis*. *Trifolium* makes a large web in bushes, but seldom stands in it. It has near by a tent above the web (fig. 402) made of leaves, drawn together and lined with silk, connected with the center of the web by a strong thread, and it usually remains in this tent with one foot on the thread, so that it feels when anything is caught. The spiders mature in September,

FIGS. 403, 404. Epeira trifolium, enlarged twice. — 403, female. 404, male.

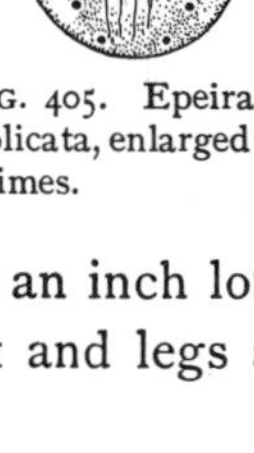

when the males may sometimes be seen about the nests of the females. In October they lay their eggs and all die before winter.

FIG. 405. Epeira displicata, enlarged four times.

Epeira displicata. — Large females are quarter of an inch long, but they are usually smaller. The cephalothorax and legs are brownish yellow, without markings. The abdomen is oval and light yellow or crimson, the latter color more common in the young. Sometimes there are two white lines in the middle.

At the sides of the hinder half of the abdomen are three pairs of round black spots surrounded by lighter rings (fig. 405). The under side of the abdomen is a little darker than the upper side, with no distinct markings.

The male has the legs and cephalothorax darker brown than the female, and the black spots on the abdomen larger and surrounded more distinctly with white, which sometimes forms a stripe on each side. The tibiæ of the second legs are not thickened. The webs are usually small and among leaves.

FIG. 406. Web of Epeira globosa in the corner of a doorway, showing the large tent at the top, from which a coarse thread runs to the center of the round web.

Epeira globosa or **triaranea.** — Length about a quarter of an inch, the male a third smaller. The abdomen is round and as wide as long, and in the female large for the size of the spider.

The front half of the abdomen is nearly covered by four white, yellow, or pink spots, partly united into a rectangular figure surrounded by an irregular black line (fig. 407). The hinder

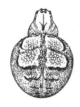

half has three or four pairs of black spots. The general color is light brownish yellow. The cephalothorax has a fine middle line from the eyes to the dorsal groove and indistinct dark marks at the sides of the head. The first and second legs have slightly darker rings at the end and middle of each joint, the third and fourth pairs at the ends of the joints only. The male is marked like the female and

FIG. 407. Epeira globosa, enlarged four times.

has the tibia of the second legs slightly curved and thickened with large spines on the inner side.

This spider makes a very large tent, out of which a strong thread runs to the center of the round web (fig. 406). From the tent a loose and irregular web extends downward, sometimes covering half of the round web (fig. 406). Opposite the thread leading to the tent, a segment of the round web is left open or partly open without any sticky threads.

Epeira labyrinthea. — This spider makes a large irregular web in which is a tent connected by a thread with the small round web below, much as in *Epeira globosa*. The female is a fifth of an inch long. The abdomen is oval and not unusually large, as it is in *globosa* (fig. 408). The cephalothorax is long, dark brown in the middle and lighter at the sides, and almost white in front around and behind the eyes. The legs are white, with narrow dark brown rings at the ends of the joints and wider yellow rings on patella and femur of the first and second pairs. The abdomen is marked with four long white spots in front and a dark brown middle band behind. At the sides the abdomen

FIG. 408. Epeira labyrinthea, enlarged four times.

Fig. 409. Web of Epeira labyrinthea with large irregular web around the nest. One-third the real size.

is light brown or yellow. On the under side the ends of the mandibles and the maxillæ are black. The sternum is black, with a white middle stripe. The abdomen has a short middle white stripe surrounded by a large dark spot, and there are several yellow spots along the sides and around the spinnerets.

The round web of this spider is not large, generally three or four inches in diameter, but the irregular part above and partly covering it may be much larger, sometimes as much as six inches across, where the shape of the surrounding plants allows it (fig. 409). One segment at the upper part of the round web is partly open, as in *globosa* (p. 173) and Zilla (p. 185), and here a strong thread passes to the nest, which is often covered by a large spreading tent. In the last of the summer several small, flat, brown cocoons are strung together in the irregular web above the tent (fig. 410), which is then smaller and less regularly made.

Epeira gibberosa. — A small and light-colored species living among grass and in bushes in open fields. The adult female is from a sixth to a quarter of an inch long, and the male smaller. The cephalothorax and legs are light greenish yellow, and the abdomen gray, or light yellow covered with lighter

Fig. 410. Web of Epeira labyrinthea with string of cocoons in the upper part over the spider's nest. One-third the real size.

spots and black and yellow markings (fig. 411). The abdomen is marked with two parallel lines on the hinder half and three smaller black spots in front, the latter often absent. The parallel lines are sometimes broken up into rows of spots, and these may form part of several transverse black and yellow marks. The cephalothorax has a narrow black line in the middle from the dorsal groove nearly to the eyes. The feet are black toward the claws, and the spines of the legs are long and black. The first and second femora have a longitudinal black line on the under side. The abdomen is oval, half longer than wide. The cephalothorax is high in the middle and slopes forward toward the eyes almost as steeply as backward (fig. 412). The web (fig. 413) is horizontal or inclined, with a round well-defined central portion, in the middle of which is sometimes a round opaque screen that nearly covers the spider. In the finished web there is usually no trace of the temporary spiral, but sometimes, as in the figure, a little of it is left, showing how it starts abruptly from the closer spirals that form the center of the web. The outer spirals are very fine and close together and the number of rays unusually large, sometimes as many as sixty.

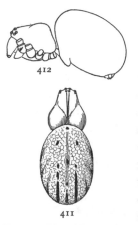

FIGS. 411, 412. Epeira gibberosa, enlarged eight times. — 411, back of female. 412, side view to show humps on the cephalothorax.

Epeira placida. — This is a small spider, about a fifth of an inch long, with the longest legs about a quarter of an inch. The cephalothorax is high in the middle where it rests against the abdomen very much as it is in *gibberosa* (fig. 412). The abdomen is oval, and widest behind. The legs are comparatively short and tapering, and the femora thick. The cephalothorax is brownish yellow, with three brown stripes. The legs are the same color, a little darker at the ends of the joints. The abdomen has a middle brown stripe, narrow in front and widening to the middle, from which it extends to the spinnerets, keeping about the same width, with a row of black spots on the edge at each side and a pair of white spots in the

FIG. 413. Web of Epeira gibberosa, showing the round center of the inner spiral, the great number of rays, and the closeness of the spirals. Torn in several places by use. Half the real size.

middle (fig. 414). The sides of the abdomen are white or yellow, and underneath it is brown, with two white stripes in the middle and four white spots around the spinnerets. The male is marked like the female and has no peculiar modifications of the legs. This spider matures early, sometimes before the first of June in Massachusetts, and half-grown young are

found in the autumn. The web is like that of *gibberosa*, with
a large, round, and close inner spiral from which, in the unfinished web, the temporary spiral starts abruptly. The web is
made in low bushes and may be vertical or inclined.

Epeira scutulata. — A light yellow spider, a sixth to a fifth of
an inch long, with the abdomen angular behind and at the

sides and as wide as long (fig. 415). The cephalothorax is half as wide in front as it is behind,
and the lateral eyes are as far from the middle
eyes as they are from each other. The front
legs are a fourth longer than the second. The
general color is light yellow, the legs darker at
the ends of the joints, with long black spines.
The head has a few brown or red marks behind
the eyes and back to the dorsal groove, but these
are often entirely absent. The

FIG. 414. Epeira
placida, enlarged
eight times.

abdomen is lighter across the front between
the two corners, and there is sometimes a
distinct white transverse stripe. In front of
each corner is a black spot, and there is
generally a row of small black spots around
the front of the abdomen, and two rows behind
converging toward the spinnerets. In the
hinder rows of spots the middle pair are
generally longest, and sometimes these are
the only pair present. The under side has no
distinct markings. The epigynum is dark at
the sides, and the finger is short and flat at the
end and turned a little outward. The male

FIG. 415. Epeira scu-
tulata, enlarged four
times.

has the legs longer, and the cephalothorax wider behind. The
abdomen is not much larger than the cephalothorax and less
angular than in the female. The colors are the same as in the
female, some individuals being light and some dark.

Epeira parvula. — A common spider all over the country, with the abdomen wide in front and bluntly pointed behind, gray and brown colors and a great variety of markings. The length is quarter to three-eighths of an inch, with the abdomen two-thirds as long and as wide across the front. The abdomen is as high behind as it is in front, and the pointed end is sometimes turned a little upward, as it is in *conica*. The

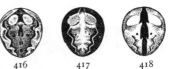

FIGS. 416, 417, 418. Markings of the abdomen of Epeira parvula, enlarged twice.

front of the head is narrow, not more than half as wide as the back of the thorax. The front legs are half longer than the body. The cephalothorax is gray, darker at the sides, and sometimes with a few black spots. The legs are irregularly marked with rings and spots, and the femora are dark toward the end. The abdomen is commonly gray, with a tapering scalloped middle stripe and a distinct dark middle spot and two large light spots at the front end (fig. 416). Sometimes

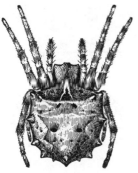

FIG. 419. Epeira stellata, enlarged four times.

there is a middle narrow dark stripe the whole length of the abdomen (fig. 418), and sometimes all the middle is white or light yellow. The males have the head a little narrower and more pointed, the legs longer, and the second tibiæ slightly thickened, but not curved. The webs are in low bushes.

Epeira stellata. — A brown spider, a quarter to a third of an inch long and nearly as broad, with pointed humps around the abdomen. The cephalothorax is wide in front, and the lateral eyes are on the outer sharp corners. The legs are short and usually drawn up and partly concealed under the abdomen. The abdomen has a sharp point in front that extends over the cephalothorax as far as the base of the first legs, and a large point behind, with a smaller one under it. At the sides are five pairs of points, and over the first of these another pair a little higher on the back. The

FIG. 420.   Unfinished web of Epeira stellata with the spider hanging near the center.
Half the real size.

cephalothorax is brown, lighter in the middle and darker at the sides, and covered with short gray hairs. The abdomen is marked with lighter and darker spots of brown, the front part generally dark with a very light middle spot, and the hinder half showing traces of the usual middle stripe of Epeira. The legs have dark rings at the ends and middle of the joints. It lives among low bushes a foot or two from the ground all over the country. This spider, as well as several other species, often leaves a web unfinished with the inner spiral still covering a large part of it, as in fig. 420.

Epeira verrucosa. — Common in the South and as far north as Long Island, N.Y. The body is about a quarter of an inch long. The abdomen is narrow behind but not pointed, and in front nearly as wide as long. The middle is nearly covered by a triangular light spot, — white, yellow, or pink in different spiders, — surrounded by a darker color of various shades of brown or gray. The cephalothorax is yellow or light gray, with sometimes some darker spots in the middle. The legs are colored like the thorax, with darker rings at the ends of the joints and in the middle of the first and second femora. The spines are slender and colored like the hairs. The abdomen has a prominent tubercle behind, at the end of the light spot, and under it in the middle line two others. At the sides near the posterior end are two pairs of tubercles, and some-

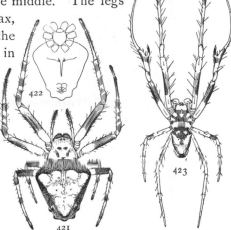

FIGS. 421, 422, 423. Epeira verrucosa. — 421, female enlarged twice. 422, under side of female. 423, male enlarged twice.

times two other pairs farther forward, and two at the corners of the light spot. The colors of the under side are as variable as those above, — sometimes light without distinct markings, and sometimes almost black at the sides, on the sternum, and around the spinnerets. The epigynum (fig. 422) has a slender pointed finger reaching halfway to the spinnerets.

The male (fig. 423) has the head narrower than the female, and the abdomen as small as the cephalothorax. The legs are longer and more slender, with the metatarsus of the second pair curved inward, and a long forked spine on the inside of the tibia of the same legs.

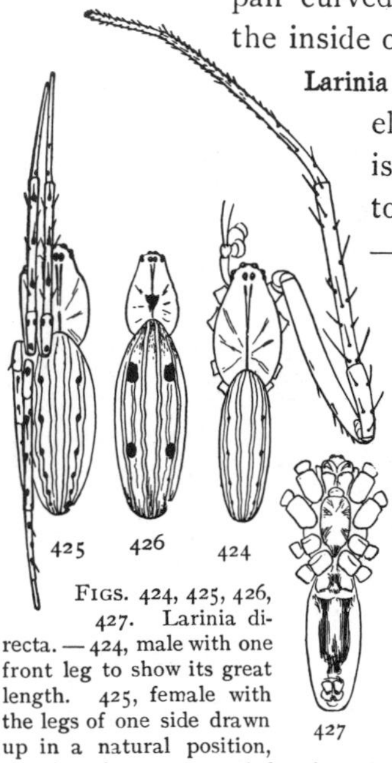

Larinia directa. — This resembles a much elongated *Epeira pratensis* (p. 167). It is about as long as *pratensis*, a quarter to a third of an inch, but very slender, — not much more than a quarter as wide as long (fig. 425). The general color is yellowish but pale and translucent, marked with very distinct black spots. The spots are usually in six pairs on the abdomen, sometimes so small as to be hardly visible, sometimes so large as to be the most distinct part of the spider. In some individuals there is a row of black spots on the upper side of each leg, so that when these are drawn up over the back hardly anything is visible except the spots. In some individuals the first and third pairs of spots on the abdomen are very large and the others very small (fig. 426). The sternum is nearly twice as long as wide, with the sides of the front half parallel. It is darker at the sides. On the under side of the abdomen are two parallel dark stripes. In the male (fig. 424) the front legs are nearly three times the length of the body, but neither the first nor

425   426   424

427

FIGS. 424, 425, 426, 427. Larinia directa. — 424, male with one front leg to show its great length. 425, female with the legs of one side drawn up in a natural position, showing the spots. 426, female with four large spots on the back. 427, under side. All enlarged four times.

the second pair is curved or thickened. It is found in South
Carolina, Georgia, and Alabama.

Cyclosa conica or **caudata.** — This spider may be known by the
blunt conical hump at the hinder end of the abdomen, extending upward and backward over the spinnerets (figs. 428, 429).
Full-grown females are about quarter of an inch long. The
color is a mixture of gray and white, different individuals varying from almost white to almost black. The cephalothorax
is longer than wide, the front part narrow, and the top of the
front of the head extended forward beyond
the base of the mandibles. The hump on
the abdomen varies considerably in size,
and is generally about half as long as the
rest of the abdomen and slopes gradually
into it. In light individuals the markings
of the abdomen are obscure, but usually
there is a distinct dark middle stripe,
widest near the base of the hump. The

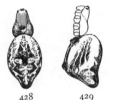

428   429

FIGS. 428, 429. Cyclosa
conica, enlarged four
times.

under side is black, with a pair of very distinct light spots
across the middle. The cephalothorax is dark gray or black
without stripes, sometimes a little lighter around the eyes.
The legs are white, with dark rings at the end of each joint
and in the middle of each except the femora. On the first
and second femora the dark rings are very wide, covering
sometimes more than half the joint. The males have the
cephalothorax darker and narrower in front, and the abdomen
smaller, with only a slight hump. The spider seems to live all
the time in the web. The inner spiral is large and widens
gradually from the center outward. There is usually a line of
silk across the web, in which are fastened parts of dead insects
and other rubbish and, in the middle of the summer, the cocoons
of eggs. The spider, standing in the middle of this band where
it crosses the center of the web, looks like part of the rubbish.

When an old web is torn down this band of rubbish is left in place, and the new web made across it.   A peculiarity of the web of this spider is that the inner spiral has one, and sometimes two, loops in it, making it wider than it is high (fig. 430).

FIG. 430.   Half-finished web of young Cyclosa conica, showing sticks and rubbish across the lower half.   The inner spiral has a loop in the left side.

THE THREE SPECIES OF THE GENUS ZILLA

We have three species of Zilla, the females of which are so much alike that it is almost impossible to tell them apart. The males also resemble each other closely except in their palpi, which are distinctly different in the different species. They are of moderate size, the largest about three-eighths of an inch long, and in general appearance resemble the genus Steatoda of the Therididæ (p. 119).   The abdomen is large and oval and a little flattened.   The legs are slender and of moderate length, like those of Epeira.   The head is rounded in front, and the lateral eyes are not separated farther from the middle pairs than they are from each other. The mandibles are large and thickened in the middle toward the front. The epigynum and the spinnerets are both small. The color of all the species is gray, with sometimes a little yellow or pink in the lighter parts. The cephalothorax has usually, but not always, a dark border at the sides and a middle dark line that widens and becomes lighter toward the eyes. The abdomen has a wide middle stripe like Epeira, scalloped at the sides and crossed at the hinder end by two or three pairs of transverse spots. In front it is almost white or tinted with pink or yellow, and narrows almost to a point, with a much darker spot each side. The sides of the abdomen are marked with oblique dark marks that extend underneath. The sternum has a light middle stripe. Under the abdomen is a dark middle stripe, with light each side of it.

Fig. 431. Female Zilla atrica, enlarged four times.

The legs are pale, with narrow gray rings at the end and middle of each joint. These three species seem to be the same as three found in Europe, — Z. atrica, Z. x-notata, and Z. montana. Atrica is found at Ipswich and Salem on the coast of Massachusetts, x-notata at Woods Hole on the south coast of Massachusetts, and montana in the White Mountains and Adirondacks.

Fig. 432. Middle of web of Zilla atrica with the open segment and thread to the nest at the left.

Wherever found they are in large numbers, atrica and x-notata living on the outside of houses, and montana in trees and rocks.

The webs of Zilla (fig. 432) have a segment left without cross threads, sometimes for its whole length, and sometimes only the part of it nearest the center. Opposite this open segment a thread leads from the center of the web to the nest (fig. 433),

FIG. 433.   Tubular nest of Zilla atrica.

which is a tube of silk open at both ends.

The differences between the palpi of the males are very plain. In *atrica* the palpi (fig. 434) are as long as the whole body, with the femur and tibia both slightly curved and the tarsus and palpal organ small and like that of *x-notata*. In *x-notata* (fig. 435) the palpus is as long as the cephalothorax, and the tarsus and palpal organ small and round. The front legs are a fourth longer than in *atrica*. In *montana* (fig. 435*a*) the palpus is still shorter, the tibia thicker, and the tarsus and palpal organ larger. There is little difference in the shape of the epigynum of the different species, but that of *montana* is twice as large as that of *x-notata* or *atrica*.

Singa pratensis. — The Singas are small Epeiridæ a sixth or fifth of an inch long, with smooth bodies and bright colors. They live among grass and other small plants in low open ground. When full grown the females of *S. pratensis* are a fifth of an inch long, with the abdomen oval and marked with a double white stripe in the middle and a single one on each side. The cephalothorax is yellow, with a little black between the middle eyes not extending to the lateral pairs.

The legs are yellow, without rings or other markings. The abdomen is yellow brown, darker toward the hinder end, with white or light yellow stripes. The under side is the same yellow-brown color, darker in the middle, with two narrow,

curved, light lines from the spiracles to the spinnerets. The males are marked in the same way and have a smaller abdomen and longer spines on the legs.

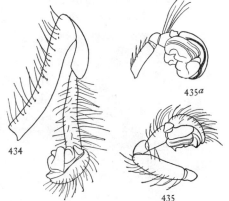

Singa variabilis. — This is a little smaller than *pratensis*, usually about a sixth of an inch long. The legs and cephalothorax are bright orange

FIGS. 434, 435, 435*a*.   Male palpi of Zilla. — 434, Zilla atrica.   435, Zilla x-notata.   435*a*, Zilla montana.

color. The front of the head between the eyes is black. The abdomen is usually entirely black, but occasionally has bright yellow markings (fig. 436) arranged somewhat as in *pratensis*. Sometimes there

FIG. 436.   Markings of the back of Singa variabilis.

is a wide middle stripe, with narrower ones at the sides and two underneath. Sometimes there are only the two lateral stripes, and there are all variations between these markings. The males are colored in the same way and have the same varieties. They are smaller than the males of *pratensis*, but have the palpal organs as large or larger.

THE GENUS ACROSOMA

These are small spiders, with the abdomen extended back half its length beyond the spinnerets, brightly colored, flattened above, and furnished with several pairs of pointed processes. The cephalothorax is longer than in Epeira and

FIG. 437. Web of Acrosoma spinea.

Argiope and widest in the middle. The legs are slender and have only fine and soft hairs. The webs (fig. 437) are inclined and have a hole in the middle surrounded by several turns of smooth thread; when hanging in it the spiders look like burrs or seeds. At a slight alarm they will sometimes drop to the ground and hide under the nearest shelter.

Acrosoma mitrata. — This is a smaller species than *rugosa* or *spinea*. The abdomen does not extend as far backward as in the other species, but comes farther forward so as to cover half the cephalothorax (fig. 438). The abdomen is truncated behind, with two pairs of pointed processes at the corners, one pair below the other. In front, the abdomen is a little narrowed over the thorax. The legs and cephalothorax are brown, as in the other species. The abdomen is light yellow, darker behind, with two or three pairs of black spots along the middle and five or six dark elongated spots along the sides.

FIG. 438. Acrosoma mitrata, enlarged four times.

The under side is black mixed with yellow spots, as in the other species. Common as far north as Connecticut.

Acrosoma rugosa. — This has five pairs of spines on the abdomen, three pairs in the same places as those of *spinea* and the other two pairs behind and under the last of the three. All the humps and spines are about the same size. The cephalothorax and legs resemble those of *spinea*, but the legs are shorter. The colors are white, yellow, and brown in spots and marks like those of *spinea*, some individuals being almost white, and others as nearly black. The males have a long slender abdomen without humps or spines. This is a common spider as far north as Connecticut, where it is occasionally found.

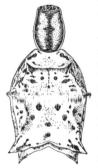

FIG. 439. Acrosoma rugosa, enlarged four times.

Acrosoma spinea. — This spider is distinguished from all the common species by the shape of its abdomen, which is narrow in front and has two long spreading points behind (fig. 440). There is a pair of smaller spines on the front of the abdomen and another near the middle of each side. The middle of the abdomen is white or bright yellow.   The spines are black at the points and bright red at the base.   There are several black spots on the back, and gray marks at the sides.   The under side of the abdomen is darker than it is above and marked with black and yellow spots.   The cephalothorax and legs are light brown, the thorax with lighter edges.

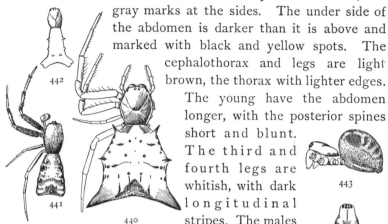

The young have the abdomen longer, with the posterior spines short and blunt. The third and fourth legs are whitish, with dark longitudinal stripes. The males are smaller than the females and resemble the young.

FIGS. 440, 441, 442.   Acrosoma spinea. — 440, female enlarged four times. 441, male enlarged four times.   442, young less than half grown.

The abdomen is a little widened behind and has in place of the spines three pairs of low humps. The front legs are dark, and the hinder legs light, as in the young.   The web (fig. 437) has a hole in the middle, across which the spider hangs.

Meta menardi. — This spider lives in caves and similar cool and shady places in various parts of this country and also in Europe.   In general appearance, especially when young, it reminds one of Linyphia.   The abdomen is longer than wide, high in front, and tapering a little behind (fig. 445). The eyes are near together, the

FIGS. 443, 444, 445.   Meta menardi, enlarged four times. — 443, 444, half-grown young. 445, back of adult female.

lateral eyes almost as near the middle pairs as they are to each other.   The mandibles are long, thickened in front near the base, and slightly turned outward at the ends and strongly toothed on the inner side about the claw. The maxillæ are also long and a little widened at the ends. The dorsal groove is very deep. The legs are long, the front pair twice the length of the body. The full-grown female is half an inch in length, the male a third shorter, but with legs nearly as long. The general color is gray, the lighter parts translucent and yellowish. The cephalothorax has three gray stripes, more distinct in the young, a middle stripe from the eyes to the dorsal groove, and one on each side of the thorax. In the young (fig. 444) the markings of the abdomen are two large dark spots near the front end and several other pairs, becoming smaller toward the hinder end. In adults these mark ings unite into a middle stripe more like Epeira, with a light middle spot in front and several middle spots and pairs of spots diminishing

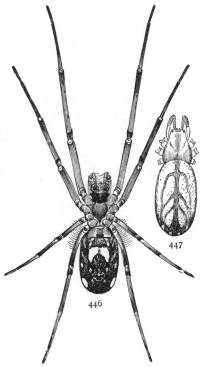

447

446

FIGS. 446, 447. Argyroepeira hortorum, enlarged four times. — 446, under side of female. 447, back of female.

backward. The legs have gray rings at the ends and middle of the joints. The webs are horizontal or inclined, according to the shape of the rocks on which they are built. They resemble the webs of Tetragnatha, having a small central spiral with a round hole in the middle, across which the spider holds herself. This spider matures late in the autumn or early in the summer, and makes large, loose, and transparent cocoons, hung near the webs.

Argyroepeira hortorum. — This is a green and silver-white spider, with slender legs and a long abdomen resembling

Tetragnatha. The body of the female is about a quarter of an inch long, the abdomen twice as long as wide, and blunt at both ends (fig. 447). The first pair of legs are twice as long as the body, the second a fourth shorter (fig. 446). The legs are bright green, darker toward the ends. The cephalothorax is green, with a darker stripe in the middle and one on each side. The upper part of the abdomen is silver white, with a dark line through the middle, giving off four pairs of branches at the sides. At the sides of the abdomen are yellow stripes extending

Fig. 448.   Argiope riparia in the middle of the web. Natural size.

downward, and toward the hinder end two bright copper-red spots. The colors of the under side are as bright as those above and are more plainly seen as the spider hangs in its web. The basal joints of the legs are light in color, and the sternum and mouth parts dark. The abdo men is green, darker from front to back, where it is almost black around the spinnerets. In the middle is a large double spot of bright copper red, and the red spots at the end of the body show as plainly from below as from above, and around the middle spot are several small spots of bright yellow. The hairs and spines of the legs are so fine that they do not much affect the general color. On the front side of the femur of the fourth leg there is a fringe of long hairs extending half its length. The males are half as large as the females, with longer and more slender legs and palpi, and the same colors. The webs are nearly horizontal, with a small hole in the center, and under the round web is often a large irregular web. The round web may be a foot in diameter, or it may be so small as hardly to cover the spider. The webs have a large number of rays, and the spirals are very close together, as in the webs of *Epeira* gibberosa (fig. 413). The smooth central part of the web is circular and very regularly woven, show ing usually no trace of the beginning of the temporary spirals, and

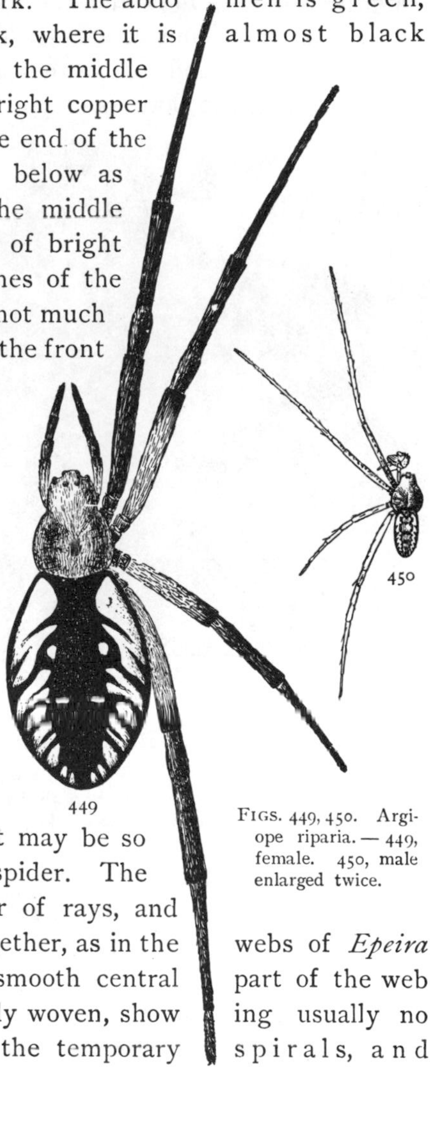

449

450

FIGS. 449, 450. Argiope riparia. — 449, female. 450, male enlarged twice.

between it and the sticky circles there is a wide space in which is nothing but the bare rays.

Argiope riparia. — This and the next species are among the largest and most conspicuous of the round-web spiders. It lives among grass and low bushes in open fields and meadows, especially along the borders of ponds and ditches. It matures

FIG. 451.   Middle of web of Argiope riparia, natural size.   The large inner spiral ends at *b* and the outer spiral at *a*.   At *c, c,* are thickened spots on the rays where the inner spiral was attached while the web was making.

in the northern states about the first of August.   Large females are nearly an inch long, with the front legs longer than the body (fig. 449).   The cephalothorax is nearly as wide as long and covered with silvery white hairs, except around the eyes.   The front legs are entirely black, and the others are black, except the femora, which are light red or yellow.   The abdomen is oval, a little pointed behind and square in front, with two small humps at the corners. There is a black stripe in the middle of the abdomen, narrowed between the humps and widened in the middle, where it includes two pairs of yellow spots. Along

FIG. 452. Rudimentary web of male Argiope riparia of the natural size. Part of the web of the female at the left shows the difference between the webs of the two sexes.

the sides are two bright yellow bands or rows of irregular spots. The color underneath is black, with a yellow stripe on the sternum and two wide yellow stripes on the abdomen, with small yellow spots between and at the sides. The young differ considerably from the adults. Until nearly full grown

the legs are distinctly marked with dark rings on the ends
and middle of each joint. When very young the abdomen is
slender, the color is pale, and the markings gray, without the
strong black and yellow of the adult. The male (fig. 450) is

Fig. 453. Web of Argiope riparia in an oval opening among plants from which the
leaves have been drawn away by the spider. At the left of the web is a screen of
irregular threads.

only a fourth as long as the female, similarly colored, but with
the markings less distinct and the palpi very large. In the middle of the summer they live near the webs of the females, where
they make small and imperfect webs of their own (fig. 452).
The females make webs, sometimes two feet in diameter, with

a zigzag band (fig. 448) of white silk up and down across the middle, and a round thick spot where the spider stands. The inner spiral of these webs is very large, covering a quarter of their diameter (fig. 452). The outer spiral comes very near

it, but the spider sometimes passes through the narrow space between them from one side of the web to the other. The web is usually a little inclined, and on one or both sides sometimes has a screen of irregular threads two or three inches distant from it (fig. 453), but these are often absent. These spiders have no nest and stand all the time in the center of the web (fig. 448). Sometimes the spider draws away the grass and leaves so as to make an oval opening large enough for the web (fig. 453). In September the eggs are laid in large pear-shaped cocoons with a brown paper-like surface, hung by threads among the grass and bushes (fig. 454). The young hatch during the winter and remain in the cocoon until May. The adult spiders disappear in October and probably all die before winter.

FIG. 454. Egg cocoon of Argiope riparia in marsh grass. Natural size.

Argiope transversa. — This species is a little smaller than *riparia*. It lives in the same places and matures a little later, about September 1. The abdomen is more pointed than that of *riparia* (fig. 455). The ground color is white or light yellow, and is crossed by a great number of black transverse lines, which are sometimes obscured, especially in

young spiders, by a thick covering of silvery-white hairs.   The
cephalothorax is covered with white hairs through which the
dark markings on the sides show indistinctly.   The legs are
light yellow, with black bands at the ends and middle of each
joint.   The femora of the first legs are sometimes entirely

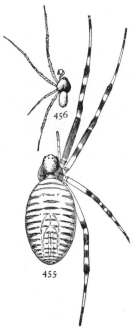

black.   The young have the back entirely
white.   The markings of the under side
are similar to those of *riparia*.   The male
(fig. 456) is colored like the female, but is
only a fourth as large.   The legs are yellow, marked with black spots, but have no
rings.   It has the same habits as *riparia*.
It remains in its web later in the season,
and makes a cocoon flattened on the top
(fig. 458) instead of narrowed to a neck,
like those of *riparia*.

This species often makes its web in
marsh grass, which it draws away and
fastens with silk (fig. 457).   As the surrounding grass becomes long and weak,
it sometimes falls away, leaving the web
in a basket of grass fastened firmly
enough together to remain standing.

FIGS. 455, 456.   Argiope transversa. — 455, female.   456,
male.   Both enlarged
twice.

THE GENUS TETRAGNATHA

The Tetragnathas are slender, usually
straw-colored spiders, living in their webs
among the long grass in meadows and near water.   The legs
are slender, the cephalothorax narrow, and the abdomen long and
cylindrical.   The mandibles are large in both sexes, and in the
males are very long and furnished with long teeth at the end
and along the inner margin.   When pairing, the male and

female hold each other by the ends of the mandibles. The eyes are in two rows nearly equal and parallel, and the distance between the lateral pairs varies in different species. The palpi are long and slender in both sexes, and in the males their

FIG. 457. Web of Argiope transversa in an opening among marsh grass, covered above by wilted ends of grass leaves.

proportions differ according to the species. The legs are also long and slender, and vary in length from *grallator*, where the female has the first legs ten times as long as the cephalothorax, to *laboriosa*, in which they are seven times as long. The webs are generally inclined and may be nearly horizontal or nearly vertical, according to the place where they are made (fig. 459). The inner spiral is small and has a hole in the middle (fig. 460). The spider stands in the web with the legs extended forward and backward close to each other, except at the ends, where they are turned outward (fig. 459). On account of their similar size and color, the species look at first sight much alike, but there are differences in the arrangement of the lateral eyes and the length of the legs, palpi, and mandibles.

FIG. 458.   Egg cocoon of Argiope transversa in marsh grass.

Tetragnatha grallator. — This spider grows to be half an inch long, with the first legs an inch and a half. The mandibles of the female are as long as the cephalothorax, and those of the male longer (figs. 461, 465). In both sexes they are inclined forward, so as to be nearly horizontal and spread apart at the ends. The lateral eyes are near together, so that they almost touch, and the upper row when seen from above is nearly straight. The palpi of both sexes are over one and a half times as long as the cephalothorax, and in the males sometimes twice as long (fig. 465). The patella and tibia together are nearly as long as the femur. The color is sometimes light yellow, but often gray, with a broken middle stripe of darker gray on the abdomen, and three stripes on the cephalothorax. The abdomen is generally enlarged a little in the front third (fig. 461). The males are smaller and more slender than the females, with longer legs and mandibles.

Tetragnatha extensa. — Female a quarter to three-eighths of an inch long, with the first leg three-quarters of an inch. The abdomen is shorter than in *grallator*, about twice as long as the cephalothorax, and not as much widened in front (fig. 462).

FIG. 459.   Web of Tetragnatha in tansy plants, showing the spider in its usual position.

The mandibles are two-thirds as long as the cephalothorax and not much inclined forward. The lateral eyes are near together. The colors are often dark, dull yellow brown or gray, with

three lines on the cephalothorax and a middle dark stripe
on the abdomen, with a light silvery stripe on each side.

The male is smaller and more slender, with the legs longer.
The male palpi are one-half longer than the cephalothorax, the
femur forming nearly half its length (fig. 466).

Tetragnatha laboriosa. — A little smaller than *extensa*, with
shorter legs and mandibles, the latter short enough in the

FIG. 460.   The same web shown in Fig. 459, treated so as to show the inner spiral
and the hole in the middle of the web.

female to be almost vertical (fig. 463).   The abdomen is proportionally longer than in *extensa*, usually in the females three

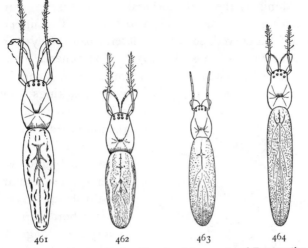

FIGS. 461, 462, 463, 464.   Backs of females of four species of Tetragnatha. —
461, grallator.   462, extensa.   463, laboriosa.   464, straminea.

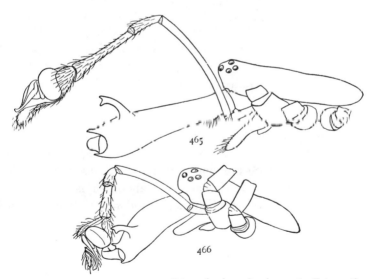

FIGS. 465, 466.   Cephalothorax, mandible, and palpus of males. — 465, Tetragnatha
grallator.   466, Tetragnatha extensa.

times as long as the cephalothorax. The first legs are about seven times as long as the cephalothorax. The upper row of eyes is a little curved, so that the lateral pairs of eyes are as far apart as the middle ones (fig. 467). The general color is light yellow. The abdomen is silvery white, with some indistinct

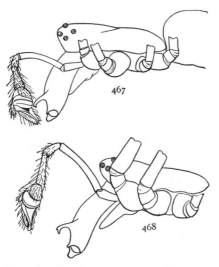

gray markings along the middle, and dark stripes on the under side. In the males the mandibles (fig. 467) are short compared with the other species, and are about two-thirds as long as the cephalothorax, and the tibia is very little longer than the patella.

Tetragnatha straminea. — A quarter to three-eighths of an inch long, about the same size as *laboriosa*, and the same color. The legs, palpi, and mandibles are all a little longer than in *laboriosa*,

Figs. 467, 468. Cephalothorax, mandibles, and palpus of male. — 467, Tetragnatha laboriosa. 468, Tetragnatha straminea.

and the lateral eyes are farther apart than the middle pairs (fig. 464). In the males the abdomen is shorter and smaller, and the legs longer. The male palpi (fig. 468) are one and a half times the length of the cephalothorax. In females the abdomen is usually three times as long as the cephalothorax and more slender than in *laboriosa*.

THE CINIFLONIDÆ, OR CRIBELLATA

This group comprises several families that differ greatly in form and habits, but agree in having peculiar spinning organs, different from those of all the other spiders. They have the usual six spinnerets and in addition the cribellum (fig. 469), a flat, wide spinning organ, close in front of the other spinnerets

and covered with finer spinning tubes. Besides this additional spinning organ they have on the hind legs the

469

FIGS. 469, 470. — 469, cribellum. 470, calamistrum of Amaurobius sylvestris.

calamistrum (fig. 470), a row of hairs that is used to draw out a loose band of silk from the spinnerets. Most of our species belong to the genera Dictyna and Amaurobius and resemble Tegenaria (pp. 96–99) in their feet with three claws, in the arrangement of the eyes, and in their general form and color. The others belong to the small and peculiar genera Filistata, Hyptiotes, and Uloborus.

THE GENUS DICTYNA

The Dictynas are all small spiders, not more than a sixth of an inch in length, but are brightly colored and live in webs in open places, where they cannot fail to be seen by any one

470

who looks for spiders. They are not easily frightened, and so
their habits can be more easily watched than those of many
larger kinds. The heads are high, arching up from the eyes to
the highest part opposite the first legs (fig. 476). The eyes are

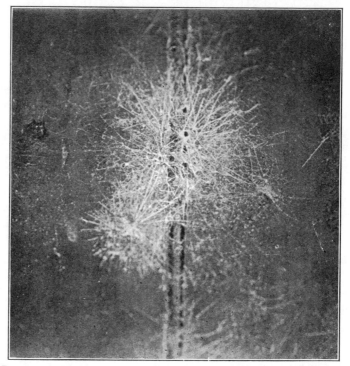

FIG. 471. Webs of Dictyna on the side of a house. The nests were in the groove
between the boards, and the webs radiated irregularly from them, crossing each
other in all directions so as to appear like parts of one web.

higher and the front of the head is more nearly vertical than in
Amaurobius (fig. 489). The head is about half as wide as the
thorax and distinctly marked off from it and usually lighter
colored. The abdomen is sometimes marked with light yellow
on a gray ground, as in Amaurobius, or with a light middle

stripe of various shapes, bordered with brown or gray (fig. 487). The whole body is covered with fine hairs, and there are often long white hairs in rows on the cephalothorax. The cribellum is large for the size of the spiders and can generally be plainly seen just in front of the other spinnerets. The calamistrum is not so easy to see, but it covers about half the length of the fourth metatarsus. The peculiarities of the species of these spiders are more strongly marked in the males. The mandibles

FIG. 476. WEB OF AMAUROBIUS IN THE CORNER OF A WINDOW PANE.

of both sexes are long and a little curved forward at the ends (fig. 476), but in the males they are sometimes so long that the distance from the ends of the mandibles to the top of the head is as great as the length of the cephalothorax, and the lower ends are turned forward at a sharp angle with the upper part. The mandibles of the males are curved apart in the middle, and they have at the base a short tooth projecting forward (fig. 477). The palpi of the males have a process on the tibia, usually near the base, on the end of which are two spines (fig. 478).

There is not much difference in size between the sexes, but they are often very differently colored, and the males do not have the cribellum and calamistrum, or have only rudiments of them. Some species live on walls and fences, making large webs

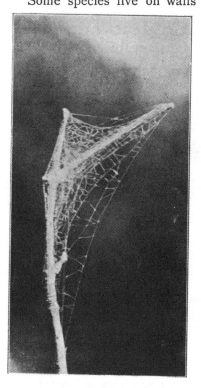

FIG. 473.   Web of Dictyna on the
end of a twig.

that become conspicuous from the dust which they collect. Others prefer the tops of plants like stiff grass and the tops of golden-rod and spiræa. Others, like *volupis* (fig. 474), prefer leaves and the ends of growing branches. The webs are usually irregular, but sometimes are nearly round and formed by threads radiating from the spider's hole, crossed irregularly by other threads (fig. 471).

Dictyna volupis. — This species and *frondea* are brighter colored and more slender than *muraria* and *volucripes* (fig. 484) and live among the leaves of bushes. The female *volupis* has the legs pale, almost white, and the cephalothorax light brown, darker at the sides and light on the head (fig. 474). The abdomen is yellow in the middle and brown, sometimes red, at the sides. The middle yellow portion forms a regular figure differing much in different individuals. The male is quite differently colored. The cephalothorax, which is larger, is bright orange brown, without much difference between the head and the sides (fig. 475). The legs are light orange, darker than those of the female. The abdomen is dark reddish brown, sometimes over the whole back, but usually with a yellow irregular middle spot smaller than that of the female. The ends of the male palpi are dark colored and as large as the spider's head (fig. 475). The hairs are very fine and light colored and do not modify the color as much as they do in the brown species. The length of *volupis* is not over an eighth of an inch. The abdomen is oval and not as wide or high as in *volucripes* and *muraria*. The head of the male is high, and the mandibles almost as long as the cephalothorax (fig. 476). The lower half is turned sharply forward and flattened out at the end. The mandibles are light orange brown, so that their shape is more readily seen than in the dark species. The tooth on the front of the base of the mandibles is very large in this species (fig. 477).

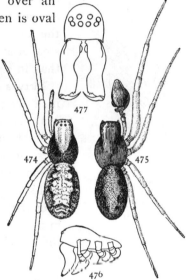

FIGS. 474, 475, 476, 477, 478. Dictyna volupis. — 474, female. 475, male. Both enlarged eight times. 476, side of male. 477, front of head of male enlarged sixteen times, showing curved mandibles. 478, palpus of male.

Dictyna frondea. — This resembles *volupis* and is likely to be mistaken for it. It is a little smaller, not over a tenth of an inch long, and there is less difference between the sexes. The legs are pale, and the cephalothorax light brown, lighter on the head. The abdomen is gray at the sides, not as red as in *volupis,* and the middle light stripe is narrower and not as bright yellow (fig. 479).   The sternum and under side of the

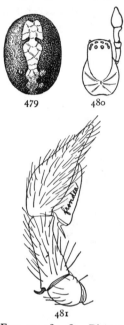

abdomen are gray, as dark as the upper part and sides, while in *volupis* they are generally lighter.   The males have the cephalothorax larger, and that and the legs a little brighter colored than in the female, and the abdomen darker.   The mandibles are not as long as in the male *volupis,* and the ends of the male palpi are much smaller and the tibia longer and straighter than in *volupis* (fig. 481).

Dictyna cruciata. — About a tenth of an inch long, with the abdomen large and oval, as in *muraria.*   The cephalothorax is light brown above and below, and the legs the same color, but still lighter.   The abdomen is gray beneath and at the sides, and silvery white on the back, sometimes over the whole upper surface, but oftener

FIGS. 479, 480, 481. Dictyna frondea. — 479, markings of the abdomen enlarged eight times.   480, cephalo-thorax and palpus of male. 481, palpus of male.

in a stripe widened in the middle so as to form a white cross on a gray ground (fig. 482). The males are darker

colored, with the light spot on the abdomen smaller.   The male palpi are short and slender, the ends large and rounded and carried close to the head (fig. 483).

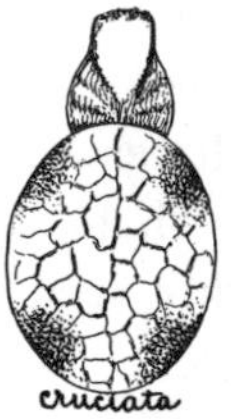

Dictyna volucripes and **muraria.** — These two gray spiders are the common Dictynas on

FIGS. 482, 483.   Dictyna cruciata. — 482, female enlarged eight times. 483, cephalothorax and palpi.

walls and fences and on the ends of grass and weeds, where they make webs shaped according to the places where they

live, having in some part of the web a hole in which the spider
usually hides (fig. 473).   Some allied species make nearly circular webs on walls, with the hole
near the center, and gather so much
dust as to appear like a spot of dirt
(fig. 471).   *Volucripes* is about a
sixth of an inch in length, and
muraria an eighth of an inch.
Volucripes is browner in color and more common
on plants, and *muraria* is grayer and more common on fences.   Both species are marked much
alike.   The cephalothorax is dark brown, partly
covered with light gray hairs, some of which
form roughly three stripes on the head.   The
abdomen is large and round, in some
females nearly as wide as long.   The front
half has a middle dark spot of various
shapes, and the hinder half two rows of

485   486

FIGS. 484, 485, 486. Dictyna volucripes. — 484,
female enlarged eight
times. 485, tibia of male
palpus of Dictyna volu-
cripes. 486, tibia of
male palpus of Dictyna
muraria.

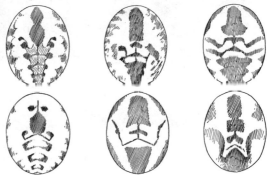

FIG. 487.   Varieties of marking on the abdomen of
Dictyna muraria.

spots connected in
pairs with a middle
line, forming a figure much like the markings of several
species of Epeira (figs. 484, 487).   The legs are dark gray or
brown, covered with fine hairs, the first pair not much longer

than the body. In the females the mandibles are a little thickened in the middle. In the male they are elongated and turned forward at the ends and curved apart in the middle, and have a small tooth on the front near the base. The palpi of the males

Fig. 488. Web of Amaurobius sylvestris on a rough conglomerate rock. The spider had a nest in a crack at one side.

(figs. 485, 486) are short, with the patella as wide as it is long and wider than the femur and tibia. The tarsus is half longer than wide and pointed at the end. In the tibia there is a little difference between the species that can be seen by looking at the palpi from the side; in *volucripes* there is a stout process

at the base as long as the tibia itself and pointing upward at a
right angle with it (fig. 485) ; in *muraria* the corresponding process is short and turned forward, and the tibia seems proportionally longer (fig. 486).   The cribellum in both these species

is large and can easily
be seen in front of the
other spinnerets. The
calamistrum extends
over half the length of
the fourth metatarsus,
which in *volucripes* is
slightly curved.

Amaurobius sylvestris.
— This is the common
Amaurobius all over
the northern part of
the country. It resem-

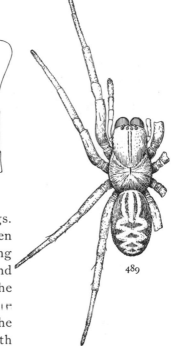

bles our species of Tegenaria (figs.
228, 233) and may easily be mistaken
for them.   It does not have long
upper spinnerets like Tegenaria, and
the eyes are lower on the front of the
head.   The females (fig. 489) are
two-fifths of an inch long, and the
males a third of an inch, but with
much longer legs.   The head of the
female is almost as wide as the middle of the thorax, and the eyes cover
half its width.   The front row of eyes

FIGS. 489, 490. Amaurobius sylvestris. — 489, female enlarged four
times.   490, male palpus without
the terminal joint to show the
processes of the tibia.

are within their diameter of the front of the head.   The head
is low in front and higher halfway between the eyes and the
dorsal groove.   The mandibles are much swelled at the base in
front, as they are in *Tegenaria medicinalis*.   The abdomen is

oval, widest behind, and usually as long as the cephalothorax or longer. The legs are not more than a fourth longer than the body, and slender for so large a spider. The cephalothorax is dark brown, darkest in front, and the legs are a little lighter brown, without markings. The abdomen is gray, with

a double row of oblique yellow or white markings on the hinder half and two curved marks of the same color on the front. These spots sometimes run together, so that the whole middle of the abdomen is light colored. The males have the head narrower and the thorax wider

FIG. 491.   Fresh part of the web of Amaurobius sylvestris.

and all the legs longer than the female, and the cephalothorax and

mandibles are not so dark colored. The male palpi have the patella as short as wide, and the tibia very short and wide, with a short hook on the outer and a longer and more slender one on the inner side, as shown in fig. 490. The epigynum has a small middle lobe inclosed by two lateral lobes that meet behind, and by this the female can be distinguished from the next species, — *Amaurobius ferox*. The cribellum (fig. 469) is sometimes covered by a fold of the skin, so that it is not readily seen. The calamistrum (fig. 470) is a close row of curved hairs on the upper side of the

FIG. 492.   Tibial joint of male Amaurobius ferox for comparison with that of Amaurobius sylvestris (fig. 490).

fourth metatarsus, about half its length. In the male the cribellum is rudimentary, and there is no calamistrum.

This spider makes a large loose web under stones and sticks (fig. 488). In the parts freshly made the loose bands of silk can be seen running irregularly about on the other threads (fig. 491).

Amaurobius ferox. — This lives in houses and is probably an imported species, as it is more common in Europe. It grows a little larger than *sylvestris* (fig. 489), and the head is a little more narrowed in front of the legs. The colors and markings are much as in *sylvestris,* but the abdomen is often darker, and the middle light stripe on the front more distinct. The epigynum has a larger middle lobe, and the lateral lobes are straighter and do not meet in the middle. The males are colored like the females and have the thorax wider and the legs longer. The palpi of the male have the tarsus short and round. The tibia (fig. 492) has only a small short hook on the inner side, and a large blunt process on the outer side. The male palpi and the epigynum distinguish these easily from the last species.

FIG. 493. Amaurobius americana, enlarged four times.

Amaurobius (Titanœca) americana. — Quarter of an inch long and deep black, except the cephalothorax, which is dull orange color, but covered, like the rest of the body, with long black hairs (fig. 493). Some individuals have a few light gray spots in pairs on the abdomen. The shape of the cephalothorax and abdomen are like *Amaurobius sylvestris,* and the legs are of the same proportional length and stouter. The palpi

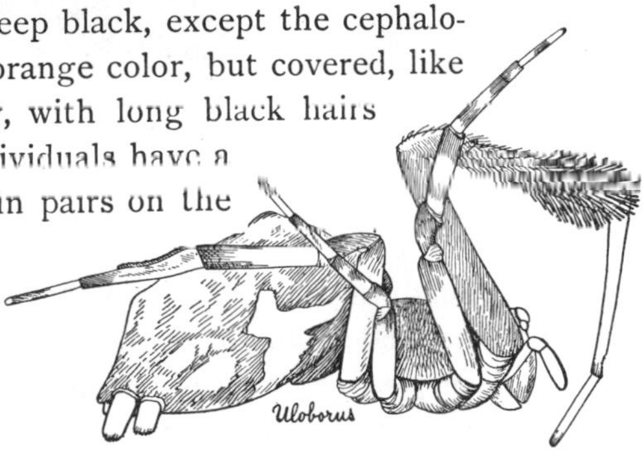

FIG. 494. Female Uloborus plumipes, enlarged eight times, showing the tuft of hairs on the front legs and the calamistrum on the fourth legs.

of the female have the tibia and tarsus a little thickened. The metatarsus of the fourth legs has the calamistrum more distinct than in others of the family, and the metatarsus appears thicker up and down than it is sidewise. The male has the legs longer, particularly the first pair, of which the tibia and metatarsus are more elongated than the other joints, and have many small spines on the under side. The male palpi have the tarsus

Fig. 495. Horizontal web of Uloborus near the ground, one side attached to a fallen tree. The outer spiral is finished over only half the diameter of the web. A line of loose silk runs across the web, and in the middle is a peculiar zigzag spiral. The figure is about the real size.

large and round, supported by a wide and very complicated tibia. It lives under stones in the hottest and dryest places.

Uloborus plumipes. — Uloborus makes a round web, like those of the Epeiridæ, and when hanging in it resembles a Tetragnatha. The adult female is about a quarter of an inch long, and narrow like Tetragnatha. The cephalothorax is low in front and extends forward, in the middle, beyond the mandibles, and the back part is widened and swelled up on each side where the abdomen extends over it (fig. 494). The abdomen is slightly notched in front and covers the cephalothorax a quarter of its length. The abdomen is widest and thickest in the front third and has there a pair of humps. The eyes are in two rows, those of the upper row largest and on the top of the head, with the lateral pair farthest back. The front row are on the edge of the head close to the mandibles. The first pair of legs is the longest and is twice as long as the second. It has at the end of the tibia a brush of long coarse hairs. The colors are various shades of brown, from very light to almost black. The cephalothorax has a light middle stripe. The legs have the joints light in the middle and black at the ends, except the first leg, which sometimes has the tarsus and metatarsus white, and the rest of the leg dark brown. The fourth metatarsus is curved in on the outer side, where the calamistrum is placed. The male is smaller

FIG. 496. Web of young Uloborus in a raspberry bush. The lower half of the web is much wider than the upper. A band of silk runs across the middle and draws up with it some of the lower spirals. Half the real size.

than the female, the legs are longer, the abdomen is smaller and less distinctly humped, the first legs do not have the brushes on the tibia, and the fourth legs do not have the calamistrum. The webs resemble those of Epeira and Tetragnatha, and are horizontal or inclined. They are often left unfinished, with several turns of the wide temporary spiral still in them (fig. 495). Sometimes there are zigzag lines of loose silk across the center or in a middle spiral, and when the eggs are laid the long cocoons are fastened in a line of silk across the web (fig. 497). When this is done the center of the radii of the web is usually at the upper part, instead of in the middle, and the whole web is one-sided. It is found all over the country, usually in shady woods, in bushes, or in the lower branches of trees, especially in the lower dead branches of pines.

FIG. 497. Web of old Uloborus. The spider is in the middle and at the left are three egg cocoons. One-third the real size.

Hyptiotes cavatus. — This peculiar spider resembles in shape and color the end of one of the dead pine branches among which it lives. It is a sixth of an inch long. The cephalothorax is as wide as long, highest in the middle, and hollowed behind under the abdomen. The abdomen is oval, thickest behind, and flattened in front, and has on the back four pairs of slight elevations, on which are a few stiff hairs (fig. 498). The legs are short and thickest in the middle, tapering toward the claws. The hind metatarsi are curved in at the calamistrum (fig. 499). The eyes are arranged as in Uloborus, but are farther apart and farther back on the cephalothorax.

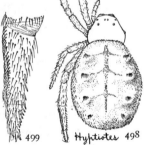

FIG. 498, 499. Hyptiotes cavatus. — 498, f e m a l e enlarged eight times. 499, end of hind leg, showing calamistrum.

The male is half as large as the female, the abdomen smaller, and the humps lower.

The web (fig. 500) consists of four rays crossed by a dozen or more threads. The point where the rays meet is attached

FIG. 500.   Webs of Hyptiotes in the top of a bush.   Half the real size.

to a thread which extends to the spider's roost, usually the end of a twig.   Here it holds on by the hind feet and draws the thread tight with the fore feet.   When an insect strikes the web the spider lets go with the hind feet and is jerked forward by the contraction of the web, and slides along toward its center, where it finds the prey and takes it out of the web to its perch.   The making of this web has been described by Wilder in the *Popular Science Monthly* in 1875.   The cross threads are made separately, beginning with the longest.   They are begun

on the upper ray, the spider walking toward the center, combing out the threads with its hind legs, until it reaches a point where it can cross to the next.   It is found all over the country, usually in the pine woods.

Filistata hibernalis. — One of the most common house spiders in the southern states, making webs in corners and on walls and fences (fig. 501).   The body is about half an inch long, but the legs are so long and stout that it appears much larger.   The first leg, which is the longest, is about twice the length of the body.   The palpi are as long as the cephalothorax and thicker than in most spiders.   The maxillæ are inclined toward each other so that they meet in front of the labium.   The cephalothorax is flat and narrowed in front between the palpi, and the mandibles are small.   The eyes are in one group, close together. The color is dark gray, without any markings, and the whole body is covered with fine short hairs.   The calamistrum is very

FIG. 501.   Filistata hibernalis, enlarged twice.

short, and near the base of the fourth metatarsus, where it can easily be seen.   The web is like that of Dictyna, radiating irregularly from the spider's hiding place, and when this is on a flat wall forms sometimes a circle a foot or more in diameter, which becomes filled with dust and is enlarged and thickened as the spider grows.

SELECTED READINGS

Comstock, J. H. *The Spider Book: A Manual for the Study of Spiders and Their Near Relatives.* Edited by W. J. Gertsch. Ithaca: Cornell Univ. Press, 1948. $6.00. Illus. 729 p.

Gertsch, Willis J. *American Spiders.* Princeton: D. Van Nostrand Co., 1949. $7.95. Illus. 285 p.

Kaston, B. J. *How to Know the Spiders.* Edited by Harry E. Jacques. Dubuque: Wm. C. Brown Co. $3.00, pap. $2.50. Illus. 224 p.

INDEX

Abdomen, the posterior half of the
  body, x.
Acrosoma, 188.
  mitrata, 189.
  rugosa, 189.
  spinea, 190.
Adult characters of spiders, xi.
Agalena nævia, 93.
Agalenidæ, 91.
Age of spiders, xv.
Agrœca pratensis, 11.
Air-sacs, x.
Air-tubes, x.
Amaurobius americana, 215.
  ferox, 215.
  sylvestris, 213.
Anatomy of spiders, viii–xi.
Anyphæna calcarata, 13.
  incerta, 12.
  rubra, 13.
  saltabunda, 14.
Argiope, 194.
  cocoons of, 197, 666.
  riparia, 194.
  transversa, 198.
  webs of, 192, 194, 196, 199.
Argyrodes, 123.
  fictilium, 126.
  nephilæ, 125.
  trigonum, 124.
Argyroepeira hortorum, 191.
Ariadne bicolor, 123.
Asagena americana, 122.
Attidæ, 41.
Attus palustris, 42.

Bathyphantes, see under Linyphia, 143,
  145.
Bites of spiders, viii.
Breathing holes, x.

Cælotes, see under Tegenaria, 99.
Calamistrum, 205.
Catalogue of American spiders, viii.
Cephalothorax, viii.
Ceratinalla fissiceps, 152.
  lætabilis, 151.
Ceratinopsis interpres, 153.
Chiracanthium viride, 21.
Ciniflonidæ, 205.
Claws, x.
Clubiona, 15.
  canadensis, 17.
  crassipalpis, 16.
  excepta, 19.
  ornata, 18.
  rubra, 18.
  tibialis, 16.
Cobwebs, xvi.
Cocoons, xiv.
Colors, xi.
Coriarachne depressa, 34.
  versicolor, 34.
Cornicularia directa, 152.
Coxa, the first joint of the leg, viii.
Crab spiders, see Thomisidæ, 24.
Cribellata, 205.
Cribellum, 205.
Cyclosa conica, 183.
Cyrba tæniola, 63.

223

Daddy longlegs, see Pholcus, 128.
Dendryphantes, 53, 54.
  æstivalis, 54.
  militaris, 53.
Dew on cobwebs, 107, 108.
Dictyna, 206–211.
  cruciata, 210.
  frondea, 210.
  volucripes, 211.
  volupis, 209.
Diplostyla, see under Linyphia, 147.
  concolor = Linyphia concolor, 147.
  nigrina = Linyphia nigrina, 147.
Dolomedes sexpunctatus, 85.
  tenebrosus, 87.
Dorsal groove, viii.
Drapetisca socialis = Linyphia socialis, 145.
Drassidæ, 1.
Drassus saccatus, 6.
Dysdera interrita, 22.
Dysderidæ, a family of spiders with six eyes, 22.

Ebo latithorax, 37.
Eggs of spiders, xiv.
Epeira, 160–180.
  angulata, 164.
  caudata or conica, see Cyclosa, 183.
  cinerea, 165.
  corticaria, 165.
  directa, see Larinia directa, 182.
  displicata, 172.
  domiciliorum, see trivittata, 167.
  gibberosa, 175, 176.
  globosa, 173.
  insularis, 169.
  labyrinthea, 174.
  marmorea, see insularis, 169.
  nordmanni, 163.
  parvula, 179.
  patagiata, 160, 161.
  placida, 176.

Epeira pratensis, 167.
  sclopetaria, 160, 161.
  scutulata, 178.
  silvatica, 164.
  stellata, 179.
  strix, 160, 161.
  thaddeus, 170.
  triaranea, see globosa, 173, 174.
  trifolium, 171, 172.
  trivittata, 166.
  verrucosa, 181.
Epeiridæ, 154.
Epiblemum scenicum, 60.
Epigynum, xi.
Erigone, 148.
  autumnalis, 151.
  dentigera, 149.
  longipalpis, 149.
Ero thoracica, 132.
Euryopis funebris, 127.
Eyes of spiders, ix.

Feet, x.
Femur, viii.
Filistata hibernalis, 220.
Flat webs, 134; see Agalenidæ, 91; Linyphia, 100.
Flower spiders, see Misumena, 25.
Flying spiders, Erigone, 151.
  Lycosa, 68.

Geotrecha bivittata, 8.
  crocata, 7.
Gnaphosa brumalis, 3.
  conspersa, 2.
Gossamer, 149.
Ground spiders, Lycosidæ, 67.
  Drassidæ, 1.

Habrocestum auratum, 43, 44.
  peregrinum, 45.
  splendens, 46.
Hahnia bimaculata, 105.

Hahnia cinerea, 106.
Hairs, xi.
Hasarius hoyi, 63, 64.
Head, viii.
Helophora insignis, see Linyphia insignis, 146.
House spiders, xii.
Hunting spiders, xv.
Hyctia pikei, 62.
Hyptiotes cavatus, 218.

Icius elegans, 57, 58.
    mitratus, 57.
    palmarum, 56.

Jumping spiders, see Attidæ, 41.

Labium, x.
Larinia directa, 182.
Latrodectus mactans, 122, 123.
Legs, viii.
Linyphia, 134.
    bucculenta = trilineata, 143.
    coccinea, 140.
    communis, 138.
    concolor, 147.
    insignis, 146.
    mandibulata, 139.
    marginata, 136.
    minuta, 144.
    nebulosa, 143.
    nigrina, 147.
    phrygiana, 141, 143.
    socialis, 145.
    trilineata, 143.
Linyphiadæ, 134.
Lungs, x.
Lycosa carolinensis, 73, 74.
    cinerea, 73, 74.
    communis, 75.
    kochii, 74.
    nidicola, 69.
    nidifex, 70, 72, 73.

Lycosa ocreata, 77.
    polita, 70.
    pratensis, 69.
    scutulata, 76.
Lycosidæ, 67.
Lyssomanes viridis, 65.

Mævia vittata, 59.
Male spiders, xi.
Mandibles, viii.
    of Tetragnatha, 203, 204.
Markings, xi.
Marptusa familiaris, 61.
Marx, George, list of spiders of North America, viii.
Maxillæ, x.
Meta menardi, 190.
Metatarsus, viii.
Micaria aurata, 8.
    longipes, 8.
Mimetus interfector, 132.
Misumena, 25.

Names of spiders, vii.
Neon nellii, 47.
Nests of spiders, xiv.
Number of spiders, vii.

Ocyale undata, 88.
Oxyopes salticus, 88.
    viridans, 89, 90.

Palpal organ, xi.
Palpi, viii.
Pardosa, 78.
    albomaculata = greenlandica, 79.
    albopatella, 83.
    brunnea = glacialis, 80.
    glacialis, 80.
    greenlandica, 79.
    lapidicina, 78.
    montana = tachypoda, 81.
    nigropalpis, 82.

Pardosa pallida, 81.
    tachypoda, 81.
Patella, viii.
Pellenes, see Habrocestum, 44–46.
Peucetia, see Oxyopes viridans, 89, 90.
Phalangium, 128.
Phidippus multiformis, 48, 49.
    mystaceus, 50.
    tripunctatus, 51.
Philodromus, 35.
    lineatus, 37.
    ornatus, 36.
    pictus, 37.
    vulgaris, 35.
Pholcus phalangioides, 128, 129.
    cornutus, 130.
Phrurolithus alarius, 9, 10.
Pirata piraticus, 84.
Plexippus puerperus, 52.
Pœcilochroa variegata, 4.
    bilineata, 4.
Poison of spiders, viii.
Prosthesima atra, 5.
    ecclesiastica, 5.
Pythonissa imbecilla, 3.

Round cobwebs, 155–159.

Saitis pulex, 43.
Salticus scenicus, see Epiblemum sceni-
    cum, 60.
Scales, xi.
Scytodes thoracica, 131.
Sight of spiders, ix.
Singa pratensis, 186.
    variabilis, 187.
Spinnerets, x.
Spintharus flavidus, 127.
Spiral threads of cobwebs, 155–159.
Steatoda borealis, 119.
    corollata, 121.
    guttata, 120.
    marmorata, 120.

Steatoda triangulosa, 121.
Stemonyphantes, see Linyphia trili-
    neata, 143.
Sternum, x.
Synemosyna, 64.

Tarantula, see Lycosa carolinensis,
    73, 74.
Tarsus, viii.
Tegenaria, 96–103.
    complicata, 102.
    derhamii, 96–98.
    longitarsus, 102, 104.
    medicinalis, 99.
Tetragnatha, 198–204.
    extensa, 201.
    grallator, 200.
    laboriosa, 202.
    straminea, 204.
Thanatus coloradensis, 39, 40.
    lycosoides, 39, 40.
Therididæ, 107.
Theridium, 110.
    differens, 114.
    frondeum, 116, 117.
    globosum, 113.
    murarium, 115.
    rupicola, 113.
    spirale, 116.
    tepidariorum, 111, 112.
    unimaculatum, 118.
    verecundum = Latrodectus mac-
    tans, 122.
Theridula sphærula, 127, 128.
Thomisidæ, 24.
Thorax, viii.
Tibellus duttonii, 39.
Tibia, viii.
Titanæca, see Amaurobius americana,
    215.
Tmarus caudatus, 38.
Tracheæ, x.

Trachelas ruber, 19, 20.
Trochanter, viii.

Uloborus plumipes, 216, 217.

Winter habits of spiders, xv.

Xysticus, 30.
    gulosus, 31.
    limbatus, 31.

Xysticus nervosus, 32.
    quadrilineatus, 33.
    stomachosus, 30.
    triguttatus, 33.
    versicolor, 34.

Zilla, 184–186.
    atrica, 185.
    montana, 186.
    x-notata, 186.

A CATALOG OF SELECTED

DOVER BOOKS

IN ALL FIELDS OF INTEREST

A CATALOG OF SELECTED
DOVER BOOKS
IN ALL FIELDS OF INTEREST

DRAWINGS OF REMBRANDT, edited by Seymour Slive. Updated Lippmann, Hofstede de Groot edition, with definitive scholarly apparatus. All portraits, biblical sketches, landscapes, nudes. Oriental figures, classical studies, together with selection of work by followers. 550 illustrations. Total of 630pp. 9⅛ × 12¼.
21485-0, 21486-9 Pa., Two-vol. set $29.90

GHOST AND HORROR STORIES OF AMBROSE BIERCE, Ambrose Bierce. 24 tales vividly imagined, strangely prophetic, and decades ahead of their time in technical skill: "The Damned Thing," "An Inhabitant of Carcosa," "The Eyes of the Panther," "Moxon's Master," and 20 more. 199pp. 5⅜ × 8½. 20767-6 Pa. $4.95

ETHICAL WRITINGS OF MAIMONIDES, Maimonides. Most significant ethical works of great medieval sage, newly translated for utmost precision, readability. Laws Concerning Character Traits, Eight Chapters, more. 192pp. 5⅜ × 8½.
24522-5 Pa. $5.95

THE EXPLORATION OF THE COLORADO RIVER AND ITS CANYONS, J. W. Powell. Full text of Powell's 1,000-mile expedition down the fabled Colorado in 1869. Superb account of terrain, geology, vegetation, Indians, famine, mutiny, treacherous rapids, mighty canyons, during exploration of last unknown part of continental U.S. 400pp. 5⅜ × 8½. 20094-9 Pa. $8.95

HISTORY OF PHILOSOPHY, Julián Marías. Clearest one-volume history on the market. Every major philosopher and dozens of others, to Existentialism and later. 505pp. 5⅜ × 8½. 21739-6 Pa. $9.95

ALL ABOUT LIGHTNING, Martin A. Uman. Highly readable nontechnical survey of nature and causes of lightning, thunderstorms, ball lightning, St. Elmo's Fire, much more. Illustrated. 192pp. 5⅜ × 8½. 25237-X Pa. $5.95

SAILING ALONE AROUND THE WORLD, Captain Joshua Slocum. First man to sail around the world, alone, in small boat. One of great feats of seamanship told in delightful manner. 67 illustrations. 294pp. 5⅜ × 8½. 20326-3 Pa. $4.95

LETTERS AND NOTES ON THE MANNERS, CUSTOMS AND CONDITIONS OF THE NORTH AMERICAN INDIANS, George Catlin. Classic account of life among Plains Indians: ceremonies, hunt, warfare, etc. 312 plates. 572pp. of text. 6⅛ × 9¼. 22118-0, 22119-9, Pa., Two-vol. set $17.90

THE SECRET LIFE OF SALVADOR DALÍ, Salvador Dalí. Outrageous but fascinating autobiography through Dalí's thirties with scores of drawings and sketches and 80 photographs. A must for lovers of 20th-century art. 432pp. 6½ × 9¼. (Available in U.S. only) 27454-3 Pa. $9.95

THE BOOK OF BEASTS: Being a Translation from a Latin Bestiary of the Twelfth Century, T. H. White. Wonderful catalog of real and fanciful beasts: manticore, griffin, phoenix, amphivius, jaculus, many more. White's witty erudite commentary on scientific, historical aspects enhances fascinating glimpse of medieval mind. Illustrated. 296pp. 5⅜ × 8¼. (Available in U.S. only) 24609-4 Pa. $7.95

FRANK LLOYD WRIGHT: Architecture and Nature with 160 Illustrations, Donald Hoffmann. Profusely illustrated study of influence of nature—especially prairie—on Wright's designs for Fallingwater, Robie House, Guggenheim Museum, other masterpieces. 96pp. 9¼ × 10¾. 25098-9 Pa. $8.95

LIMBERT ARTS AND CRAFTS FURNITURE: The Complete 1903 Catalog, Charles P. Limbert and Company. Rare catalog depicting 188 pieces of Mission-style furniture: fold-down tables and desks, bookcases, library and octagonal tables, chairs, more. Descriptive captions. 80pp. 9⅜ × 12¼. 27120-X Pa. $6.95

YEARS WITH FRANK LLOYD WRIGHT: Apprentice to Genius, Edgar Tafel. Insightful memoir by a former apprentice presents a revealing portrait of Wright the man, the inspired teacher, the greatest American architect. 372 black-and-white illustrations. Preface. Index. vi + 228pp. 8¼ × 11. 24801-1 Pa. $10.95

THE STORY OF KING ARTHUR AND HIS KNIGHTS, Howard Pyle. Enchanting version of King Arthur fable has delighted generations with imaginative narratives of exciting adventures and unforgettable illustrations by the author. 41 illustrations. xviii + 313pp. 6⅛ × 9¼. 21445-1 Pa. $6.95

THE GODS OF THE EGYPTIANS, E. A. Wallis Budge. Thorough coverage of numerous gods of ancient Egypt by foremost Egyptologist. Information on evolution of cults, rites and gods; the cult of Osiris; the Book of the Dead and its rites; the sacred animals and birds; Heaven and Hell; and more. 956pp. 6⅛ × 9¼. 22055 9, 22056 7 Pa., Two-vol. set $22.90

A THEOLOGICO-POLITICAL TREATISE, Benedict Spinoza. Also contains unfinished *Political Treatise*. Great classic on religious liberty, theory of government on common consent. R. Elwes translation. Total of 421pp. 5⅜ × 8½. 20249-6 Pa. $7.95

INCIDENTS OF TRAVEL IN CENTRAL AMERICA, CHIAPAS, AND YUCATAN, John L. Stephens. Almost single-handed discovery of Maya culture; exploration of ruined cities, monuments, temples; customs of Indians. 115 drawings. 892pp. 5⅜ × 8½. 22404-X, 22405-8 Pa., Two-vol. set $17.90

LOS CAPRICHOS, Francisco Goya. 80 plates of wild, grotesque monsters and caricatures. Prado manuscript included. 183pp. 6⅞ × 9⅜. 22384-1 Pa. $6.95

AUTOBIOGRAPHY: The Story of My Experiments with Truth, Mohandas K. Gandhi. Not hagiography, but Gandhi in his own words. Boyhood, legal studies, purification, the growth of the Satyagraha (nonviolent protest) movement. Critical, inspiring work of the man who freed India. 480pp. 5⅜ × 8½. (Available in U.S. only) 24593-4 Pa. $6.95

CATALOG OF DOVER BOOKS

ILLUSTRATED DICTIONARY OF HISTORIC ARCHITECTURE, edited by Cyril M. Harris. Extraordinary compendium of clear, concise definitions for over 5,000 important architectural terms complemented by over 2,000 line drawings. Covers full spectrum of architecture from ancient ruins to 20th-century Modernism. Preface. 592pp. 7½ × 9⅜. 24444-X Pa. $15.95

THE NIGHT BEFORE CHRISTMAS, Clement C. Moore. Full text, and woodcuts from original 1848 book. Also critical, historical material. 19 illustrations. 40pp. 4⅝ × 6. 22797-9 Pa. $2.50

THE LESSON OF JAPANESE ARCHITECTURE: 165 Photographs, Jiro Harada. Memorable gallery of 165 photographs taken in the 1930s of exquisite Japanese homes of the well-to-do and historic buildings. 13 line diagrams. 192pp. 8⅜ × 11¼. 24778-3 Pa. $10.95

THE AUTOBIOGRAPHY OF CHARLES DARWIN AND SELECTED LETTERS, edited by Francis Darwin. The fascinating life of eccentric genius composed of an intimate memoir by Darwin (intended for his children); commentary by his son, Francis; hundreds of fragments from notebooks, journals, papers; and letters to and from Lyell, Hooker, Huxley, Wallace and Henslow. xi + 365pp. 5⅜ × 8. 20479-0 Pa. $6.95

WONDERS OF THE SKY: Observing Rainbows, Comets, Eclipses, the Stars and Other Phenomena, Fred Schaaf. Charming, easy-to-read poetic guide to all manner of celestial events visible to the naked eye. Mock suns, glories, Belt of Venus, more. Illustrated. 299pp. 5¼ × 8¼. 24402-4 Pa. $8.95

BURNHAM'S CELESTIAL HANDBOOK, Robert Burnham, Jr. Thorough guide to the stars beyond our solar system. Exhaustive treatment. Alphabetical by constellation: Andromeda to Cetus in Vol. 1; Chamaeleon to Orion in Vol. 2; and Pavo to Vulpecula in Vol. 3. Hundreds of illustrations. Index in Vol. 3. 2,000pp. 6⅛ × 9¼. 23567-X, 23568-8, 23673-0 Pa., Three-vol. set $41.85

STAR NAMES: Their Lore and Meaning, Richard Hinckley Allen. Fascinating history of names various cultures have given to constellations and literary and folkloristic uses that have been made of stars. Indexes to subjects. Arabic and Greek names. Biblical references. Bibliography. 563pp. 5⅜ × 8½. 21079-0 Pa. $9.95

THIRTY YEARS THAT SHOOK PHYSICS: The Story of Quantum Theory, George Gamow. Lucid, accessible introduction to influential theory of energy and matter. Careful explanations of Dirac's anti-particles, Bohr's model of the atom, much more. 12 plates. Numerous drawings. 240pp. 5⅜ × 8½. 24895-X Pa. $6.95

CHINESE DOMESTIC FURNITURE IN PHOTOGRAPHS AND MEASURED DRAWINGS, Gustav Ecke. A rare volume, now affordably priced for antique collectors, furniture buffs and art historians. Detailed review of styles ranging from early Shang to late Ming. Unabridged republication. 161 black-and-white drawings, photos. Total of 224pp. 8⅜ × 11¼. (Available in U.S. only) 25171-3 Pa. $14.95

VINCENT VAN GOGH: A Biography, Julius Meier-Graefe. Dynamic, penetrating study of artist's life, relationship with brother, Theo, painting techniques, travels, more. Readable, engrossing. 160pp. 5⅜ × 8½. (Available in U.S. only) 25253-1 Pa. $4.95

CATALOG OF DOVER BOOKS

AMERICAN CLIPPER SHIPS: 1833–1858, Octavius T. Howe & Frederick C. Matthews. Fully-illustrated, encyclopedic review of 352 clipper ships from the period of America's greatest maritime supremacy. Introduction. 109 halftones. 5 black-and-white line illustrations. Index. Total of 928pp. 5⅜ × 8½.
25115-2, 25116-0 Pa., Two-vol. set $21.90

TOWARDS A NEW ARCHITECTURE, Le Corbusier. Pioneering manifesto by great architect, near legendary founder of "International School." Technical and aesthetic theories, views on industry, economics, relation of form to function, "mass-production spirit," much more. Profusely illustrated. Unabridged translation of 13th French edition. Introduction by Frederick Etchells. 320pp. 6⅛ × 9¼. (Available in U.S. only) 25023-7 Pa. $8.95

THE BOOK OF KELLS, edited by Blanche Cirker. Inexpensive collection of 32 full-color, full-page plates from the greatest illuminated manuscript of the Middle Ages, painstakingly reproduced from rare facsimile edition. Publisher's Note. Captions. 32pp. 9⅜ × 12¼. (Available in U.S. only) 24345-1 Pa. $5.95

BEST SCIENCE FICTION STORIES OF H. G. WELLS, H. G. Wells. Full novel *The Invisible Man*, plus 17 short stories: "The Crystal Egg," "Aepyornis Island," "The Strange Orchid," etc. 303pp. 5⅜ × 8½. (Available in U.S. only)
21531-8 Pa. $6.95

AMERICAN SAILING SHIPS: Their Plans and History, Charles G. Davis. Photos, construction details of schooners, frigates, clippers, other sailcraft of 18th to early 20th centuries—plus entertaining discourse on design, rigging, nautical lore, much more. 137 black-and-white illustrations. 240pp. 6⅛ × 9¼.
24658-2 Pa. $6.95

ENTERTAINING MATHEMATICAL PUZZLES, Martin Gardner. Selection of author's favorite conundrums involving arithmetic, money, speed, etc., with lively commentary. Complete solutions. 112pp. 5⅜ × 8½. 25211-6 Pa. $3.95

THE WILL TO BELIEVE, HUMAN IMMORTALITY, William James. Two books bound together. Effect of irrational on logical, and arguments for human immortality. 402pp. 5⅜ × 8½. 20291-7 Pa. $8.95

THE HAUNTED MONASTERY and THE CHINESE MAZE MURDERS, Robert Van Gulik. 2 full novels by Van Gulik continue adventures of Judge Dee and his companions. An evil Taoist monastery, seemingly supernatural events; overgrown topiary maze that hides strange crimes. Set in 7th-century China. 27 illustrations. 328pp. 5⅜ × 8½. 23502-5 Pa. $6.95

CELEBRATED CASES OF JUDGE DEE (DEE GOONG AN), translated by Robert Van Gulik. Authentic 18th-century Chinese detective novel; Dee and associates solve three interlocked cases. Led to Van Gulik's own stories with same characters. Extensive introduction. 9 illustrations. 237pp. 5⅜ × 8½.
23337-5 Pa. $5.95

Prices subject to change without notice.

Available at your book dealer or write for free catalog to Dept. GI, Dover Publications, Inc., 31 East 2nd St., Mineola, N.Y. 11501. Dover publishes more than 400 books each year on science, elementary and advanced mathematics, biology, music, art, literary history, social sciences and other areas.